FOOD, CULTURE & SOCIETY

AN INTERNATIONAL

JOURNAL OF

MULTIDISCIPLINARY

RESEARCH

Volume 15 | Issue 2 | June 2012

Subscription Information

2012. Volume 15. 4 issues.
Free online subscription to institutional subscribers.
Electronic access through www.ingentaconnect.com

Subscription Rates
Print. Institutional (1 year): £455/US$889; (2 year): £663/US$1,422.
Online Only. Institutional (1 year): £387/US$755; (2 year): £620/US$1,207.
Single issues: £32/US$60.
Membership Rates
Individual (1 year): £50/US$89; (2 year): £80/US$142.
Student (1 year): £33/US$60. Proof of student status to be provided. Please email Eleanor Graves, *eleanor.graves@bloomsbury.com*, or fax to: +44 (0)1865 791165.
Members of the ASFS receive the journal as part of their membership fee.

Ordering Options

Online: www.bergpublishers.com
By Email:
    custserv@turpin-distribution.com
By Mail: Berg Publishers
    c/o Turpin Distribution
    Stratton Business Park
    Pegasus Drive
    Biggleswade SG18 8TQ
    United Kingdom
By Phone: +44 (0)1767 604 951
By Fax: +44 (0)1767 601 604

Inquiries

Editorial: Julia Hall,
julia.hall@bloomsbury.com
Production: Ken Bruce,
ken.bruce@bloomsbury.com
Advertising and subscriptions: Eleanor Graves, *eleanor.graves@bloomsbury.com*

Reprints can be obtained from the publisher at the appropriate fees. Write to: Eleanor Graves, Berg Publishers, 50 Bedford Square, London WC1B 3DP, UK

ISSN: 1552-8014

Published by Berg Publishers on behalf of ASFS. Berg Publishers is an imprint of Bloomsbury Publishing Plc.

Food, Culture & Society is indexed by Abstracts in Anthropology; Agricola; America: Historical Abstracts; America: History and Life; Anthropological Index Online (AIO); British Humanities Index; Food Science and Technology Abstracts (FSTA); International Bibliography of Book Reviews of Scholarly Literature in the Humanities and Social Sciences (IBR); International Bibliography of Periodical Literature on the Humanities and Social Sciences (IBZ); International Bibliography of Social Sciences (IBSS); Sociological Abstracts; International Food Information Service (IFIS)

Berg Publishers is a member of CrossRef
Cover and text designs by Raven Design
Typeset by Avocet Typeset, Chilton, Aylesbury, Bucks
Printed in the UK

FOOD, CULTURE & SOCIETY

VOLUME 15 | ISSUE 2 | JUNE 2012

CONTENTS

Perspectives on Teaching

FOOD, CULTURE & SOCIETY

VOLUME 15 | ISSUE 2 | JUNE 2012

From the Editors

This second issue of our fifteenth volume opens by continuing the focus on cheese that began in 15.1. In "'The Days Had Come of Curds and Cream': The Origins and Development of Cream Cheese in America 1870–1880," Jeffrey Marx's history of this very particular, very perishable cheese focuses on a period of time he describes as the cusp between the "pastoral" and "modern" periods of American dairy history, and on the particular technological, cultural and social forces that intertwine in the creation of cream cheese. Among the elements Marx explores are a rise in the demand for "fancy" cheeses among wealthy Americans; advances in transportation (particularly the capacity to ship perishable goods); and the entrepreneurial ingenuity of one man, William Lawrence. (Marx also solves for me the childhood mystery: why was it called *Philadelphia* cream cheese?)

Next, we come to the issue's special focus on the foods of the Carolinas and the Caribbean. In the first piece, "Recipes in Context: Solving a Small Mystery in Charleston's Culinary History," Donna Gabaccia and Jane Aldrich use an unlikely and ingenious combination of scholarly tools to detect the probable author of the first cookbook featuring the recipes of the Carolina Low Country, *The Carolina Receipt Book or Housekeeper's Assistant*. When traditional culinary historical methods proved insufficient to ascertain its authorship, Gabaccia and Aldrich turned to a consideration of some of the major political issues of antebellum Charleston, including states' rights, slavery and Nullification, to reach their compelling conclusion (Hercule Poirot, eat your heart out). The next article explores the emergence of the Costa Rican national dish: "*El Gallo Pinto*: Afro-Caribbean Rice and Beans Conquer the Costa Rican National Cuisine." Patricia Vega Jiménez examines the ways in which this Afro-Caribbean dish of beans and rice (which translates as "spotted rooster") became *the* national dish, overcoming its stigmatization by middle class Costa Ricans invested in a view of the nation as white and European. Jimenez traces the arrival and popularization of rice to the region, and links the ascendance of this dish to the Great Depression, a period in which "diverse factors combined to change the diet: climate, war, economy, politics, even diplomacy." The third paper of this section, "Mirrors in the Kitchen: The *New Cuban Woman* Cooks Revolutionarily," by Marisela Fleites-Lear, moves the discussion to Cuba, and to a textual analysis of several Cuban cookbooks and a magazine (*Mujeres*), to analyze the ideological role of cookery in the Cuban revolution, and the ways in which the revolution reconceptualized women. Fleites-Lear analyzes an "essential yet paradoxical element" of the "new Cuban woman"—namely, the "revolutionary cook." She separates the Cuban revolutionary period into three distinct sections, corresponding to three understandings of the relationship between Cuban women and the kitchen, and embodied, for example, in the pages of *Mujeres*. The last (present) stage of this relationship, she suggests, is characterized by an effort to "reopen the question of domesticity and to break the association between woman and kitchen." In "Nostalgia for Origins in a Fast Food Culture: Teaching with the Food Memories of Carolina College Women," author Corrie Norman describes a qualitative research project she uses in a religious studies course, in which students explore each other's food narratives as "origin stories that orient people between the sacred and the profane." Norman's students analyze narratives filled with grandmothers, Thanksgiving, and fast-food chicken, and find in them "something basic about their origin that serves to give them … a means by which to understand and articulate who they are and why they are here."

Marisa Wilson's paper, "Moral Economies of Food in Cuba," uses the concept of a moral economy—"ideas and values about what can and cannot be commoditized"—to examine the national moral economy of Cuba, and to consider the matter of food within that economy. Drawing upon field research from Tuta, a rural village in Cuba, Wilson explores the ways in which local moral economies are informed by the national moral economy, which is rooted both in traditional concepts such as hard work and asceticism, and such post-revolution ideas as subordination of individual desires to the collective entitlement. Ultimately, Wilson uses her research to argue against two totalizing theories: both the neoclassical view rooted in the demand to increase one's consumption at all costs, and "a socialist fantasy that the revolution's provision of hospitals and schools has somehow erased all Cubans' desires for plentiful consumer commodities."

Moving to Central America, Emily Yates-Doerr's article "The Opacity of Reduction: Nutritional Black-boxing and the Meanings of Nourishment," studies the way in which nutritional information is perceived by consumers in the Guatemalan highlands. Borrowing the idea of the "black box" from Bruno Latour, Yates-Doerr suggests that contemporary nutrition education in Guatemala often takes the form of "black-boxing"—"consolidating technical and historically contingent ideas about nourishment and the myriad relationships surrounding dietary practices into seemingly unproblematic terms: a vitamin, a nutrient." Her research in three sites—a rural clinic, an elementary school, and a hospital obesity program—leads her to conclude that "Despite its pretense of simplicity, the reductionism of nutritional black-boxing produces confusion." She calls for public health nutrition that is "listening to and valuing the knowledge that people already possess, even when this knowledge takes the inconvenient, ineffable form of practices, engagements, and diverse sensory experiences; even when this knowledge resists reductive simplicity."

The final paper in this issue is part of the journal's occasional series on pedagogical matters. In "(Re) Focus on Local Food Systems through Service Learning: Empowering Pedagogy in a Human Nutrition Degree Program," Laurie Wadsworth, Christine Johnson, Colleen Cameron and Marla Gaudet, discuss the work they have done to develop two courses in a nutrition education program that utilize service learning. They identify a half-dozen measures against which they show that, through service learning courses, student nutritionists develop their capacities and become empowered to act in their communities. Among the measures they discuss are the ability to form networks, mobilize resources, identify and assess problems, and ask "why" questions.

A final note: this issue of *Food, Culture and Society* should feel a bit heftier in your hands; we've been able to increase the journal length by roughly sixteen pages per issue, in response to the volume of fine contributions the journal has been receiving. We're pleased with our increased portion sizes!

Lisa Heldke
DOI: 10.2752/175174412X13233545145147

FOOD,
CULTURE&
SOCIETY

VOLUME 15

ISSUE 2

JUNE 2012

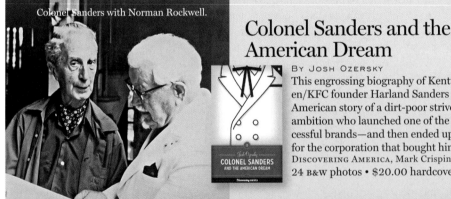

VOLUME 15 | ISSUE 2 | JUNE 2012

"The Days Had Come of Curds and Cream"

THE ORIGINS AND DEVELOPMENT OF CREAM CHEESE IN AMERICA, 1870–1880

Jeffrey A. Marx

Independent scholar

Abstract

This paper explores the earliest production of cream cheese by postcolonial Philadelphia farm families. It examines how changes in American cuisine and demographics produced the demand for "fancy" cheeses in the late nineteenth century. It shows how mechanization transformed the dairy industry as it moved from its pastoral period into the Industrial Age. This paper also traces how these changes resulted in large-scale cream cheese manufacturing efforts in the late 1870s. Finally, the critical role played by William A. Lawrence, a Chester, NY farmer, who was the first manufacturer of cream cheese in America, is also detailed.

Keywords: cream cheese, dairy, Charles Green, William Lawrence, mechanization, Neufchâtel, Philadelphia

The second half of the nineteenth century witnessed transforming changes in the American dairy industry, largely due to the mechanization of production. Technological and manufacturing innovations (small steam engines, gang presses, self-heating cheese vats, cooling cans, commercial rennet, the cream separator) caused the production of dairy goods to move from the farmhouse to the farm factory, from hand to machine, from varied quality to uniform quantity. This period also saw men displace women as butter and cheese makers, French cheeses take their place alongside English Cheddar, and dairy products shipped to market by rail rather than horse and wagon.

As radical and far-reaching as these changes were during this time, they, in turn, would be superseded in the early years of the twentieth century by new advancements in mechanical and food technology (pasteurization, homogenization,

.2752/175174412X13233545145426
s available directly from the
ers. Photocopying permitted by
only © Association for the Study of
d Society 2012

mechanical packaging, chlorofluorocarbon refrigeration, process cheese) and by changes in business organization and advertising. The close of this period would witness the diminishment of the small, independent, fluid milk, butter and cheese producers and the beginning of their absorption into large conglomerates. It would see the symbiotic relationship between dairy producers and distributors replaced by the corporate control of all facets of production and distribution. The last half of the nineteenth century, then, would serve as a crucial bridge between the dairy industry's pastoral and modern periods.[1]

While social histories have been written concerning the impact of dairy industrialization upon farm families during the second half of the nineteenth century, and while there also exist a number of histories focusing on the technological changes which occurred in the manufacture of milk, cheese and butter during this time, there are few detailed, critical histories exploring the interplay of technology upon farm family culture and of American culture upon dairy manufacturing. Moreover, those social histories which do exist treat the cheese industry as a unified whole. In fact, some individual cheeses, due to their particular nature, interacted with technology and with society in unique ways.[2]

This detailed, critical examination of the historical development of one dairy product—cream cheese—brings into sharp relief the salient technological and cultural changes that occurred in the second half of the nineteenth century and their effect upon the dairy industry. In addition, it highlights those changes in the dairy industry that, in turn, acted upon American culture. It examines the particular nature of cream cheese as a symbol of luxury during the "Gilded Age," and considers how its unique physical properties as a highly perishable dairy product influenced its production and distribution. Finally, as changes in technology and production are inextricably intertwined with the specific individuals who create, develop, introduce and market them, the critical role played by a key innovator in the early manufacture of cream cheese will also be examined.

Cream cheese, like most food products, was not invented but, rather, developed over time. Its roots—insofar as its history in America is concerned—can be found in England during the Tudor Era (1485–1603), when the English upper class enjoyed a dish called junket, consisting of pure cream curdled with rennet (the dried fourth stomach of a young, un-weaned calf), sweetened with sugar and flavored with rosewater. Soon, thereafter, in the early 1700s, cream cheeses made from cream or from whole milk mixed with cream (such as Stilton) were found in English counties. The English colonists to America brought with them a taste for these cheeses and the knowledge of how to make them.[3]

A number of different recipes both for English Stilton and cream cheese can be found in American books and periodicals beginning in the mid-eighteenth century. The 1769 *Pennsylvania Gazette*, for example, carried a recipe for cream cheese in which rennet was added to whole milk, and the curds then cured (ripened) for four to five days. *The Plough Boy* journal carried in 1821 a recipe for Pine-Apple Cheese, "also called Cream Cheese," in which cream was mixed with new milk, rennet added, and the cheese cured for six weeks. The *Encyclopaedia Americana* of 1831 offered the simplest recipe for making cream cheese: "…putting cream into a linen bag, and leaving it there till it becomes solid." An early American cookbook, Eliza Leslie's *Directions for Cookery in its Various Branches* (1837) provided a recipe for Stilton cheese, using milk, cream and rennet water, which was cured for two to three months. Leslie noted: "Cream cheeses (as they are generally called) may be made in this manner." Her 1844 edition included a specific recipe for cream cheese, again using milk, cream and rennet water, now with a curing time of four to five days. The cream cheese recipe in *Lady's Home Magazine* of 1857 was similar, but its curing time was only for a day or two.[4] Note the progressively shorter curing time as the years went by, which would later become a signature feature of American cream cheese makers.

The majority of these recipes for the making of cream cheeses originated in and around Philadelphia, which had gained for itself, by the early nineteenth century, a reputation for this cheese. An 1822–23 travelogue of a visit to Columbia called its cream cheese: "...fresh and well made, as if from Philadelphia," and an 1835 tour through Pennsylvania, in praising the food products of Philadelphia, singled out its cream cheese for attention, noting that it was produced on dairy farms and families near the city. This was echoed by the 1844 *Farmer's Encyclopaedia*, which stated: "Excellent cream cheeses [made from cream exposed to the air for three to four days] are supplied to the Philadelphia market by the neighboring Pennsylvania farmers. They are round, generally from six to ten inches in diameter, and about one inch thick."[5]

The highly perishable nature of these cream cheeses helps explain why they were initially confined to the Philadelphia area. Refrigeration, even by ice, was not yet available, and even the fastest (and most expensive) stage-wagon in the early nineteenth century took a day and a half to travel from Philadelphia to New York. That would change with the introduction and development of steamship and railroad service between Philadelphia and New York City (1832–1850). In 1841, for example, Sam Ward, in a letter to Henry Wadsworth Longfellow, mentioned that he had recently been in Philadelphia, but not for the "creamcheese." Six years later, however, *The Monthly Journal of Agriculture* noted that cream cheese (the size "about that of the bottom of a dinner-plate, and about an inch or a little more thick") originally to be found only in the Philadelphia market was arriving in New York markets as well. *Spirit of the Times*, a weekly New York City newspaper, carried an advertisement in 1848 for a Manhattan grocery store selling "Philadelphia Cream Cheeses," and in 1867, a chronicler of New York's markets noted that while cream cheese was found particularly in Philadelphia, it was sometimes sold in the markets of New York.[6]

FOOD,
CULTURE &
SOCIETY

VOLUME 15

ISSUE 2

JUNE 2012

While Philadelphia had achieved, by the early nineteenth century, a reputation for fine cream cheeses, it was not the sole location where cream cheeses were being made. New York monthly publications for farmers, such as *The Plough Boy* (1821), *The Cultivator* (1844), *The Monthly Journal of Agriculture* (1847), and *The Working Farmer* (1857) all carried recipes for cream cheese, as did recipe books published in New York in the early 1870s.[7] But for both the New York and Pennsylvania farmers, cream cheese production was still quite limited, insofar as it was being made by individuals on their farms in one-room structures, was an expensive product for consumers to buy, and was highly perishable, thus making it difficult to transport.[8]

By 1880, however, that situation would change; due, in part, to the efforts of William A. Lawrence. His success can be attributed to his willingness and ability to make good use of the opportunities that came his way, but it was also due to the technological advancements that transformed dairying; demographic shifts in urban populations; and changing consumer tastes that made those opportunities possible. He was, as will shortly be demonstrated, "a necessary link in the chain of progressive events."[9]

William Alfred Lawrence (1842–1911) was born in the town of Florida, Orange County, NY, about 65 miles north of New York City. His father worked as a carpenter, farmer and sawmill owner. In the late 1840s, the family left New York and moved to a farm in Michigan; following his father's death, however, William and the family returned to Orange County in 1852.[10] Lawrence, as a young man, was a farm laborer. By 1860 he worked for a Chester, NY, farmer, James Holbert, an elderly widower with two daughters. Lawrence probably would have spent his entire life as a farm hand, but when he was nineteen, an event occurred that would change the course of his life: in 1861 he married Holbert's daughter, Susan Theresa (1834–1871). Over the next ten years, he took over and then inherited their family farm.[11]

In 1862, Lawrence began to manufacture cheese—probably Cheddar—on the farm.[12] His cheese-making operation would have been the same as that of the Philadelphia farmers and the New York dairymen around him. The American farmers' cooperative system of making butter and cheese, whereby local farmers brought their milk to a single facility for production, was only a decade old when Lawrence began his manufacturing, and there were probably less than fifty such "factories," as they were soon to be called, in the entire state of New York at that time.[13] Thus, the quantities that Lawrence produced were, in all probability, small.

Lawrence's cheese production would also have been small, as it was more economically feasible in the 1860s for New York farmers to sell liquid milk rather than turn it into cheese. This had been the case for two decades. In 1841, a New York and Erie Railroad line had been constructed through Orange County (a station was built that year in Chester), and dairy farmers quickly discovered that they could get better prices for shipping their fluid milk to New York City rather than making it into butter and cheese. Though refrigerated railroad cars would not come into use in New York until the early 1900s, these farmers, by 1842, had solved the problem of shipping by rail during hot summer months by first cooling the milk in springs of water. (By the 1860s, the harvesting and storing of ice had been perfected and the milk was now cooled in icehouses). "In less than two years," wrote a New York reporter, "there was scarcely a farmer within reach of the railroad who did not ship his milk to New York." Given that it took, on average, ten pounds of milk to make one pound of cheese, it was not yet economically feasible in the 1860s for a farm family to concentrate all its dairy resources on cheese making. In 1865, a number of Orange County cheese factories still continued to ship the bulk of their milk and cream to the New York markets.[14]

In the early 1870s, however, the situation had changed and Lawrence made what would be a second, fortuitous decision: to leave farming behind and to go into the factory production of Neufchâtel. According to Lawrence, a Frenchman (identified by his son in 1911 as J.B. Colas) had come to Orange County and manufactured Neufchâtel but was unable to make a successful business of producing it. Lawrence bought him out and took over the business in 1873.[15]

Lawrence did so because, by this time, several factors had made it increasingly clear to New York dairy farmers that cheese could compete with the fluid milk market. First, were the economic advantages of making cheese through the factory system. Salt, bandages (wrappings), coloring and boxes could be ordered in bulk, and fewer employees were needed to produce great quantities of cheese. In addition, the standardized manufacturing techniques of the factory reduced the varied quality of "workmanship of risk" by the individual artisan, with the "workmanship of certainty." As a result, spoilage was reduced. Moreover, cheese brokers were willing to pay a little more to the factory for the ease of only having to travel and contract with one supplier rather than going from farm to farm. All these savings resulted in a gain of one or two cents per pound over cheese made on the family farm. As even the smallest of factories was manufacturing thousands of pounds of cheese per year, the profit was considerable.[16]

A second factor contributing to the rise of cheese production at this time was the rise of consumer demand, both domestic and foreign. In 1866, the American Dairymen's Association had sent to England the American dairy expert X.A. Willard, to explore the possibilities of export. By the early 1870s, more than 63 million pounds of cheese were being shipped overseas—the majority of it from New York— representing almost a ten-fold increase from a decade earlier. Though the initial impetus to seek new cheese markets was probably fueled by over-production (a common problem in the early years of mass production) there were other factors which continued to sustain the English market through the 1870s and early 1880s: the abolition of Great Britain's duty on cheese (1859); the high quality and lower prices of American cheese; and the development of ice refrigeration on steamships which reduced the amount of spoilage. Thus, between 1862 and 1865, almost four hundred new cheese factories were started in New York, a number that doubled by 1870.[17] Within the United States, there was also at this time a rising demand for all dairy products on the part of city dwellers. In the years following the Civil War, as the rural population of the United States began to decline and the urban population began to rise, fresh food needed to be brought in from the outlying farms in increasing quantities.[18]

Lawrence's decision to go into the factory production of a specific cheese, Neufchâtel, was also influenced by his time. Domestically, by the early 1870s, there was an increasing demand among a rising American upper-middle class, for "fancy cheese." This referred both to English cheese made from cream (Stilton and Cream Cheddar) and cheese whose origin was in France (Brie, D'Isigny, Camembert, Gruyère, and Neufchâtel). While, as noted above, America's earliest cuisine was based on English cooking, the beginning of the nineteenth century witnessed a fascination among the upper class with French cuisine. In 1828, Louis Eustache

FOOD,
CULTURE &
SOCIETY

VOLUME 15

ISSUE 2

JUNE 2012

Ude's *The French Cook* was published in Philadelphia, followed by other books on French cookery. In the early 1870s, émigrés fleeing the Franco-Prussian War (1870–1871) came to New York and opened up French restaurants. French cheeses thus increasingly found their way onto the menus of elegant restaurants and hotels. They were also found in upper-middle class home entertaining guides as Americans, during this period, began to engage in "pecuniary emulation: spending money to mimic the habits of wealthier people."[19]

American cheese makers were quick to meet the demand for these fancy French cheeses. Though evidence of Neufchâtel cheese-making in America is found in 1867, it seems to have been made in limited quantities. By 1873, however, a farm journal noted: "The New York market is now pretty well supplied with home-made Neufchâtel cheese from German dairies in New Jersey." Given the perishable nature of the French Neufchâtel, it is highly unlikely that American cheese makers in the 1860s and 1870s were creating their version of Neufchâtel based on the taste of imported samples. Rather, they simply sought to create a rich, soft cheese that could be molded into a cylinder, one of Neufchâtel's signature forms.[20]

(American) Neufchâtel was thus made as follows: rennet was used to curdle whole or skim milk. The curds were then poured into cotton bags that were carefully pressed to drain off the excess liquid (whey). Salt was added and the mixture then formed into small cylinders to be wrapped and shipped. There were also critical aspects of temperature, quality of rennet, firmness of curd, amount of pressing weight, proportion of salt, quality of the initial milk, etc. which had to be carefully followed and which constituted the craft of nineteenth-century cheese making. The basic recipe, however, was essentially the same as the cream cheeses that American farmers had been previously making in Philadelphia and in New York State.[21] Until it was regulated in 1907, any type of whole or skim milk soft cheese that was rolled into cylinders was known as Neufchâtel.[22]

The American Neufchâtel manufacturers also sought to speed the production time, skipping the French method of curing the cheese for weeks in favor of shipping it out for consumption as soon as it was made. In addition, to be more cost-efficient, they often used a reduced-fat base for their cheese. Cream was first separated from the whole milk and used for making butter, while the remaining skim milk was used for making the Neufchâtel. If a richer Neufchâtel was desired, inexpensive lard could be added to the skim milk mixture to replace the cream that had been removed. This practice was common in the 1880s, until regulations arose which banned the manufacture of "filled cheese." Speed of production and increased profit, rather than quality, drove these fancy cheese makers, which was emblematic of industry, in general, during the second half of the nineteenth century.[23]

Lawrence's entry into manufacturing was made possible by the existence, at this time, of equipment for the mass production of cheese: milk testers, heating vats, curd knives, gang presses capable of holding two dozen cheeses at one time, iron-clad milk cans for transporting the milk from farm to factory, and economical steam boilers and engines to power the mechanized operation. Just as American dairy farmers had, in previous years, recourse to various printed works on cheese making, so too, now, detailed manuals for the factory production of cheese were published. The report of the New York State Cheese Manufacturers' Association (1864), followed by works such as X.A. Willard's *Practical Dairy Husbandry* (1872) and L.B. Arnold's *American Dairying* (1876), included plans for the layout of the cheese factory, discussions of the pros and cons of the newly-introduced cheese factory equipment, and the temperatures at which the milk was to be heated and the cheese cured.[24]

Both the equipment for handling large quantities of cheese and the availability of technical instructions helped reduce huffing (bloating), leakiness, and skippers (insects), which resulted in unusable products. They helped create a uniform product not just on the part of the local factory but throughout the state. Though experienced cheese makers were still necessary, not everyone who worked in the production of cheese now needed to be an artisan. The craft of cheese making in the pastoral period, once part of the knowledge base of all dairy farm households, especially of women, now slowly began to be in the hands first of men and then of "specialists." By the modern period, this would result in chemists and food technicians in charge of cheese production and the banishment of farmers from this endeavor.[25]

Lawrence's production of Neufchâtel was small the first year. Each cake of Neufchâtel was first rolled in manila tissue paper to hold its shape. (By 1880, white parchment paper was utilized).[26] Then, the wrapped cheeses were packed in used starch, soap or raisin boxes that were obtained from grocers. Each box held between 112 and 248 cakes, with straw stuffed into the empty spaces to protect the cheeses from damage during transportation. Soon, after a period of experimentation, uniform boxes were manufactured which held one hundred rolls. Two boxes of Neufchâtel were produced a day, utilizing no more than two hundred quarts of cream.[27]

Some time after he acquired the Neufchâtel business (1873), Lawrence was approached by the New York grocery firm, Park & Tilford, which *The New York Times* called, "…the very *beau ideal* of what a really first class grocery store should be." The owners, according to Lawrence, told him that they were looking to put a richer and more delicate cheese on the market. Lawrence studied the subject for some time and then, in essence, made Neufchâtel with cream added to it. Whole milk was curdled using rennet and the curd poured into cotton bags that were carefully pressed to drain off the excess whey. Now cream, together with salt, was added to the mixture, which was pressed and wrapped in manila tissue paper. The primary difference between American Neufchâtel and this new product was thus in the percentage of fat; Neufchâtel having about 4 percent fat and this cheese about 6 percent. Lawrence called his product, "Cream Cheese." (The amount of milk fat would rise over the years, so that, by the 1920s, cream cheese consisted of a 33 percent milk fat content, resulting in a sweeter and smoother cheese very different from Lawrence's original.)[28]

Unlike Neufchâtel, which was produced in cylinder molds, Lawrence's cream cheese was manufactured in square shape. At this time, cheese makers in New York were beginning to move away from manufacturing round cheeses such as Cheddar, due to the expense involved in the construction of the round wooden hoops

FOOD, CULTURE & SOCIETY

VOLUME 15

ISSUE 2

JUNE 2012

used as molds, and experimenting instead with square and rectangular cheeses whose molds were more economical to make. In addition, more square and rectangular cheeses than round ones could be packed into shipping boxes. Whereas, in the pastoral period, a difference in shape would not be a significant economic issue given the small quantities produced, now, as mass production entered the cheese-making enterprise, the ability to trim costs on each item produced became a significant factor. Beginning at this time, the economics of mass production altered the traditional shape of cheese. It presaged the modern period when not just the shape but the organic nature of cheese would be changed through the invention of process cheese created to lengthen shelf life and reduce spoilage.[29]

Lawrence faced a number of risks in going into the mass production of cream cheese. First were the general problems associated with the cheese factory. The quality of the milk delivered could vary greatly from farmer to farmer based on the feed that the cows received; inclement weather could slow down the morning or evening delivery of milk, resulting in spoilage; poor cleaning of the farmers' milk cans and pails could contaminate a load of milk; and unscrupulous suppliers could water down the milk they delivered. Second were the problems associated specifically with the manufacture of cream cheese. Here, Lawrence faced the same problems that had confronted the makers of cream cheeses in the Philadelphia area during the first half of the eighteenth century. Cream cheese was expensive to make because it required additional ingredients (cream) and was more complicated to manufacture. (The curd needed to be chilled before it was pressed to reduce the amount of fat that might be lost). It was not easy to mold and wrap given its soft form. In addition, though uniformity of product helped to reduce spoilage, nonetheless, cream cheese was a highly perishable product due to its higher water content. This meant that the lucrative English market would not be available for cream cheese export. Though ice refrigeration was available on some steamships to Great Britain, it still took time to ship the cheese to New York City for loading and then, on the other side of the Atlantic, to ship it from port to market. Only hard cheeses could withstand the length of the journey.[30] (The perishable nature of cream cheese also explains why Wisconsin cheese makers did not produce the "fancy cheeses." The shipping time to the Eastern seaboard—both for New York and New England consumption as well as for British export—while not a factor for their American, Edam, Gouda and Swiss cheese, was a deciding factor for the fresher cheeses).

Yet Lawrence already had some experience in running a cheese factory and working with a soft, perishable cheese. In addition, cream cheese would fetch a good price as a "fancy cheese," and he already had a retailer willing to purchase the product. Lawrence's move into this market would prove to be a shrewd one, as the price for cream cheese would, within ten year's time, overshadow the other "fancy cheeses." In 1889 Muenster sold for 13 cents a pound, Domestic Swiss for 13 to 15 cents a pound, Parmesan for 23 cents a pound, while cream cheese sold for 30 cents a pound.[31]

By the mid-1870s, the economic advantages of Neufchâtel and cream cheese were evident to other Orange County dairymen.[32] One of them was Charles H.

Green, another Chester farmer. Green (1844–1918) was the son of a North Fork, Long Island, farmer who had migrated by 1844 to Quincy, Illinois, where Charles was born. In 1851–1852 his father moved the family back to New York, and they settled on a large farm in Chester where Charles worked as a farm laborer until at least 1870. By 1875, he was involved in the creamery business on his father's farm, quite possibly manufacturing Neufchâtel.[33] By 1880, he was manufacturing cream cheese. In 1883, Green received an award from the New York State Agricultural Society for his Neufchâtel cheese. That year, he was manufacturing about three thousand packages of 5 oz. Neufchâtel cheese a day. In 1893, under his World Brand and Globe Brand labels, he produced 680,312 pounds of cheese (five times the amount produced by Lawrence). Yet, in 1894, Green left the cheese manufacturing business for unknown reasons.[34]

Green's involvement in cream cheese manufacturing is mentioned here as cream cheese histories written since 1980 state that Lawrence did not buy a Neufchâtel business, but rather stole the formula for Neufchâtel from Green. These accounts, told more than one hundred years after the facts and based on unsubstantiated "local lore," claim that Green, in the 1870s, brought a Swiss maker of cheese to Chester to make Neufchâtel or that a friend of Green's, from Switzerland, brought along the recipe. Lawrence, who was said to be either a neighbor or a young stable hand (!) of Green's, was eavesdropping through a window and overheard them discussing the formula. He went home, doubled (perhaps accidentally) the amount of cream used in the Neufchâtel formula and created cream cheese.[35] (The accidental element is particularly unbelievable as any cheese maker would know that increased cream yields increased richness.) Note, however, that these tales told by Lawrence's detractors a hundred years later still confirm the central parts of Lawrence's story: that the formula for Neufchâtel was brought to the Chester area by a foreign cheese maker; that he derived cream cheese from Neufchâtel; and that he was the first to manufacture it.[36]

In 1877, in order to distinguish his cheese products from his competitors, Lawrence created a brand consisting of the silhouette of a cow facing left, next to the words, "Neufchâtel & Cream Cheese." (This was probably so he could use the same brand for both types of cheese.) He stenciled his brand in black ink on the sides of the boxes.[37]

Mass manufacturing had now made branding necessary, as a uniform technology created relatively little difference between products.[38] Within two decades, as the

FOOD,
CULTURE &
SOCIETY

VOLUME 15

ISSUE 2

JUNE 2012

Fig 1: America's First Brand of Cream Cheese—William A. Lawrence's Neufchatel and Cream Cheese Trade Mark, 1881 (in use from 1877)
Source: Neufchatel and Cream Cheese Trade Mark from Lawrence, W.A. (1881) *Trade-Mark for Cheese*. Washington, DC: US Patent Office.

modern period began, the importance of the brand would almost completely overshadow the quality of the product.

In the late 1870s, Lawrence decided to build a larger facility for Neufchâtel and cream cheese production and sought additional capital to do so. (The cost of setting up a small cheese factory in 1875 was estimated to be between $2,000 and $5,000, not including the costs of cows, land, barn and feed).[39] He approached a wealthy Chester merchant, Samuel Satterly Durland (1840–1916), to help him out. Durland was the son of a Chester farmer, descended from Dutch settlers who had come to New York in the 1600s. At age twenty-one, Durland had left the family's farm for a brief period and worked in a general merchandise store in Warwick, NY. Upon his return to Chester, he went into the grocery business (J & SS Durland) with his half-brother, Joseph. By 1872, he had sold out his share and returned to the family farm.[40]

In 1879, Durland entered into partnership with Lawrence to operate a Neufchâtel and cream cheese factory in Chester. It seems that Lawrence handled the cheese-making operations while Durland served as the bookkeeper for the operation. They used a building on Durland's farm that abutted a creek, which provided ice in the winter to help cool the milk, as well as a place to dispose of the whey drained from the curds. In addition, it had plenty of land around it for expansion. Though, in 1880, Lawrence had no cows on his farm—his land being given over to grow onions and potatoes—Durland did have several dozen cows on his, which would have helped provide some of the milk used in the cheese manufacture.[41]

The location of Lawrence and Durland's factory was also chosen for its proximity to both the road from Chester and the road to Goshen. This made it possible for local farmers to deliver milk easily. In addition, the New York and Erie Railroad station was close by for shipping the cheese to New York City. The choice to locate the factory at a strategic crossroad was one that was followed during this time by cheese manufacturers throughout the state, altering the landscape of the farm town. Now, in addition to the church and schoolhouse, the factory was a standard landmark.[42]

A few years after the factory was built, Lawrence constructed a large home on the premises—a vestige of the pastoral period, when cheese production took place on the family farm rather than at factories located some distance away. Although it was less than twenty years since Lawrence had begun making cheese, that time, already, seemed very far away, indeed.

Acknowledgments

The quote in the title of this article is taken from J. Wilson (1842) *The Recreations of Christopher North*, p. 33. My thanks to the following individuals for their research help: Becky Tousey, Chief Archivist, Global Corporate Affairs, Kraft Foods Inc., Morton Grove, IL; Sally Nakanishi, HUC-JIR Library, Los Angeles; Cindy Stark, NY State Library, Albany; the records staff at the Otsego Court House, Cooperstown, NY; Dianne Ermilio, Mid-Atlantic Region, National Archives and Records Administration, Philadelphia; Orange County Genealogical Society, Goshen, NY; Jim Nelson, Monroe Historical Society, Monroe, NY; William Lawrence's great grandchildren, Harriet McManus and Ted Talmadge; and especially Clifton Patrick, Chester, NY Town Historian. Finally, my thanks to my wife, Susan, for her loving support so I could go back in time and wander, for a while, in the farm fields and cheese factories of nineteenth-century America.

Jeffrey A. Marx is a visiting lecturer at Hebrew Union College-Jewish Institute of Religion in Los Angeles. He is the author of, "Give Me My Childhood Again: The Grand Street Boys' Association 1915–1945" (American Jewish Archives, 1991) and "Jewish Agricultural Colonies in Kansas" (*Avotaynu*, 2010). He is currently working on a history of the Breakstone Brothers Dairy of New York. 1448 18th St., Santa Monica, CA 90404, USA (rabjmarx@gmail.com).

Notes

1   Edwards (2006: 38–43); Giedion (1940: 31, 40, 50, 95); Lampard (1963: 126–7, 197–204, 220–1); Levenstein (1988: 29, 37, 42, 43); McIntosh (1995: 92); Mott (1897); Wilde (1988: 92–3).

2   For an overview of the changes that occurred in the second half of the nineteenth century, see Selitzer (1976). For a detailed account, see Lampard (1963) and McMurry (1995).

3   Cooley (1872: 322); Defoe (1724: 283–4); Hickman (1995: 22); Letheby (1872: 33); Mingay (1984: 99); Philp (1870: 171); P.W.H.J. (1872); Weaver (2004: xxxviii, xxxix, 325); M.T. Wilson (1984 [1957]); C. Wilson (2002). Weaver (2004: 325,326) suggests that Dutch colonists may have also brought cream cheese recipes with them to America.

4   *American Farmer* (1825); Eden (2008: 26–7); *Godey's Lady's Book* (1865); *Lady's Home Magazine* (1857:139); Leslie (1837: 391 and 1844: 447–8); Lieber (1831: 488); Monk (1798); *Pennsylvania Gazette* (1769); Stewart (1888: 369–70). Philadelphia was also known for another dairy product called Rahmkasse, produced by German farmers, consisting of curds with cream mixed in. *Phenix Cheese Co. v. S. Ridgway Kennedy, et al.* 5/18/1915, US District Court, Eastern District of PA; Royall (1829: 171); Youman (1872: 126).

5   Duane (1826: 324); Johnson (1844: 317); Letters on Pennsylvania, excerpted from Nicklin (1835).

6   Armstrong (1819: 164); DeVoe (1867: 404); Elliot (1938: 301); *Monthly Journal of Agriculture* (1847); Scharf and Westcott (1884: 2,159, 2,170, 2,183); *Spirit of the Times* (1848). My thanks to Anne Mendelson for pointing out the Sam Ward letter to Longfellow.

7   Allen (1871: 390); Armstrong (1819: 164); Henderson (1870: 58); *Monthly Journal of Agriculture* (1847); *Plough Boy, and Journal of the Board of Agriculture* (1821: 326); Sheldrick (1844); *Working Farmer* (1857).

8   Raguet (1840: 32); Willard (1872: 304).

9   Arnold (1876), commenting on the role that Jesse Williams played in the "creation" of the cheese factory (quoted in Lampard 1963: 93). In the 1880s, Alvah Reynolds would also play a key role in the development of cream cheese, when he wrapped Lawrence's cheese in foil imprinted with his Philadelphia brand and marketed this product throughout New York City. Testimony of Alvah Reynolds, in *International Cheese Company v. Phenix Cheese Company*, 3/26/1906, Supreme Court, Otsego County, NY.

10   *Portrait and Biographical Record of Rockland and Orange Counties, New York* (1895: 793);

FOOD,
CULTURE &
SOCIETY

VOLUME 15

ISSUE 2

JUNE 2012

1850 US Census: Berrien County, MI, "Thomas H. Lawrence"; *Middletown Times Press* (1911). See also the Lawrence Mausoleum, in Warwick, NY.

11 The 1860 US Census shows Lawrence as a farmhand, living on the Holbert farm. According to the 1870 US Census, he was still living on the farm but now owned $4,000 worth of real estate, while his father-in-law was listed as a retired farmer. William and Susan had one son, Theodore F. (1862–1947), who later went into business with his father in the firm, W. A. Lawrence & Son. Following Susan's early death in May 1871, Lawrence married a local widow, Mary (May) Murray. See death records of James Holbert and S. Teresa Holbert, 1871 (copies held by the Chester Historical Society); Holbert, "Little Sister's Quilt" (Textile Collection, Smithsonian National Museum of American History, Washington, DC); Interview with Harriet McManus, Potomac, MD, April 8, 2010; *Portrait and Biographical Record of Rockland and Orange Counties, New York* (1895: 793); 1870, 1910, 1920, 1930 US Census: Orange County, NY, "Theodore Lawrence"; 1880 US Census: Orange County, NY, "Thos. F. Lawrence"; 1860, 1870, 1880, 1900, 1910 US Census: Orange County, NY, "William Lawrence."

12 *Middletown Times Press* (1911); *Portrait and Biographical Record of Rockland and Orange Counties, New York* (1895: 793); Selitzer (1976: 51). See also *International Cheese Company v. Phenix Cheese Company*; testimony of Theodore Lawrence in *Lawrence et al. v. P. E. Sharpless Co.*, 11/17/1911 and 1/25/1912, US Circuit Court, Eastern District PA, DC 637.

13 Though the number of cheese factories in New York would soon radically increase, reaching over four hundred by 1865, an 1871 list of cheese and butter factories in Orange, NY, does not list Lawrence as a manufacturer, suggesting that Lawrence's cheese production was small throughout the 1860s. Bolles (1889: 130, 131); Colby and Williams (1914: 107); Gilbert (1896: 36); Hough (1867: 415); New York State Cheese Manufacturers' Association (1864: 1–33); Selitzer (1976: 67, 69); Stamm (1991: 47); Wickson (1875); Wilde (1988: 90); Willard (1872: 535); 1870, 1880 US Census: Orange County, NY: "William Lawrence." For an excellent account of the factory system, see McMurray (1995: 123–47).

14 Anderson (1953: 37–41, 48–51, 63); Dillon (1941: 2–3); Giedion (1948: 220–2); Hough (1867: 415); Lampard (1963: 127); Mott (1897); New York State Cheese Manufacturers' Association (1864: 8); James Durland in Ruttenber and Clark (1980: 623); Selitzer (1976: 38–9); Willard (1872: 345). It is ironic that James Durland, a Chester farmer, who was one of the earliest farmers to give up cheese production in order to ship milk by train to New York City, would have a son, Samuel, who, nearly forty years later, would give up milk production in order to manufacture cheese with Lawrence.

15 Gilbert (1896: 27); testimony of Theodore Lawrence, in *Lawrence et al. v. P. E. Sharpless Co.* Lawrence's son stated that Lawrence bought the business from Colas in 1862, which cannot be correct. I have been unable to find any record in the US Census of a J.B. Colas or Collas in Orange County, New York, or in the United States from 1850 to 1900. Theodora Talmadge, Lawrence's great-granddaughter, stated, over one hundred years later, that John Roach, a crippled immigrant whom Lawrence had befriended, was the one who gave him the Neufchâtel recipe. Genna (2004: 49); 1880 US Census: Orange County, NY, "John Roach."

16 Bolles (1889: 130, 131); Giedion (1948: 195); Lampard (1963: 94, 97); McMurry (1995: 128, 135–7); Pye (1968: 20–4); Wilde (1988: 72–4).

17 Anderson (1953: 60–1); Bolles (1889: 131–2); Giedion (1948: 215, 219); Gilbert (1896: 19, 20); Lampard (1963: 95, 122); McMurry (1995: 134). The dairy industry was not unique

in its search for overseas markets. "By the mid–1880s producers of farm machinery locomotives, elevators, typewriters, and pharmaceuticals had substantial sales in Europe and elsewhere" Edwards (2006: 47).

18 Anderson (1953: 37); Giedion (1948: 41–2).

19 Edwards (2006: 96–7), paraphrasing Thorstein Veblen's *The Theory of the Leisure Class* (1899). Gilbert (1896: 26, 27); Grimes (2009: 10, 93); Levenstein (1988: 10–19); Smith (2007a: 238); Willard (1872: 303, 478).

20 *American Agriculturist* (1873: 419); Flint (1867: 81); Harland (1871: 268); *Medical Summary* (1885); State Board of Health of Massachusetts (1904: 492); Thom and Fisk (1918: 94); Blake (1870: 210). While the 1865 NY State Census noted that there were (at least) three factories producing French cheese, it did not state which kind. Hough (1867: 415).

21 Michels (1915: 76); *NY State Dairy Commissioner* (1886: 279); Publow (1909: 6–9); Stewart (1888: 340); Stocking (1917: 434–8); US Department of Agriculture (1911: 38–9). For an excellent presentation of the details of nineteenth century cheese making, see Willard (1872). For a presentation of Neufchâtel cheese-making in the early twentieth century, see Matheson and Cammack (1918) and US Department of Agriculture (1918).

22 Emmons and Tuckey (1967: 107); Harland (1871: 268); Richard L. Sweezy's letter to W.A. Lawrence & Son, November 24, 1906, Complainant's Exhibit 17, in *Lawrence et al. v. P. E. Sharpless Co.*; *P.E. Sharpless Co. v. Levin et al*, June T, 1919, C.P. No. 5, No. 2323 in Equity, Philadelphia County; US Department of Agriculture (1910); "Mrs Washington" (1886:256).

23 *American Agriculturist* (1873: 419); Arnold (1876: 334); Edwards (2006: 61); Gilbert (1896: 23, 41–2); NY State Dairy Commissioner (1886: 279–80); Pirtle (1926: 105); VanSlyke and Price (1927: 249); Wickson (1875: 824–5). In 1883, Lawrence's factory would be under investigation for such adulteration. Martin (1884: 266–7); *New York Times* (1883).

24 Arnold (1876: 281–3, 297–300, 305–6, 308–9, 313, and ads at end of book); New York State Cheese Manufacturers' Association (1864: 9–13, 22–24, 29); Wilde (1988: 92–3); Willard (1872: 370–1, 397, 399–404, 406–9). For early examples of farmers' manuals, see Fessenden (1840), Johnson (1844) and NY State Agricultural Society (1859).

25 McMurry (1995: 63, 65, 79–84, 150, 168–71); Monk (1798); *Plough Boy, and Journal of the Board of Agriculture* (1821: 326); Sheldrick (1844); Wickson (1875: 818, 823).

26 Gilbert (1896: 28); Alvah Reynolds testimony, in *International Cheese Company v. Phenix Cheese Company*; testimony of Albert F. Leonhard and Theodore Lawrence, in *Lawrence et al. v. P. E. Sharpless Co.*, 1/25/1912; Martin (1884: 266).

27 Gilbert (1896: 27–9); Lawrence (1881); *Middletown Times Press* (1911).

28 Testimony of William Lawrence and Alvah Reynolds, in *International Cheese Company v. Phenix Cheese Company*; Lundstedt (1954); Matheson and Cammack (1918), ii; Mendelson (2008: 297–8); Publow (1909: 9–10); Scharf (1886: 742); Stocking (1917: 438–40). It is unknown where the manufacturing took place. A 1947 history of Chester stated that Lawrence manufactured Neufchâtel and cream cheese in the cellar of Joseph Durland's store in West Chester. A 2008 article on Lawrence stated that he developed the formula for cream cheese in the basement of his home. Levy (1947: 59); Interview with Ted Talmadge, Chester, NY, June 2010; Patrick (2008).

29 Wilde (1988: 70–1, 142–3); *Middletown Times Press* (1911).

30 Lampard (1963: 98–100); Pecht (1894: lines 41–6); Publow (1909: 9); Thom and Fisk (1918: 108–9).

FOOD,
CULTURE &
SOCIETY

VOLUME 15

ISSUE 2

JUNE 2012

31 Exhibit M, p. 3, in *International Cheese Company v. Phenix Cheese Company*; *Journal of Commerce and Commercial Bulletin* (1889).

32 The Monroe Cheese Company is one example. *Goshen Democrat* (1879); *Journal and Republican* (1874, 1879).

33 Beers (1875: 140); *Cemeteries of Chester, New York* (1977: 45); Charles H. Green obituary in untitled Chester newspaper dated December 1918 (Chester Historical Society); Gravestone of Huldah Board Green, Chester Cemetery; Village of Chester Centennial Commission (1992: 150); 1860, 1870 US Census: Orange County, NY: "Charles Green." Though the Village of Chester Centennial Journal Committee stated that Green's cream cheese and Neufchâtel manufacturing could be dated to the 1860s, this is not borne out by his listed profession in the 1860 and 1870 US Census of New York. I have been unable to locate any evidence that dates Green's cheese-making before 1875.

34 Testimony of Alvah Reynolds, in *International Cheese Company v. Phenix Cheese Company*; Martin (1884: 266); New York State Agricultural Society (1889); NY State Department of Agriculture (1894: 665; 1895: 1179); H. Predmore's Genealogy Files, 1955–1978 (Goshen, NY: Orange County Genealogical Society); Village of Chester Centennial Commission (1992: 150); 1880, 1900, 1910 US Census: Orange County, NY: "Charles Green."

35 Genna (2004: 49); Interview with Clifton Patrick, Chester, NY, May 2010; Patrick (2008); H. Predmore's Genealogy Files, 1955–1978 (Goshen, NY: Orange County Genealogical Society); Letter from Mrs. Florence C. Salisbury, 11/17/1984 and from Mrs. Myrtle Edwards, 5/8/1985 quoted in Stamm (1991: 181); L.W. White note 3/5/1992 (Chester Historical Society). Unfortunately, this legend can now be found in authoritative works on food and on dozens of food sites on the internet. See, for example, Allen (2007), and Marks (2010: 109, 110).

36 Lawrence's claims as to when he manufactured Neufchâtel and cream cheese must be weighed carefully. In general, the later his statements, the earlier the year that he claimed he manufactured the cheese. In 1881, he stated that he created a brand for his Neufchâtel cheese in 1877. In 1895, he stated that he bought the Neufchâtel business in 1873. In 1911, his son, Theodore, stated that his father had bought the business in 1862. The same thing is true for his statements concerning his cream cheese manufacture. In 1881, he stated that he created a brand for his cream cheese in 1877. In 1895, he stated that sometime after 1873 he created cream cheese. In 1905, he stated that in 1872 he created cream cheese. Though there is no evidence to corroborate Lawrence's assertion that he began production of Neufchâtel and cream cheese in or before 1872–73, I believe it is reasonable to state that Lawrence was making Neufchâtel by 1875 (when his business was listed as "Cheese Manufactory") and was the first to manufacture cream cheese by 1877 (as stated in his 1881 trademark registration). Beers (1875: 14); Gilbert (1896: 27); *Goshen Democrat* (1880); testimony of William Lawrence and Alvah Reynolds in *International Cheese Company v. Phenix Cheese Company*; Lawrence (1881); testimony of Theodore Lawrence, in *Lawrence et al. v. P. E. Sharpless Co.*, 11/17/1911; *Middletown Times Press* (1911); White (1880).

37 Lawrence (1881).

38 Giedion (1948: 132–3); Levenstein (1988: 35).

39 Lampard (1963: 106–8); Stewart (1888: 312–13); Wickson (1875: 818); Willard (1872: 371).

40 Lathrop (1903, plates 19, 20); McCready (1898: 73–4); *Middletown Press* (1890?); Nikkel (1985: 14, 23); Predmore (1965: 208); Reynolds (1913: 189); Ruttenber and Clark (1980:

624); 1850, 1880, 1900, 1910 US Census: Orange County, NY: "Samuel Durland"; 1870 US Census: Orange County, NY, "SS Durland"; 1880, 1900 US Census: Orange County, NY: "William Lawrence." See also the gravestone of James and Amelia Durland, at Chester Cemetery, Chester, NY.

41 Beers (1875: 140); Chester, NY, Fire Insurance Map (Sanborn Map Co. 1894); the personal recollections of G.S. Banker, in Durland (1901); Gilbert (1896: 27); Lathrop (1903, plates 19, 20); testimony of Theodore Lawrence, in *Lawrence et al. v. P. E. Sharpless Co.*, 1/25/1912; McCready (1898: 73-4); Patrick (2008); Ruttenber and Clark (1980: 623); Village of Chester Centennial Commission (1992: 149); 1880 US Census, Non-Population Schedules: Orange County, NY, "Samuel Durland" and "William Lawrence"; 1910 US Census: Orange County, NY: "Samuel Durland" and "William Lawrence." Though B.D. Gilbert reported (in 1896) that Lawrence purchased the Neufchâtel business with a partner in 1873, Durland stated (in 1898) that the partnership was not formed until 1879. Lawrence's son, Theodore, stated (in 1912) that the partnership started between 1880–85. I suspect that B.D. Gilbert, in his 1895 interview with Lawrence, wrongly assumed that Lawrence had, from the beginning, operated with his current partner. Lawrence's son, Theodore, stated (in 1912) that Durland only drew a salary and did not receive any profits from the business, which does not seem likely, especially as the firm was called, "Lawrence & Durland" and was located on Durland's farm. It is more likely that Durland simply received a salary as bookkeeper when he was bought out by Lawrence in 1895.

42 Chester, NY, Fire Insurance Map (Sanborn Map Co. 1894); McMurry (1995: 152–3); *Portrait and Biographical Record of Rockland and Orange Counties, New York* (1895: 793).

References

Allen, G. 2007. Cream Cheese. In A.T. Smith (ed.) *The Oxford Companion to American Food and Drink*. New York: Oxford University Press: 175–6.

Allen, R.L. 1871. *New American Farm Book* (revised by L.F. Allen). New York: Orange Judd and Co.

American Agriculturist. 1873. Neufchâtel Cheese. *American Agriculturist* 32(11): 419.

American Farmer, The. 1825. For Making Cream Cheese. *American Farmer* 7(18): 148.

Anderson, O.E. 1953. *Refrigeration in America: A History of New Technology and its Impact*. Princeton, NJ: Princeton University Press.

Armstrong, J. 1819. *A Treatise on Agriculture; Comprising a Concise History of its Origin and Progress, the Present Condition of the Art, Abroad and at Home, and the Theory and Practice of Husbandry Which Have Arisen Out of the Present State of Philosophical Attainments in Europe*. Albany, NY: J. Buel.

Arnold, L.B. 1876. *American Dairying: A Manual for Butter and Cheese Makers*. Rochester, NY: Rural Home Publishing Co.

Beers, F.W. 1875. *County Atlas of Orange, New York, 1875*. Chicago, IL: Andreas Baskin & Burr.

Blake, W.P. (ed.). 1870. *Reports of the US Commissioners to the Paris Universal Exposition, 1867*. Vol. 1. Washington, DC: Government Printing Office.

Bolles, A.S. 1889. *Industrial History of the United States*. Norwich: The Henry Bill Publishing Co.

Cemeteries of Chester, New York. 1977. Monroe, NY: Library Research Associates.

Colby, F.M. and Williams, T. (eds.). 1914. *The New International Encyclopeadia*, Vol. V. New

FOOD,
CULTURE &
SOCIETY

VOLUME 15

ISSUE 2

JUNE 2012

York: Dodd, Mead and Co.

Cooley, A.J. 1872. *Cooley's Cyclopaedia of Practical Receipts*. London: J&A Churchill.

Defoe, D. 1724. *A Tour Through England and Wales: Divided into Circuits or Journies: Vol. 1*. New York: E.P. Dutton & Co. Inc.

DeVoe, T.F. 1867. *The Market Assistant, Containing a Brief Description of Every Article of Human Food Sold in the Public Markets of the Cities of New York, Boston, Philadelphia and Brooklyn*. New York: Riverside Press.

Dillon, J.J. 1941. *Seven Decades of Milk*. New York: Orange Judd Publishing Co., Inc.

Duane, W. 1826. *A Visit to Colombia, in the Years 1822 & 1823, by Laguayra and Caracas, Over the Cordillera to Bogota, and thence by the Magdalena to Cartagena*. Philadelphia, PA: Thomas H. Palmer.

Durland, F. 1901. *Recollections of Early Chester*. Chester, NY: Chester Historical Society.

Eden, T. 2008. *The Early American Table: Food and Society in the New World*. DeKalb, IL: Northern Illinois University Press.

Edwards, R. 2006. *New Spirits: Americans in the Gilded Age, 1865–1905*. New York: Oxford University Press.

Elliot, M.H. 1938. *Uncle Sam Ward and His Circle*. New York: Macmillan.

Emmons, D.B. and Tuckey, S.L. 1967. *Cottage Cheese and Other Cultured Milk Products*. New York: Chas. Pfizer & Co., Inc.

Fessenden, T.G. 1840. *The Complete Farmer and Rural Economist; Containing a Compendious Epitome of the Most Important Branches of Agricultural and Rural Economy*. Philadelphia, PA: Thomas, Cowperthwaite, & Co.

Flint, A. 1867. *The Physiology of Man; Designed to Represent the Existing State of Physiological Science as Applied to the Functions of the Human Body*. New York: D. Appleton & Co.

Genna, M.E. 2004. Chester's Own Cheese. *The Valley Table*. No. 23 (March–May): 49–50.

Giedion, S. 1948. *Mechanization Takes Command: A Contribution to Anonymous History*. New York: Oxford University Press.

Gilbert, B.D. 1896. *The Cheese Industry of the State of New York*. US Department of Agriculture Bulletin No. 15. Dairy No. 6. Washington, DC: Government Printing Office.

Godey's Lady's Book. 1865. Cream Cheese. *Godey's Lady's Book* 52 (April): 369.

Goshen Democrat. 1879. No Title. April 24. Monroe Cheese Co. File, Monroe Historical Society.

Goshen Democrat. 1880. No Title. February 5. Monroe Cheese Co. File, Monroe Historical Society.

Grimes, W. 2009. *Appetite City: A Culinary History of New York*. New York: North Point Press.

Harland, M. 1871. *Common Sense in the Household: A Manual of Practical Housewifery*. New York: Charles Scribner & Co.

Henderson, W.A. 1870. *How to Cook, Carve and Eat; or Wholesome Food, and How to Prepare it for the Table*. New York: Leavitt & Allen Bro's.

Hickman, T. 1995. *The History of Stilton Cheese*. Stroud: Alan Sutton Publishing Ltd.

Hough, F.B. (ed.). 1867. *Census of the State of New York 1865*. Albany, NY: Charles VanBenthuysen and Sons.

Johnson, C.W. 1844. *The Farmer's Encyclopaedia, and Dictionary of Rural Affairs, Embracing All the Most Recent Discoveries in Agricultural Chemistry*. Philadelphia, PA: Gouverneur Emerson, Carey and Hart.

Journal and Republican. 1874. Cheese. *Journal and Republican*, April 22, p. 1.

Journal and Republican. 1879. Making Cream Cheese. *Journal and Republican*, May 28, p. 1.

Journal of Commerce and Commercial Bulletin. 1889. May 20.

Lady's Home Magazine, The. 1857. Cream Cheese. *Lady's Home Magazine* 10 (September): 139.

Lampard, E. E. 1963. *The Rise of the Dairy Industry in Wisconsin: A Study in Agricultural Change 1820–1920*. Madison, WI: The State Historical Society of Wisconsin.

Lathrop, J.M. 1903. *Atlas of Orange County, New York*. Philadelphia, PA: A.H. Mueller & Co.

Lawrence, W.A. 1881. *Trademark for Cheese*. #8,147. Washington, DC: US Patent Office.

Leslie, E. 1837. *Directions for Cookery in its Various Branches*. Philadelphia, PA: E.L. Carey & A. Hart.

Leslie, E. 1844. *Directions for Cookery in its Various Branches*. Philadelphia, PA: E.L. Carey & A. Hart.

Letheby, H. 1872. *On Food*. New York: William Wood and Co.

Levenstein, H.A. 1988. *Revolution at the Table: The Transformation of the American Diet*. New York: Oxford University Press.

Levy, S.J. 1947. *Chester, NY: A History*. Chester, NY: Chester Chamber of Commerce.

Lieber, F. (ed.). 1831. *Encyclopaedia Americana: A Popular Dictionary of Arts, Sciences, Literature, History, Politics and Biography, Brought Down to the Present Time; Including a Copious Collection of Original Articles in American Biography; on the Basis of the Seventh Edition of the German Conversations-Lexicon: Vol. VIII*. Philadelphia, PA: Carey and Lea.

Lundstedt, E. 1954. Manufacture of Quality Cream Cheese. *Journal of Dairy Science* 37(2): 243–45.

Marks, G. 2010. *Encyclopedia of Jewish Food*. Hoboken, NJ: John Wiley & Sons, Inc.

Martin, E. 1884. Report on the Manufacture of Neufchâtel Cheese and its Adulterations, at the Factories of Charles H. Green, Chester, Orange County, and Lawrence & Durland, Chester, Orange County. In State Board of Health of New York, *Fourth Annual Report of the State Board of Health of New York*. Albany, NY: Weed, Parsons and Co., pp. 266–7.

Matheson, K.J. and Cammack, F.R. 1918. *Neufchâtel and Cream Cheese: Farm Manufacture and Use*. Farmers' Bulletin No. 960. Washington DC: US Department of Agriculture.

McCready, R. H. 1898. *The First Presbyterian Church, Chester, NY, 1798–1898*. Chester, New York.

McIntosh, E. N. 1995. *American Food Habits in Historical Perspective*. Westport, CT: Praeger.

McMurry, S. 1995. *Transforming Rural Life: Dairying Families and Agricultural Change, 1820–1885*. Baltimore, MA: Johns Hopkins University Press.

Medical Summary. 1885. The Genuine Articles. *Medical Summary: A Monthly Journal of Practical Medicine, New Preparations, Etc.* 7(5): 84.

Mendelson, A. 2008. *Milk: The Surprising Story of Milk Through the Ages*. New York: Alfred A. Knopf.

Michels, J. 1915. *Milk and Milk Products in the Home*. Farmingdale, NY: privately published.

Middletown Press (1890?). Chester's Old Store History. W.S. Durland Collection, Chester Historical Society.

Middletown Times Press. 1911. William A. Lawrence Succumbs to Paralysis. March 31.

Mingay, G.E. 1984. The East Midlands. In J. Thirsk (ed.) *The Agrarian History of England and Wales: 1640–1750*, Vol. V i. Cambridge: Cambridge University Press, pp. 89–128.

Monk, J. 1798. Method of Making Stilton Cheese. *The Weekly Magazine of Original Essays, Fugitive Pieces, and Interesting Intelligence* 2(18): 155.

Monthly Journal of Agriculture. 1847. Cream-Cheese—How to Make It. *Monthly Journal of Agriculture* 2(12): 554.

Mott, E. 1897. An Idea Worth Millions. *New York Sun*, November 21.

"Mrs Washington." 1886. *The Unrivalled Cook-Book and Housekeeper's Guide*. New York:

FOOD,
CULTURE &
SOCIETY

VOLUME 15
ISSUE 2
JUNE 2012

Harper & Brothers.

New York State Agricultural Society. 1859. *Transactions of the NY State Agricultural Society. Vol. 18, 1858*. Albany, NY: Charles Van Benthusen.

New York State Agricultural Society. 1889. *Transactions of the NY State Agricultural Society. Vol. 34, 1883–1886*. Albany, NY: The Troy Press Co.

New York State Cheese Manufacturers' Association. 1864. *Extracts From the Report of the New York State Cheese Manufacturers' Association, Rome, NY, January 7, 1864*. Albany, NY: Van Benthuysen's Steam Printing House.

New York State Dairy Commissioner. 1886. *Second Annual Report*. Albany, NY: Weed Parsons and Co.

New York State Dept. of Agriculture. 1894. *Annual Report of the NY State Dept. of Agriculture. 1(1), 1893*. Albany, NY: J.B. Lyon.

New York State Dept. of Agriculture. 1895. *New York State Dept. of Agriculture, 2nd Annual Report, 1894*. Albany, NY: J.B. Lyon.

New York Times, The. 1883. Using Lard Instead of Cream. *New York Times*, December 11, p. 2.

Nicklin, P. 1835. A Pleasant Peregrination through the Prettiest Parts of Pennsylvania. *The Southern Literary Messenger*. 2(1): 445–50.

Nikkel, M.E.J. 1985. *A Record of the Edwards, Durland and Allied Families*. Goshen, NY: Orange County Historical Society.

P.W.H.J. 1872. Cream Cheese. *The English Mechanic and World of Science* 15(380): 415.

Patrick, C. 2008. Wheys and Means of Chester's Cheese History. *The Chronicle*, December 4.

Pecht, J.B. 1894. M*achine for Molding Neufchâtel Cheese*. #518,625. Washington, DC: US Patent Office.

Pennsylvania Gazette, The. 1769. A Receipt for Making Cream Cheese. *Pennsylvania Gazette*, May 25.

Philp, R.K. 1870. *Best of Everything*. London: W. Kent & Co.

Pirtle, T.R. 1926. *History of the Dairy Industry*. Chicago, IL: Mojonnier Bros. Co.

Plough Boy, and Journal of the Board of Agriculture, The. 1821. Cheese Making. *Plough Boy, and Journal of the Board of Agriculture* 2(41): 326.

Portrait and Biographical Record of Rockland and Orange Counties, New York. Vol. II. 1895. New York: Chapman Publishing Co.

Predmore, H. 1965. *The Chester (NY) Presbyterian Church, A History 1799–1965*. Monroe, NY: Library Research Associates.

Publow, C. A. 1909. *Fancy Cheeses for the Farm and Factory*. Bulletin 270. Ithaca, NY: Cornell University Agricultural Experiment Station of the College of Agriculture.

Pye, D. 1968. *The Nature and Art of Workmanship*. Cambridge: Cambridge University Press.

Raguet, C. 1840. *The Principles of Free Trade, Illustrated in a Series of Short and Familiar Essays*. Philadelphia, PA: Privately Printed.

Reynolds, C. (ed.) 1913. *Genealogical and Family History of Southern New York and the Hudson River Valley: Vol. 1*. New York: Lewis Historical Publishing Company.

Royall, A. 1829. *Mrs. Royall's Pennsylvania, or Travels Continued in the United States: Vol. I*. Washington, DC: privately published.

Ruttenber, E.M. and Clark, L.H. 1980. *History of Orange County, New York: Vol. 2*. Interlaken: Heart of the Lakes Publishing.

Scharf, J.T. 1886. *History of Westchester County, NY*. Philadelphia, PA: L.E. Preston & Co.

Scharf, J.T. and Westcott, T. 1884. *History of Philadelphia 1609–1884: Vol. III*. Philadelphia,

PA: L.H. Everts & Co.

Selitzer, R. 1976. *The Dairy Industry in America*. New York: Magazines for Industry.

Sheldrick, A. 1844. Cream Cheese. *The Cultivator.* April. 1(4): 134.

Smith, A.F. 2007a. French Influences on American Food. In *The Oxford Companion to American Food and Drink*. New York: Oxford University Press: 237–9.

Smith, A.F. (ed.). 2007b. *The Oxford Companion to American Food and Drink*. New York: Oxford University Press.

Spirit of the Times. 1848. Advertisement: Groceries, &c. November 18, p. 18.

Stamm, E.R. 1991. *The History of Cheese Making in New York State*. Endicott, NY: Lewis Group Ltd.

State Board of Health of Massachusetts. 1904. *35th Annual Report of the State Board of Health of Massachusetts*. Boston, MA: Wright & Potter Printing Co.

State Board of Health of New York. 1884. *Fourth Annual Report of the State Board of Health of New York*. Albany, NY: Weed, Parsons and Co.

Stewart, H. 1888. *The Dairyman's Manual*. New York: Orange Judd Co.

Stocking, W. A. 1917. *Manual of Milk Products*. New York: Macmillan.

Thirsk, J. (ed.). 1984. *The Agrarian History of England and Wales: 1640–1750. Vol. V i.* Cambridge: Cambridge University Press.

Thom, C. and Fisk, W. W. 1918. *The Book of Cheese*. New York: Macmillan.

US Department of Agriculture. 1910. Notice of Judgment No. 566, Food and Drugs Act. In *Annual Reports of the US Department of Agriculture*. Washington, DC: Government Printing Office.

US Department of Agriculture. 1911. *Experiment Station Work* 4(1). Washington, DC: Government Printing Office.

US Department of Agriculture. 1918. *The Manufacture of Neufchâtel and Cream Cheese in the Factory*. Bulletin No. 669. Washington, DC: Government Printing Office.

VanSlyke, L. L. and Price, W. V. 1927. *Cheese*. New York: Orange Judd Publishing Company, Inc.

Village of Chester Centennial Commission. 1992. *The Village of Chester 1892–1992 Centennial Journal*. Pennsylvania, PA: Jostens Printing and Publishing.

Weaver, W. 2004. *A Quaker Woman's Cookbook: The Domestic Cookery of Elizabeth Ellicott Lea*. Mechanicsburg, PA: Stackpole Books.

White, G. 1880. *Cheese-Press*. #228,291. Washington, DC: US Patent Office.

Wickson, E.J. 1875. Butter and Cheese. *Harper's New Monthly Magazine*. 51(306): 813–27.

Wilde, M.W. 1988. *Industrialization of Food Processing in the United States, 1860–1960*. Unpublished PhD thesis. University of Delaware.

Willard, X.A. 1872. *Willard's Practical Dairy Husbandry*. New York: D.D.T. Morre.

Wilson, J. 1842. *The Recreations of Christopher North*. Edinburgh: William Blackwood and Sons.

Wilson, C. 2002. Cheesecakes, Junkets, and Syllabubs. *Gastronomica, The Journal of Food and Culture* 2(4): 19–24.

Wilson, M.T. 1984 [1957]. The First American Cookbook. In *The First American Cookbook: A Facsimile of "American Cookery," 1796 by Amelia Simmons*. NY: Dover Publications, Inc, pp. vii–xi.

Working Farmer, The. 1857. To Make Cream Cheese. *Working Farmer* 9(10): 226.

Youman, A.E. 1872. *A Dictionary of Every-Day Wants Containing Twenty Thousand Receipts in Nearly Every Department of Human Effort*. New York: Frank M. Reed.

FOOD,
CULTURE &
SOCIETY

VOLUME 15

ISSUE 2

JUNE 2012

195

FOOD, CULTURE & SOCIETY

VOLUME 15 | ISSUE 2 | JUNE 2012

Recipes in Context

SOLVING A SMALL MYSTERY IN CHARLESTON'S CULINARY HISTORY

Donna Gabaccia

University of Minnesota

Jane Aldrich

Independent scholar

Abstract

This paper makes novel use of digital archives and the history of publishing to reveal the previously unknown author of the first cookbook published by a woman in the Carolinas. The traditional tools of the culinary historian, including textual analysis and biographical research, proved insufficient to identify the author of The Carolina Receipt Book *(1832). The researchers therefore situated the cookbook within the social and intellectual milieu of antebellum Charleston—not only the traditional female networks of domestic literature and charitable works, but also the masculine politics of Nullification, slavery and states' rights, which led ultimately to the Civil War. The paper analyzes how an elite Southern family sought to erase the historical memory of the volume in order to assure cultural predominance for its own female members.*

Keywords: historical memory, culinary history, history of publishing, female authorship, Nullification

Introduction

Resting on the shelves of the Charleston Museum is the first female-authored low-country cookbook, *The Carolina Receipt Book or Housekeeper's Assistant* (hereafter *Carolina Receipt Book*), published in 1832. The identity of its author, listed only as an anonymous "Charleston Lady," has remained unknown for 175 years.[1]

The mystery has persisted because few have even bothered to ask who the author was. That is itself odd, given the considerable scholarly and popular attention that Charleston's early foodways attract and the fascination of readers of culinary history with famous "firsts." For more than three decades, readers and

.2752/175174412X13233545145183
s available directly from the
ers. Photocopying permitted by
only © Association for the Study of
d Society 2012

cooks have had access to attractive reprints and editions of many other early Charleston recipe collections. These editions linked the eighteenth-century culinary manuscripts of Eliza Lucas Pinckney (1722–1793) and her daughter Harriott Pinckney Horry (1748/49–1830)[2] to the very well known *Carolina Housewife*—which is not, as many believe, the first but rather the second cookbook by a local woman, published in Charleston in 1847).[4] The author of that anonymously printed cookbook was identified already in 1855[4] as Sarah (Sally) Rutledge (1782–1855), a woman tightly connected through kinship to Pinckney and Horry.[5] As it was republished in 1963 and 1979, Rutledge's 1847 cookbook—rather than the earlier one penned in 1832 by the anonymous "Charleston Lady"—has exemplified historical low-country cuisine, an important variation on regional Southern cuisine. Why should this be so when the existence of the earlier cookbook is also widely acknowledged, at least by scholars and local specialists? Why had no one before us bothered to ask who the author of the 1832 cookbook might have been?

In this paper, we tackle the issue of the authorship of the *Carolina Receipt Book*. More importantly, we ponder the pioneering cookbook's long-term neglect in a region fascinated with its elite, gentry female recipe writers. Looking for its unknown author demonstrated to us first the excitement and then the limits of the most commonly used techniques of culinary history. Faced with a methodological dead-end, we turned to the very different methods developed by historians of print culture. By doing so, we came to understand female culinary writings in Charleston in new ways. For Charleston's white women, publishing cookbooks was more than a quiet assertion of leadership and skill in their separate, domestic sphere. Publishing also subtly reflected and expressed women's political, religious and class loyalties in the same medium—print—that created, debated and spread sectional identities among Southern men in the 1830s and 1840s. For the female descendants of the elite Pinckney/Rutledge family, including Anna Wells Rutledge (1906–1996, the editor of a widely-read modern edition of the 1847 cookbook), the crafting of a family history of culinary excellence, focused on cookbook writing, served yet another purpose. It worked to perpetuate a declining local dynasty's sense of cultural centrality even after a century and a half of persistent cultural challenges from outside its immediate circle of intimacy.

Among those outside challengers was the otherwise modest and likeable compiler of the *Carolina Receipt Book*. A newcomer to Charleston, this woman adopted the city as her permanent home, and she loved it dearly. Despite her efforts, the surviving evidence suggests that the older, female elite of Charleston were not eager to celebrate her culinary accomplishments, neither during her lifetime nor over the century that followed. This is why the 1832 author did not become known as the "first" Charleston cookbook writer. The compiler of the *Carolina Receipt Book* ate, cooked, and wrote about rice. But it was the Pinckney and Rutledge women who survived and triumphed as originators of the local cuisine in the culinary history of the coastal Carolinas. They did so, as the local saying continues to assert, like the Chinese—not just by eating rice but also by worshiping their own ancestors.

Genealogical and Textual Clues

While little-known to readers of popular cookbooks, the *Carolina Receipt Book*'s existence is no secret to specialists. Anna Wells Rutledge described the work in the annotated "Preliminary Checklist of Early Carolina Cookbooks" that she included in her modern edition of Sarah Rutledge's 1847 cookbook. Tellingly, Rutledge tentatively attributed authorship of the *Carolina Receipt Book* to Harriott Horry Pinckney (1776–1866), another member of the famed Pinckney/Rutledge circle.[6] Pride in kinship alone explains this attribution, for little textual or other evidence points toward her as author.[7]

Harriott Horry Pinckney was the granddaughter of Eliza Lucas Pinckney and a namesake of her aunt, Harriott Pinckney Horry, with whom she had lived as a child, after the death of her mother (who was also the sister of Sarah Rutledge's deceased mother). As cousins and unmarried women, Sarah Rutledge and Harriott Horry Pinckney sometimes traveled together and in late life they also shared a home.[8] Descendants remembered Harriott Horry Pinckney as cheerful, pious and interested in the moral reform of the seamen of Charleston's harbor.[9] Because she lived until 1866—long enough to experience exile from Charleston and the losses that followed the Civil War—Harriott Horry Pinckney also became an important focus of memory for subsequent generations of Pinckneys and Rutledges, including Anna Wells Rutledge.[10]

Unfortunately, the editorial motives, authorial voice and recipes of the 1832 cookbook do not suggest a close connection between its author and Charleston's better-known circle of elite, recipe-writing kinswomen. The author of the *Carolina Receipt Book* wrote at least in part to raise money, although she assured readers she sought no gain for herself: the "profits of the work ... are destined to objects of public usefulness," she promised, hoping this motive would "secure for it a still larger extent of patronage."[11] Almost certainly the profits from the book were destined for charitable work—work Charleston's women had been undertaking at least since 1790. In 1847, Sarah Rutledge would make no such promise in writing her *Carolina Housewife*.[12] As Rutledge reportedly "lavished thousands" from an "overflowing purse" on her own chosen charities, she had no need to publish a cookbook in order to raise money for it.[13] As for Harriott Horry Pinckney, whom Anna Wells Rutledge believed to be the author? She was by far the wealthiest woman in Charleston, having inherited a city mansion, plantations, and slaves from her father at the time of his death in 1825.

The author of the 1832 cookbook also struck an exceedingly modest tone in addressing her potential readers. In her preface she noted that she "presents her little work to the public with much diffidence. Unused to the art of composition, she places the chief merit of her book in its usefulness." This desire for usefulness and this reference to a publication as work—both twice repeated—were used by the author to establish a bond between herself and women readers who "like herself, are engaged in the cares and duties of rearing a family."[14] In keeping with its theme of usefulness and the word of cookery, the *Carolina Receipt Book* offered a sequence of simple recipes for soup, meat, vegetables, breads, sauces, eggs and desserts, arranged more or less in the order they might appear on a modest,

FOOD,
CULTURE&
SOCIETY

VOLUME 15

ISSUE 2

JUNE 2012

weekday family dinner table. Most recipes required only limited numbers of ingredients and a few steps of preparation. Indeed, some scarcely seemed like recipes at all. To prepare a breast of veal, stewed, for example, the author offered the advice that the veal be "stewed till quite tender, and smothered with an onion sauce."

Even if the decidedly modest and conventional Harriott Horry Pinckney had possessed the culinary interests and writerly skills of her kinswomen (and unfortunately we have almost no evidence that she did; unlike one of her sisters, she was not much of a writer), she would scarcely have prefaced her cookbook with comments about the "cares and duties" of "rearing a family." In 1832 Harriott Horry Pinckney was 56 years old, unmarried, and living in a large mansion with her widowed and unmarried sisters. Two years earlier, census takers had found her in possession of a staff of twenty-eight servants—three free black men and twenty-five slaves, among them a large group of females who presumably undertook most of the practical "duties" and work of the household, including the everyday cooking. "Sally" Rutledge was similarly unburdened with the cares and duties of family life. In 1847, as she prepared the *Carolina Housewife* for publication, she was 65 years old; three years later, she was living with her Pinckney cousins, and local census takers listed her three female slaves as additions to her cousin's household slave staff of twenty-three.

In her own 1847 cookbook, Rutledge differed sharply from the 1832 author by assuming an authoritative voice and beginning with the somewhat confrontational statement that "We call this [book] 'House and Home,'[15] because a house is not a home, though inhabited, unless there preside over its daily meals a spirit of order, and a certain knowledge of the manner in which food is to be prepared."[16] Rutledge wrote for women she imagined as younger or inferior in culinary education to herself. She also made clear the source of her authority. "It rarely happens," she emphasized, "that more than one woman in three generations takes the pains to collect and arrange receipts; and if her descendants are many, the greater part lose the benefit of her instruction." Alas, Rutledge continued, the manuscripts of grandmothers "cannot be in the possession of more than one family in ten." Hers was clearly one of that small minority of families and she was proud of the fact.

Rutledge was far less concerned with managing a family, and a family budget, than with highlighting the skills of women as hostesses.[17] Perhaps fearing that readers might find some of the recipes of *Carolina Housewife* too complex, Rutledge insisted that "our own cooks" (presumably a reference to slave labor) had successfully used her recipes without recourse to an elaborate "*abattrie de cuisine*." Most revealing of Rutledge's concerns was her ironic recounting of a supposedly "valuable receipt" given to her by "an experienced housekeeper" for "throwing an illusion over an indifferent dinner to which company is suddenly brought home:" the guest should be presented, she wrote, with "A clean table-cloth and a smiling countenance."[18] Rutledge clearly did not approve of such carelessness and lack of preparation.

As a good culinary historian of the 1950s, Anna Wells Rutledge had compared the recipes of the 1832 *The Carolina Receipt Book* with those in Sarah Rutledge's

1847 *The Carolina Housewife* and had concluded from the exercise that "the contents do not suggest any connection" between the two authors.[19] Here, she may have over-stated her case, but only slightly. Of the 126 recipes in the earlier publication, four are identical to or very similar to those in Rutledge's cookbook—"potato biscuit," "Wafers" (Rutledge's "Rice Wafers Number 2"), "Rice Cakes," and "Flannel Cake" (Rutledge's White Flannel Cake"). It is striking that two of the four shared recipes featured rice, which is, of course, the ingredient that—along with shrimp and crabs (also represented in both books)—is the most distinctive marker of low-country foodways even today.[20]

Our comparisons with the earlier recipes of the mother/daughter pair of Eliza Lucas Pinckney and Harriott Pinckney Horry revealed many similarities with the *Carolina Housewife* but almost none with the *Carolina Receipt Book*. Sarah Rutledge in 1847 emphasized that her book drew on "the family receipt books of friends and acquaintances, who have kindly placed their manuscripts at the disposal of the editor."[21] Those recipes included at least four that had originated in Eliza Lucas Pinckney's mid-eighteenth century collection (and were subsequently entered into Harriott Pinckney Horry's book of receipts)—"To Pott Beef Like Venison," "To Dobe a Rump of Beef," "To Caveach Fish/Mackerel," and "Mushroom Catchup and Powder" along with 24 additional recipes from Harriott Horry's late-eighteenth-century collection.[22] It is unlikely that Rutledge's cousin Harriott Horry Pinckney, had she written the 1832 cookbook, would have ignored the culinary expertise of her close relatives, yet that is exactly what the author of the *Carolina Receipt Book* seems to have done: she offered only two recipes that bore even the slightest resemblance to those in Pinckney's and Horry's collections. One was a substantially simplified and revised version of the older Pinckney's "to dress a Calves Head in imitation of Turtle" (or, as the 1832 publication called it, "mock Turtle)." The second was a recipe for "India pickles," which slightly resembled Harriott Horry's recipe "To Make Atzjar."[23]

The authors of both the 1832 and 1847 cookbooks admitted they were mere compilers, drawing on many sources. For Rutledge, these sources included translations from German, Russian and French recipes. The borrowing and reprinting of recipes was (and still is, even in our age of concerns about plagiarism) exceedingly common among cookbook writers. Fortunately, digitized versions of early cookbooks now make it possible to identify such borrowing with greater accuracy, and also, in this case, with surprising results. While several borrowings connected Rutledge to Philadelphia cookbook writer Eliza Leslie,[24] the 1832 cookbook compiler turned instead to New England publications. From Lydia Maria Child's *Frugal Housewife*, the *Carolina Receipt Book* reprinted many household injunctions, including those to make one's own bread and cake and to do one's own mending once a week; to count towels, sheets, spoons, occasionally; to wrap knives and forks in paper, not wool; to avoid throwing away breadcrusts; and to wash one's hair in New England Rum.[25] The decided simplicity of her recipes also resembled those of the *Frugal Housewife*, even without direct borrowings.

The compiler of the *Carolina Receipt Book* also took from a Boston writer her advice about domestic order and about the management of the servants. The

FOOD,
CULTURE &
SOCIETY

VOLUME 15

ISSUE 2

JUNE 2012

201

cookbook counseled readers to "Do everything at the proper time; Keep everything in its proper place" and to "avoid all appearances toward *familiarity* [emphasis in original] with our servants: which, to a proverb, is accompanied by *contempt*, and soon breaks the neck of obedience." Both instructions were copied with great precision from Robert Roberts's *House Servant's Directory*, published in Boston in 1827.[26] Historians have recently recognized how many Southerners knew of and even participated in the literary culture of New England in the 1830s.[27] But borrowing from *The House Servant's Directory* in this case seems especially noteworthy because the book had been penned by a free, African-American man who worked as a butler to Christopher Gore, the Governor and Senator from Massachusetts. It was one of the earliest publications of any sort by an African-American, although it was also more of a guide to housework than a collection of recipes. Regardless, it is unlikely that any woman of Charleston's plantation elite would have deemed Roberts's advice as authoritative enough to copy it.

The usual methods of culinary history thus suggested that the compiler of the *Carolina Receipt Book* not only came from outside the elite family circle of Pinckney, Horry and Rutledge recipe collectors but that she was both an outsider to Charleston (possibly with roots in or connections to New England) and a woman with unconventional thoughts on the authority of African-Americans. With these tantalizing hints, unfortunately, the methods of culinary history had also reached their limits. To find the author of the *Carolina Receipt Book* required a search that extended well beyond recipes, cookbooks and histories of Southern cooking and dining. By seeking instead to embed the 1832 culinary text in its historical context and to give it a publication history, we discovered a fascinating, gendered and political backdrop to the cookbook's publication. We also discovered the female outsider—in fact, Boston-born—who seemed its most plausible author.

Historical Context: Solving a Culinary Mystery

According to the local newspaper, the *Charleston Courier*, the *Carolina Receipt Book* ("price, 75 cents") was first offered for sale at a "Ladies' Fair" held May 18–20, 1832, at the Hall of the South Carolina Society. Careful attention to divisions among Charleston's male voters, its women benevolent workers, and its book and newspaper printers suggested further that the cookbook's author was a woman with close ties to a group of moderate Unionists during Charleston's dramatic and tumultuous Nullification crisis of previous years.[28]

The Charleston Ladies' Fair of 1832 was clearly an expression of what Barbara Bellows has termed "benevolence among slaveholders." Between admissions (25 cents) and sales of handicrafts and books, the fair netted more than $1,500—a very substantial amount for the time. Unlike women's benevolent work (which had deep local roots), public fundraising campaigns by Charleston's women were new, innovative and controversial. Today, historians associate both fairs and fundraising cookbooks mainly with northern benevolent workers. According to Beverly Gordon, ladies fairs and bazaars emerged first in England, and then became common in New England after Josepha Hale in 1830 suggested women begin to support a flagging campaign to finance a Bunker Hill monument. Gordon found no other ladies fairs in her research in Charleston and very few anywhere else in the antebellum South.[29] But, in fact, Charleston's ladies organized several bazaars and fairs in the early 1830s, including one in 1833 to support Harriott Horry Pinckney's favorite cause, the city's seamen.[30] Sold at the earlier 1832 fair, the *Carolina Receipt Book* may well be the earliest extant example of a fundraising or charitable cookbook. Most scholars have attributed such cookbooks instead to the initiative of northern women supporting charities and hospitals during and just after the Civil War.[31]

Timing alone suggests it was the Nullification crisis of 1830–1832 that moved Charleston's benevolent women into the new public arena of fundraising, encouraging a shift from private recipe collecting into print culture. By 1830, several models for female-authored cookbooks existed, even in the South. As we have seen, Charleston's women read and owned earlier cookbooks published in Virginia, Boston, New York and Philadelphia. But only in 1832 did they finally take this step themselves. Many scholars have pointed to cookbook writing as a female and culinary expression of groups in formation, and both the *Carolina Receipt Book* and the *Carolina Housewife* fit this mold.[32] Both works claimed to represent regional Carolina—not Charlestonian, not Southern—cooking. Both clearly acknowledged their interests in regional distinctiveness. The author of the 1832 *Carolina Receipt Book* claimed to have observed "a deficiency of articles, peculiarly appropriate to the climate or the habits of Carolinians."[33] Fifteen years later, the *Carolina Housewife* offered rice bread recipes from Weenee, Ashley and Beaufort as well as "Carolina Rice and Wheat Bread."[34] A newspaper advertisement for Rutledge's cookbook noted its recipes were "particularly adapted to our situation &c," citing also Rutledge's claim that it included "nearly one hundred dishes in which rice or corn form a part of the ingredients."[35]

Culinary solidarity in Charleston emerged amidst passionate male polemics over Nullification—a state's right to reject (nullify) federal legislation, notably tariffs (but potentially also abolitionist legislature), to which it might object. This "crisis" proved particularly intense in Charleston because it highlighted sharp cleavages within local society, cleavages that played out in women's lives, too, and notably in the organizational lives of the female benevolent activists of the city. Since the 1790s, Jeffersonian voters in the Carolina upland had challenged the political leadership of coastal elites in general, and the Federalist Pinckney/Rutledge political alliance in particular.[36] Presbyterian and Episcopalian plantation owners disdained upcountry yeomen and their evangelical or "enthusiastic" religiosity. Within Charleston, the cleavages were just as sharp but somewhat different. There, commercial and professional families, many with ties to New England, differed both religiously and in their family and social customs from the urban-dwelling planter elite with their deep rural roots. By the early 1830s, the men of Charleston had divided into two main political camps. Radical "Nullifiers"—an alliance of "town-dwelling planters, petty shopkeepers and mechanics," according to Nullification's most important historian—were willing to risk severance of South Carolina's place in the republic and even imagine civil war over the tariff issue, whereas Unionist moderates ("heavily supported by the East Bay mercantile community") hoped to

FOOD,
CULTURE &
SOCIETY

VOLUME 15

ISSUE 2

JUNE 2012

defend localism, including even the local institution slavery, within the existing constitutional framework.[37]

The Pinckney women openly supported the most radical of the Nullifiers. Harriott Horry Pinckney and her sisters did not attend meetings or give speeches. Instead, they loaned their family name and their own pens to the radicals' cause. Already in 1830, Harriott's older sister Maria Henrietta Pinckney (whom a niece later described as being "of masculine intellect") had written a political tract called "The quintessence of long speeches, arranged as a political catechism," "by a lady, for her god-daughter,"[38] to explain the issues of states' rights to the next, female generation of Rutledges, the grandchildren of Harriott Pinckney Horry. A year later, on July 4, 1831, radical Nullifiers marched through the nighttime streets of Charleston to the Pinckney mansion, where a banner "Millions for defense, not a cent for tribute" (the famous words supposedly uttered by their father Charles Cotesworth Pinckney during the XYZ Crisis in Paris in 1795)[39] "was presented, in the names of Pinckney's three daughters, with the motto inscribed in Gold" from the balcony. Soon thereafter Maria Henrietta Pinckney christened the sisters' home "Nullification Castle."[40] If needlework could signal women's political loyalties during tumultuous times, might not a cookbook do the same?

Of course, Charleston's women rarely battled as openly as men did. Still, their charitable work reflected the divisions playing out more dramatically among male citizens. Women may have agonized more over their divisions but they nevertheless divided into separate and competing benevolent societies and they also split over how best to support the largest group of urban poor in their hometown. The elite Harriott Horry Pinckney's favorite charity—moral outreach to the port's seamen—provides a case study of these more subtle distinctions. It was men of the city's commercial elite who in 1818 first organized a Marine Bible Society, to distribute scripture among seamen; the following year, women of the decidedly commercial Congregationalist Circular Church organized as the "Female Domestic Missionary Society" to support a preacher to the mariners. The Marine Bible Society then raised money for a church; its distinctive pulpit moved about as the Mariner's or Marine Church shifted location in the years that followed. In 1823, men of the commercial and professional classes again sought to create a more stable financial foundation for the church by organizing the "Charleston Port Society for Promoting the Gospel among Seamen" (CPS). It soon employed a permanent preacher. From 1836 until 1882 William B. Yates (1809–1882), a Presbyterian, served as its chaplain.[41]

Throughout these years, the Episcopalian and patrician Harriott Horry Pinckney, held apart from the CPS's work, to pursue her own agenda and lead her own benevolent work.[42] (According to CPS records, Pinckney joined the group only in 1850.) In 1826, Pinckney may have funded or helped to organize the "Ladies' Seamen's Friend Society" that advocated building a boarding house home for sailors.[43] In 1836, upon urging from Yates, the CPS sought land from the City Council to build a chapel and boarding house "on East Bay, and extending West to the Market" (near the site of Harriott Horry Pinckney's home). For whatever reason, this initiative too came to naught. But the CPS did succeed in opening a home for sailors elsewhere by 1839.[44] This did not end Pinckney's independent quest, however. In her will, she created a corporation to create a church and home to be located on her own property and under Episcopal rather than Presbyterian leadership. By the time she died in 1866, Harriott Horry Pinckney's estate was much diminished. But after financial stewardship by two successive generations of Pinckney men, the home of which she dreamed was finally built in 1916. In cooperation with the by-then financially much-diminished CPS, this church and home saw service for fifty years.[45]

Charleston's benevolent women were similarly divided. At the beginning of 1832, Charleston had not one but two societies of local women "visitors" who sought to help and to assist the sick poor of the city.[46] A Ladies Benevolent Society (LBS) had been founded in 1813; its members were the female Episcopalian elite of St. Phillip's Church, including Harriott Pinckney Horry, Harriott Horry Pinckney and her two sisters, Sarah Rutledge (later to become the author of the 1847 cookbook), Harriott Pinckney Horry's daughter, Harriott Pinckney Horry Rutledge, and the mother of William B. Yates. In 1824, a second female charitable group, the Female Charitable Association (FCA) declared its intention to minister to the poor of Charleston Neck (an outlying district inhabited by free blacks as well as by increasing numbers of German and Irish immigrants). Its first president was Caroline Howard Gilman, the wife of the minister at Charleston's Unitarian Church. Later presidents of the FCA included many Presbyterians and women from commercial or professional families.[47] The FCA ceased to exist in 1860.

No direct evidence establishes which of these two groups of benevolent women organized the 1832 fair at which the *Carolina Receipt Book* was first sold.[48] The fair may even, in fact, have sought to overcome existing divisions between the two groups, for a newspaper announcement acknowledged "the numerous and varied kindnesses … which they have received from their friends of every class and denomination."[49] In a polarized city, however, even this bland announcement hinted at the fair organizers' political alliances as it appeared in the *Charleston Courier*. Throughout the Nullification crisis, the *Charleston Courier* printed mainly the viewpoints of local Unionists. More telling, the *Courier* not only published every notice that appeared for the Ladies' Fair, it also carried all of the advertisements for the *Carolina Receipt Book*. Had female Nullifiers organized the fair, they almost certainly would have turned instead to the *Charleston Mercury*, which was edited by Henry Laurens Pinckney, a kinsman of Harriott Horry Pinckney and a vigorous supporter of the Nullifiers. (Fifteen years later it would be the *Mercury* that published advertisements for Sarah Rutledge's *Carolina Housewife*, a work it tellingly described as "to the manor born."[50])

Local printers of books such as the 1832 cookbook were just as divided by the crisis, allowing us to draw further connections between the cookbook and the local Unionists. The press of Archibald E. Miller published most writings by the Charleston Pinckneys, and by 1830 it had become a favored outlet for radical Nullifiers.[51] Miller published Maria Henrietta Pinckney's "quintessence of long speeches" and the text of the meeting that preceded the nighttime parade to "Nullification Castle." By contrast, local moderate Unionists such as James Petigru and William Drayton preferred the press of James S. Burges.[52] Burges frequently printed works on dissenting religion—for example, Samuel Gilman's 1827 defense of Unitarianism.[53] Soon after the 1832 Ladies' Fair, Burges took over publication of a struggling children's magazine edited by Gilman's wife, Caroline Gilman, the founder and first president of the FCA. It was from the press of James S. Burges that the *Carolina Receipt Book* then emerged. With these pieces of print history in place, we quickly discovered that Caroline Howard Gilman possessed the writerly traits and Boston connections that our culinary analyses of the *Carolina Receipt Book* had identified. She may have been modest in claiming she was "unused to the art of composition" (she had already published poems and edited her own journal) but such modesty, too, was characteristic of Unitarian, New England women of her generation and upbringing.

Caroline Gilman and the Carolina Receipt Book

Authorship of the *Carolina Receipt Book* by Caroline Howard Gilman (1794–1888) fits nicely with almost all the textual and contextual clues we had been able to uncover. Caroline and her husband Samuel Gilman were former residents of Boston, where Samuel had graduated from Harvard College and Divinity School.[54] At the time of the 1832 cookbook's publication, Gilman was 38 years old and the mother of five daughters. She certainly understood the cares and duties of raising a family; she had lost an infant son in 1827. Two months after the ladies' fair, she would lose a daughter of sixteen months. Being "useful" to others and doing good "work" were both important to Caroline Gilman and to her minister husband; she called attention to their importance in letters written soon after arriving in Charleston and again after her return to a devastated Charleston in 1865.[55]

Writing—for herself, for distant relatives, and for broader audiences—was a life-long devotion of Gilman's. Although her first publications were heroic poems that appeared in the *North American Review* in the 1810s, most of Gilman's writing focused on the domestic lives of women and children. After arriving as a bride in Charleston in 1819, she began compiling handwritten recipes—which would not find publication under her own name until the middle of the twentieth century.[56] By 1827, she began to publish occasional pieces, but the largest part of her considerable oeuvre, including the children's newspaper, *The Rosebud*, and a string of domestic novels and collections of poetry, followed after the 1832 cookbook.[57] In her short autobiography, Gilman insisted that her only truly innovative writing had been for children.[58] But her contemporaries disagreed, and she enjoyed a reputation as one of the leading female writers of her age.[59]

Gilman's family and husband apparently recognized her talent and encouraged her to write and to publish. This writing allowed Gilman to make modest but also badly needed financial contributions to her family. (When, in 1833, Samuel Gilman took their second daughter to Boston for medical treatment, Caroline Gilman and her younger children lived in rented rooms in order to economize. For the remainder of the decade, Samuel and Caroline Gilman worked together to pay off a mortgage on the house [11 Orange Street] that they purchased upon his return.) Like many Unitarian women of her generation, Gilman was devoted to benevolence, which she could support only with her writing and with her unpaid labor. Whether or not she helped to organize the 1832 Ladies' Fair, it is easy to hear her voice behind the *Courier*'s acknowledgment of the help the event received from "friends of every class and denomination." Gilman badly wanted the approval of all local women, including the local elite, and she worked hard to prove herself a loyal Charlestonian.

The ties of both Gilmans to New England were nevertheless longstanding, familial and literary; they maintained these connections over their entire lives. Gilman's periodicals and books found a national, not an exclusively Southern, audience. Especially interesting to note are the close connections between Gilman and the two cookbook writers from which the *Carolina Receipt Book* most liberally borrowed. Samuel Gilman's brother-in-law worked for Christopher Gore, the Massachusetts Governor who also employed the African-American author Robert Roberts. The brother of Lydia Maria Child had attended Harvard with Samuel Gilman; later, in 1819, as the minister to Gilman's sister's congregation, he performed the Gilmans' wedding ceremony. Gilman certainly knew Lydia Maria Child, and in the 1820s contributed several short pieces to Child's magazine for children, which was probably also an inspiration for Gilman's *Rosebud*.[60]

As Samuel Gilman was widely known in Charleston as a Unionist, it was almost certainly he who directed his wife to the press of James Burges in 1832. Samuel Gilman had written a "Union Ode" for a meeting of moderates on the same July 4th evening night when Nullifiers marched on "Nullification Castle" to receive their banner from the Pinckney sisters.[61] In letters written during the Nullification crisis, Caroline Gilman attempted to provide her Boston sisters and in-laws with a balanced introduction to the complex issues under debate; she referred to a silver cup given to her husband by local Unionists.[62] In her other writings, Gilman tried to overcome the divisions emerging between Southern and Northern women: their shared domestic responsibilities and duties formed a central theme in all of Caroline Gilman's publications in the 1830s. According to historian Jonathan Daniel Wells, Gilman "worked hard to promote sectional reconciliation."[63] This would have been in keeping also with her husband's commitment, as a Unitarian, to harmonious social relations and to the importance of demonstrating one's faith through an exemplary and modest life.[64]

Not all the circumstantial evidence supports Gilman's authorship, of course. We could find no obvious resemblance between the *Carolina Receipt Book* and the few early recipes of Gilman's that were published much later in 1941 (under circumstances discussed below). Nor could we find any references in Gilman's published letters to either the 1832 cookbook or to the ladies' fair where it was sold. A few recipes from the *Carolina Receipt Book* do appear in the Boston publication Gilman supposedly edited from 1837 to 1839 (although one of her biographers insists that an un-named northern woman began ghost-writing the *Lady's Annual Register and Housewife's Memorandum-Book* after the 1840 death of Gilman's infant son).

And what of the unconventional attitudes toward servants detectable in the 1832 cookbook author's decision to "borrow" from Robert Roberts's *House Servant's Directory?* Scholars have devoted much time and attention to the complex identities of Caroline and Samuel Gilman as transplanted New Englanders. Much of this

FOOD,
CULTURE &
SOCIETY

VOLUME 15

ISSUE 2

JUNE 2012

207

debate focuses on whether the Gilmans owned slaves, whether they emancipated them and whether or not Harriet Martineau's critique of the married couple—of Samuel for his reserve and of Caroline for her vigorous defense of slavery—were accurate. Although sharp disagreements remain, most scholars assume that Samuel Gilman remained more of a New Englander, who survived in antebellum Charleston only by consistently avoiding any public discussion of slavery. By contrast, Caroline Gilman clearly gave her heart to Charleston and to her Southern neighbors, allowing at least some scholars to argue she had become a defender of both slavery and states' rights. (Her children's identities, at least as revealed by their marriages, suggest a family split—two daughters married Southerners and remained in South Carolina; two married Northerners and relocated north.) Our research does not allow us to resolve this ongoing debate. We can establish only that the same woman who apparently borrowed advice on handling her servants from the African-American Robert Roberts also, in her own hand-written cookbook, attributed recipes by name to several of her presumably enslaved cooks. That kind of attribution is, to the best of our knowledge, not found in any other published cookbook of the antebellum South, and certainly not in Sarah Rutledge's *Carolina Housewife*.

While scholars debate whether Caroline and Samuel Gilman embraced the South's peculiar institution, we are more interested in the embrace of Caroline Howard Gilman by the ladies of Charleston and in how relations between Gilman and Charleston's elite, notably the Pinckney/Rutledge women, may have shaped the long-term neglect of the *Carolina Receipt Book*. Certainly, today, elite Charlestonians cherish warmer memories of Caroline than of Samuel Gilman. In her own times, too, Southern readers clearly enjoyed and subscribed to Gilman's *Rosebud*. Nevertheless, Gilman's own comments—on her relationship with the elite of Charleston and with the women of Charleston's elite —limited and ambiguous as they are—are probably worth citing.

In 1821, Gilman attempted in a letter to her sister to rank the standing of her husband's Unitarian congregation in local society and concluded it was "highly respectable but engrossing little of the fashions & aristocracy of the place." She noted, correctly that "Episcopacy takes the lead," in Charleston but when she continued "& there is unquestionably a light feeling of contempt among them for all Presbyterians & Congregationalists," her husband felt it necessary to amend this with his own comment— "I doubt it." Caroline Gilman continued, however, insisting that the family's "comparatively humble style of living" made them "forgotten by the great." Although she then found a way to transform even these comments into a positive expression of her satisfaction with her new life in Charleston, we have no reason to think her impressions of relations between Gilman's and the plantation elite of Charleston were either inaccurate or disingenuous.

Years later, in December, 1832, Caroline Gilman wrote in *The Rosebud* that she had been requested to invite the little girls of the city to dress sailors' dolls for the upcoming Seamen's Fair. The following month she reported that it would take extraordinary effort if the women's movement to create a boarding home for sailors were not to fail. Soon thereafter Gilman came as close to expressing a critique of other women as her commitment to harmony and usefulness allowed. In March of 1833, she noted that the recent Seamen's Fair—also held in the Hall of the South Carolina Society and also decorated by "ladies of the different congregations"—had been "brilliant" and "delightful" but that it had collected only $1300, an amount that did not "equal public expectation." Gilman attributed this to the fact that "some of the individuals had so short a time for preparation" or perhaps it was "because another similar call had been so lately made on our community" by the 1832 fair.

It would be false to suggest that such mild expressions of competition, or even the more intense and public male controversies over Nullification, produced open enmity between Gilman and older Charleston families like the Pinckneys and the Rutledges. On the contrary, we know that Gilman—remembering her own father—wrote a poem, "The Sailor's Daughter," for the 1833 Seamen's Fair. We know also that when the harried (and again pregnant) Gilman implored readers of *The Rosebud* in 1839 to pay their increased subscription fees "in advance," Harriott Horry Pinckney was among the first to do so. Still, Gilman and the Pinckney and Rutledge women represented competing models for Southern womanhood. Years later, as Anna Wells Rutledge tried to help her readers to enter the antebellum social milieu of Charleston, she insisted that "Miss Rutledge probably turned in her grave" when exposed in 1855 as the author of the *Carolina Housewife* for "until about 1920-odd the name of a Charleston woman appeared in print but thrice—when born, when married and when buried."[65] This was not the Charleston social milieu of Caroline Gilman. Just to the side of the page on which the *Charleston Mercury* announced sales of the *Carolina Housewife,* there appeared a small notice, but in capitals, that "MRS. C. GILMAN'S NEW WORK"—the Sybil "by Mrs. Caroline Gilman"—was also for sale.[66] Caroline Gilman's name appeared many more than three times in print while she still lived. She, her family and friends—in Charleston and in the North—seemed not to have minded in the slightest.

Conclusion: Constructing the Pinckney/Rutledge Culinary Legend[67]

Caroline Gilman is the subject of a rich, and still growing scholarly literature on her writings, whereas Sarah Rutledge, Harriott Pinckney Horry and Harriott Horry Pinckney and her sisters have attracted no biographers. Their importance is decidedly local. But their hold on the culinary history of the low country has been a secure one. At the same time, national prominence has been insufficient to make Gilman a star in Charleston's local culinary history. In introducing readers to the Charleston society that had produced the *Carolina Housewife*, Anna Wells Rutledge acknowledged that "of course 'everyone' (everyone being her friends and relations) knew" that the *Carolina Housewife* had been compiled by Sarah Rutledge. Presumably many Charlestonians in the 1830s also knew that Gilman had compiled the *Carolina Receipt Book*. How, then, we finally ask, does such knowledge disappear as the past becomes historical memory?

Anna Wells Rutledge suggested that "the better a cookbook is, the more likely its pages are to be hastily flapped, written in, and spilled upon, with the distinctly un-Darwinian result that among cookbooks it is not the fittest but the least fit that

FOOD,
CULTURE &
SOCIETY

VOLUME 15

ISSUE 2

JUNE 2012

survive."[68] It is a clever analogy, but it is not adequate to answer our question. American libraries hold at minimum 27 copies of the first edition of Sarah Rutledge's 1847 cookbook; by contrast, the *Carolina Receipt Book* in the Charleston Museum appears to be the only surviving copy. The disappearance of Gilman and the *Carolina Receipt Book* from Charleston's culinary memory may be the result of its usefulness and thus its loss of the competition for survival. More likely, it is a small consequence of persistent efforts by several generations of Charleston women to secure their Pinckney and Rutledge forebears' reputation for culinary excellence. As Barbara Bellows has recently concluded, Rebecca Brewton Motte, an accomplished in-law of the better known Eliza Lucas Pinckney (and one who also collected recipes) might, under other circumstances, have been "paired" with her as "two South Carolina Heroines of the eighteenth century." (Motte's heroism involved setting fire to her home in order to oust the occupying British forces.) Instead, Motte has been "folded into the Pinckney legacy" and remains largely unknown.[69] Is this what happened to Caroline Howard Gilman?

Why some kinship groups, and not others, produce many writers, and why some of those writers, more than others, make their families and family histories the focus of their writing are such enormously complicated questions of family and of individual psychology that we can scarcely promise to answer them here. Still, the difference between the descendants of Samuel and Caroline Gilman (who continued to add to Caroline's manuscript book of recipes but who chose not to celebrate their illustrious forebears) and the descendants of Eliza Lucas Pinckney and Harriott Pinckney Horry (who included several generations of both collectors and preservers of family papers and writers about the family) are quite striking.[70]

In the case of the Pinckneys, male and female, a series of experiences and perceptions of loss encouraged the development of a family tradition of both preserving family records and of vigorously asserting the kin group's continuing political and cultural importance long after their wealth and political influence had waned. One might begin the list of losses with the family's belief that Charles Pinckney, husband of Eliza Lucas Pinckney, had in 1752 been unfairly denied a title for which he had been nominated (and by which his descendants always honored him)—that of Chief Justice of the colony—or with the fire that destroyed all of Charles Pinckney's papers, save only his will. (Maria Henrietta Pinckney would report later that "in the language of one fully competent to judge" his simple will could still "'be read with delight by the patriot, the philanthropist, the parent and the Christian' Such was the fascination of his manner."[71]) For Charles Cotesworth and Thomas Pinckney, the sons of Charles Pinckney and Eliza Lucas Pinckney, the losses would be political ones. Firm American patriots, they cast their lot with the Federalists, and their political influence faded quickly once Jeffersonian Democrats captured leadership at both the national and state levels. (Both lost bids for the presidency.)

As for the Pinckney women of subsequent generations, they quickly began writing and celebrating their forebears. Maria Henrietta Pinckney's 1820 play may be a fictionalized account of one kinsman's naval adventures;[72] a great-niece in the 1850s would be the first to edit and publish some of the writings of Eliza Lucas

Pinckney.[73] The next generation of Pinckney/Rutledge women would continue Eliza Lucas Pinckney's tradition of compiling recipes as well as the new tradition of celebrating their women forebears, including one (Eliza Lucas Rutledge, the sister of Frederick Rutledge) who saved the family papers (including those of Eliza Lucas Pinckney and Harriott Pinckney Horry) from the 1861 fire that destroyed "Nullification Castle."[74] By 1936, the genealogically based South Carolina Society of the Colonial Dames of America took over the task of finally bringing the recipes of Eliza Lucas Pinckney into print[75] at the same time that other descendants of the early elite of Charleston, including Anna Wells Rutledge, began to transform Charleston's history into the palatable version that, to this day, attracts tourists to experience an old South cleansed of conflicts over race, class, gender and political ideology.[76] The 1979 republication of the *Carolina Housewife*, edited by Anna Wells Rutledge, might be regarded as the last in this long line of histories that celebrate Pinckney cultural leadership in part because they are written by Pinckney and Rutledge descendants.

To forge a history of Pinckney/Rutledge culinary leadership, subsequent generations had to ignore much that did not fit into this celebratory genre. Critics have repeatedly noted how the culinary works of slave-owning women rendered invisible the culinary knowledge and skill of their African-American women cooks. In her private writings, and especially in her letters, Eliza Lucas Pinckney in the eighteenth century often commented on the skills of these cooks,[77] just as she (and her daughter Harriott Pinckney Horry) noted the names of the women from whom they borrowed their recipes. But even this minimally collaborative, cross-racial and sisterly dimension of female culinary creativity disappeared as literate, white women began to use print culture to express their regional identities as low-country cooks.

In the same manner, writers of Pinckney family histories have understandably ignored family conflicts (including sharp political conflicts between close kinsmen,[78] duels over family honor,[79] a surprising defense of free labor by Thomas Pinckney,[80] and the separation from the family of wayward sons[81]). And they have almost completely ignored the contributions of outsiders—whether of the Charleston Port Society's management of a chapel and home for seamen that long predated Harriott Horry Pinckney's benevolence or of Caroline Gilman's Female Charitable Association and of her cookbook. It is surprisingly easy to empathize with such management of memory in the pursuit of family reputation and honor; most of us do the same in organizing our own memories of our kin. Less acceptable, however, are the many cases of scholars, journalists and archivists adopting without question the assertions of what are in effect, celebratory family histories.[82] To cite an extreme case, even Northerners who write today about Charleston cuisine often feel they must claim a secure place in the local Pinckney/Rutledge lineage in order to write with any authority about culinary matters.[83]

Unlike Rebecca Mott, Caroline Gilman was not quietly folded into the Pinckney legacy. On the contrary, descendants of the Pinckney and Rutledge recipe collectors and writers both marginalized Gilman and, more ironically, ensured that her writings remained available in print to twentieth-century readers. In a typewritten

FOOD,
CULTURE
SOCIETY

VOLUME 15

ISSUE 2

JUNE 2012

211

draft of what was later to become a postscript to the 1979 edition of the *Carolina Housewife*, Anna Wells Rutledge demonstrated that she knew quite a lot about Gilman and about Gilman's work, and that she had considered Gilman, at least initially, as a contributor to the culinary writings that were "strictly Charleston or South Carolina."[84] In draft, at least, Rutledge concluded, somewhat dismissively, that Gilman in the 1830s and 1840s "edited or wrote industriously, giving some attention to food," and she even called attention to the publication of the Gilman family's "New England-South Carolina receipts" in the 1941 book, *Balcony in Charleston*. At the time she wrote this draft, Rutledge was considering the possibility that it was Miss "Sally" Rutledge (and not Harriott Horry Pinckney) who had penned the 1832 *Carolina Receipt Book*. By the time she brought the 1979 edition into print, however, she had not only changed her mind about authorship of the 1832 cookbook (for reasons we cannot know) but she had also decided to remove all discussion of Gilman from her preface and from her preliminary checklist of Carolina cookbooks.

Still, it was yet another Rutledge, a cousin of Anna Wells Rutledge—the poet laureate of South Carolina, Archibald Rutledge—who agreed to provide an enthusiastic and flattering foreword to a book, *Balcony in Charleston*, that in 1941 finally printed for the first time Gilman's recipes and letters. (The book was edited by Mary Scott Saint-Amand and dedicated to the memory of her friend, Clare Jervey, Gilman's granddaughter.) In a beautiful example of the surprising symmetries of local history, Archibald Rutledge was also the last family owner of Hampton plantation—the plantation that in the 1780s had been the home of Eliza Lucas Pinckney and Harriott Pinckney Horry; it had served as a revolutionary-era refuge for both the orphaned Sarah Rutledge and Harriot Horry Pinckney and her sisters. In times to come, Rutledge wrote in his foreword, this first published collection of Gilman's writings from Charleston "would be a great source book concerning life in the Carolinas during the nineteenth century." We believe that our modest historical excursions into that world, as we went looking for the author of the *Carolina Receipt Book*, demonstrate just how prescient in his judgments this particular Rutledge had been.

A Digital Postscript

Even as this paper evolved slowly toward publication over the years, our access to the print culture of Charleston continued to improve, largely as the result of the latest revolution in the history of print technology—the digitization of historical texts, especially historical newspapers. In the year before this article went to press, the rapidly expanding digital archive of Charleston newspapers finally delivered what we had sought for so long: the culinary equivalent of a "smoking gun." While we were also excited to learn in these newly available newspapers that still earlier ladies' fairs organized by benevolent Southern women (one held in Macon, Georgia, in 1828, another in Charleston in November of 1831) had preceded the Ladies' Fair of May of 1832—making even more obvious our claims about the Southern roots of a key institution of female benevolence—it was the Ladies' Fair of 1832 that continued to draw our attention.

Here is what we learned as the digital archive expanded. On April 14 and May 12, 1832, the *Southern Patriot* and the *City Gazette* published almost identical announcements of the upcoming fair. Unlike the announcements we had viewed earlier, these two actually listed the sponsor of the Ladies' Fair. Its sponsor was "the Ladies Working Society attached to the Unitarian Church." The two newspapers, unlike the ones we had consulted previously, also told readers of the intended purpose of the ladies' fund-raising, which was to make necessary repairs to the Unitarian church headed by Samuel Gilman. If earnings from the fair exceeded the amount needed for that purpose, the two newspapers went on to report, they would provide support for the mariner's church operated by the Charleston Port Society. On May 18, 1832, the *Southern Patriot* reported on the large attendance at the fair, and commented "What an emblem of charity, to see the professors of opposite religions, bringing their contributions to one common mark, for sacred ends." There was a goal that Caroline Howard Gilman and her husband Samuel could and did support, as they did also Unionism during the height of South Carolina's Nullification crisis and the birth pains of regional, Southern and low-country patriotism.

Donna R. Gabaccia is the Rudolph J. Vecoli Chair of History and Director of the Immigration History Research Center at the University of Minnesota. She is the author of many books and articles on international migration, immigrant life in the United States, and Italian migration around the world. Among her books are *We Are What We Eat: Ethnic Food and the Making of Americans* (1998), *Italy's Many Diasporas* (2000), and *Foreign Relations: Global Perspectives on American Immigration* (2012). Department of History, University of Minnesota, 1110 Heller Hall, 271 19th Ave S., Minneapolis, MN 55455, USA (drg@umn.edu).

Jane Aldrich has an MA in history from the College of Charleston and develops public and classroom programming that illustrates the history and culture of the Carolina low-country and its broad early connections throughout the Atlantic world. Aldrich has worked extensively with local school districts, the College of Charleston, and non-profit organizations to create materials and opportunities to teach about the transatlantic slave trade, the low-country plantation system and African contributions to the development of the production of rice as a staple crop, as well as the development of the Gullah-Geechee culture and its direct connections to West Africa. Her interest in foodways includes the origins and restoration of heirloom crops, the transference of African crops and traditions into early Southern foodways, and the origins and development of low-country plantation receipts over time. 2315 Marsh Lake Court, Charleston, SC 29414, USA (aldrichjane@aol.com).

Notes

1   Its full title is *The Carolina Receipt Book or Housekeeper's Assistant in Cookery, Medicine and Other Subjects Connected to the Management of a Family* (Charleston, SC: James S. Burges, 1832). Our thanks to Julia McIver Logan and Sharon Bennett at the Charleston

Museum who made it possible to use this rare book.

2   Richard J. Hooker (ed.) *A Colonial Plantation Cookbook* (Columbia, SC: University of South Carolina Press, 1984) introduced the manuscript collections of the very well known Eliza Lucas Pinckney and her daughter, Harriot Pinckney Horry. See the earlier publication of Pinckney's recipe as *Recipe Book of Eliza Lucas Pinckney, 1756* (South Carolina Society of the Colonial Dames of America, 1936, 1936, 1956). Pinckney has attracted much attention from historians of early British North America. See, most recently, Barbara L. Bellows, "Eliza Lucas Pinckney: The Evolution of an Icon," *South Carolina Historical Magazine* 106 (April/July, 2005): 147–65. Debates about the origins of rice and the relative importance of slave know-how and white capital and innovations for the development of Carolina plantation economy and low-country cuisine have also emerged. Compare Karen Hess, *The Carolina Rice Kitchen: The African Connection* (Columbia, SC: University of South Carolina Press, 1992) and Judith A. Carney, *Black Rice: The African Origins of Rice Cultivation in the Americas* (Cambridge, MA: Harvard University Press, 2001) which offers an even more effective critique of early works that include Peter H. Wood, *Black Majority: Negroes in Colonial South Carolina From 1670 through the Stono Rebellion* (New York: Alfred A. Knopf, 1975); Daniel C. Littlefield, *Rice and Slaves: Ethnicity and the Slave Trade in Colonial South Carolina* (Baton Rouge, LA and London: Louisiana State University Press, 1981); Ira Berlin and Philip D. Morgan (eds), *Cultivation and Culture: Labor and the Shaping of Slave Life in the Americas* (Charlottesville and London: University Press of Virginia, 1993); and Joyce E. Chaplin, *An Anxious Pursuit: Agricultural Innovation in the Lower South, 1730–1815* (Chapel Hill, NC and London: University of North Carolina Press, 1993).

3   Sarah Rutledge, *The Carolina Housewife* (ed.) with an introduction and a preliminary checklist of South Carolina cookbooks published before 1935 (Columbia, SC: University of South Carolina Press, 1979). This edition of the 1847 cookbook was edited and introduced and the preliminary checklist was prepared by Anna Wells Rutledge, well known locally both as an art historian and for her interest in promoting local Charleston history. The cookbook was first published as Lady of Charleston, *The Carolina Housewife: or, House and Home* (Charleston, SC: W.R. Babcock, 1847). A new edition appeared in 1851. The book was again republished, presumably in Charleston, sometime in the 1860s (after the author had died) under Sarah Rutledge's name as *House and Home, or, The Carolina Housewife*. It reappeared in Charleston again in 1963, published by S.S.S. Publishers.

4   *The Olden Time of South Carolina by the Octogenarian Lady of Charleston, SC* (Mrs. Poyas) (Charleston, SC: S.G. Courtenay, 1855), pp. 146–47.

5   The ties between Sarah Rutledge and the Pinckney family are well known, and Anna Wells Rutledge called attention to them in her preface to the 1979 edition of *Carolina Housewife*. Sarah's mother was the sister of the wife of Eliza Lucas Pinckney's oldest son (and Harriott Pinckney Horry's brother) Charles Cotesworth Pinckney. (Both these Middletons who married into the Pinckney and Rutledge families died young.) As a girl, the motherless Sarah Rutledge lived and traveled in Europe with Charles Cotesworth Pinckney's family and she returned there again later, with her own stepmother. Consolidating family ties through marriage, Harriott Pinckney Horry's only daughter Harriott then married a fraternal cousin of Sarah Rutledge, Frederick Rutledge. The Rutledge/Pinckney kinship network is well known to historians in part because it functioned as an important political faction in the early years of the American republic. See Lorri Glover, *All Our Relations: Blood Ties and Emotional Bonds among the Early South Carolina Gentry* (Baltimore, MD:

Johns Hopkins University Press, 2000), pp. 113, 137–38.

6 According to Anna Wells Rutledge, the 1832 cookbook was found among "Pinckney material" at Runnymede Plantation on the Ashley River. The Runnymede Plantation house was destroyed in 1865, and a new house constructed there later by Charles Cotesworth Pinckney (the son of Thomas Pinckney, grandson of Eliza Lucas Pinckney and nephew of Harriott Horry Pinckney) who had purchased the land in 1862 and who subsequently oversaw the corporation established to fulfill Harriott Horry Pinckney's bequests for Charleston's seamen (see note 42 below). Charleston museum personnel suggested the donation had arrived at the museum in the early 1950s but could tell us little more about its provenance.

7 We discuss the only connection that links Harriot Horry Pinckney to the *Carolina Receipt Book* in note 42, below.

8 Christine Jacobson Carter, *Southern Single Blessedness: Unmarried Women in the Urban South, 1800–1865* (Urbana, IL: University of Illinois Press, 2006), p. 102. According to the manuscript census listings for Charleston in 1850, Harriet Horry Pinckney headed a household that included both her married sister Eliza L. Izard and her cousin Sarah Rutledge.

9 For Pinckney's interest in seamen, see Barbara Bellows, *Benevolence among Slaveholders; Assisting the Poor in Charleston, 1670–1860* (Baton Rouge, LA: Louisiana State University Press, 1993), p. 115.

10 See "To Miss Harriot Pinckney, last surviving daughter of Gen. Charles Cotesworth Pinckney on her eight-second birthday, ca. 1863," (43/1033), South Carolina Historical Society. Published in Columbia, SC, the document is incorrectly dated December 1853 in Confederate Imprints, no. 3205. The poem clearly refers to the destruction by fire of Pinckney's home in 1861, to the family's journey into inland exile during the Civil War, and to the threats of invasion and death ahead, suggesting the 1863 date. That year, however, would have been Pinckney's 87th birthday. For a selection from another birthday poem dedicated to Pinckney two years later, this time by a Middleton descendant, see Carter, *Southern Single Blessedness*, p. 17.

11 *Carolina Receipt Book*, pp. 3–4.

12 After Rutledge's death, the "Octogenarian Lady" who named her as author did assert that "she published for charitable purposes," *The Olden Time of South Carolina*, p. 147. We have been unable to determine with any certainty what Rutledge's charitable object may have been. By 1847 the Charleston Ladies Benevolent Society, to which Rutledge belonged, was almost bankrupt; newspaper notices begging for contributions appeared in the *Charleston Courier*, December 14, 1847, p. 1. In the same years, the women of the St. Phillip's Episcopal Church, to which Rutledge and most of her Pinckney and Rutledge kin belonged, had also initiated a campaign for a Church home to house and to train homeless, indigent women. Rutledge had interests in many charitable causes, including Charleston's Orphan House and Jubilee College in Tennessee (where her brother lived). See M.R.F., "In Memoriam: The Late Miss Rutledge of Charleston, South Carolina" (Nashville, TN, 1855), South Carolina Historical Society.

13 M.R.F., "In Memoriam."

14 *Carolina Receipt Book*, p. 3.

15 The original title of the work in 1847; this became its subtitle in subsequent editions.

16 *Carolina Housewife*, pp. iii–iv.

17 Hospitality is a prominent theme in every study of Southern plantation cookery. For a brief

FOOD,
CULTURE &
SOCIETY

VOLUME 15

ISSUE 2

JUNE 2012

introduction, see Joe Gray Taylor, *Eating, Drinking, and Visiting in the Old South: An Informal History* (Baton Rouge, LA: Louisiana State University Press, 1982). For early plantation mistresses, provisioning a bounteous table competed with hospitality as the focus of recipe collections; this was most visible in Eliza Lucas Pinckney's many manuscript receipts for pickling, preserving, brewing and distilling, and in Harriott Pinckney Horry's detailed directions for operating a dairy. Unlike her mother, who collected recipes for curing illness and making many kinds of household supplies, Horry collected only a few recipes for the production of household supplies, while the urban-dwelling Sarah Rutledge included none at all in her book. Still, the expectations of hostesses to provide lavish displays of food were increasing even during Harriott Pinckney Horry's later life. Thus, for example, the proportion of elaborate composed meat dishes and of desserts (especially baked ones) increased steadily across the three generations of Pinckney/Horry/Rutledge recipe collections.

18 *Carolina Housewife*, p. iv.

19 *Carolina Housewife*, p. 225.

20 In addition, one finds slight resemblances among another half dozen—compare, for example, recipes for "Fricasee of chicken" (to Rutledge's "White Fricassee") "Forcemeat," "Diet Bread," "Beer" (to Rutledge's "Pine-apple Beer"), "Bird's Nest Pudding," and "Cottage Potato Cake." We concluded there probably was some personal connection between the authors of the two cookbooks but it was neither a close one nor one based on kinship to Eliza Lucas Pinckney and Harriot Pinckney Horry.

21 *Carolina Housewife*, p. v.

22 Apparently, Sarah Rutledge especially liked Eliza Lucas Pinckney's and Horry's recipes for savory meats and sauces, while she borrowed considerably less from the older women's desserts and she completely ignored their formulas for common household products and remedies for illness.

23 This 1832 recipe for mock turtle is closer to the version offered in Mary Randolph's 1824 *Virginia Housewife* (Washington: Davis and Force, 1824).

24 It is possible that Sarah Rutledge knew Philadelphia cookbook writer Eliza Leslie (1787–1858) for members of the Pinckney and Rutledge families had close and longstanding ties to Philadelphia, Leslie's home city. At the very least, Rutledge had read (and she cited in her preface) Leslie's *Directions for Cookery, in its Various Branches*. Was Leslie also the "experienced housewife" Rutledge cited in *Carolina Housewife*? In 1853, when Leslie published *Cookery as it Should Be*, aiming for a more sophisticated and middle class readership than the one addressed in *Directions for Cookery*, she repeated Rutledge's (or her own?) anecdote about the clean table cloth and smiling countenance. It is unclear in this case who had borrowed from whom.

25 *Carolina Receipt Book*, p. 5. We used the online version (second edition, 1830) of *The Frugal Housewife, Dedicated to those who are not ashamed of economy*, p. 10. Available from: http://digital.lib.msu.edu/projects/cookbooks/html/book_06.cfm (accessed September 1, 2011).

26 The full title is *The House Servant's Directory, or A Monitor for Private Families: Comprising Hints on the Arrangement and Performance of Servants' Work* (New York: Charles S. Francis, 1827; Boston: Munroe and Francis, 1827). Available from: http://digital.lib.msu.edu/projects/cookbooks/html/authors/author_roberts.html (accessed December 13, 2011). Roberts had been born in Charleston in 1777 but lived in Boston already by 1805.

27 Jonathan Daniel Wells, *The Origins of the Southern Middle Class, 1800–1861* (Chapel Hill, NC: University of North Carolina Press, 2004).

28 Like most other authors, we began our examination of the nullification historiography in the work of William W. Freehling, *Prelude to Civil War: The Nullification Controversy in South Carolina, 1816–1836* (New York: Oxford University Press, 1965).

29 Beverly Gordon, *Bazaars and Fair Ladies: The History of the American Fundraising Fair* (Knoxville, TN: University of Tennessee Press, 1998), pp. 37, 228, note 6; see also Gordon, "Playing at Being Powerless: New England Ladies' Fairs, 1830–1930," *Massachusetts Review* 23:1 (1986): 144–60.

30 See also notes on a German fair, *The Rosebud*, November 10, 1832; "Seamen's Fair," *The Rosebud*, March 2, 1833; Rea Bryant Aldous, "The First Bazaar of the Unitarian Church of the Charleston, S.C., 1836" (Charleston, SC: Archives Committee of the Woman's Alliance, 1960).

31 Lynne Ireland, "The Compiled Cookbook as Foodways. Autobiography," *Western Folklore* 40:1 (1981): 107–14. In describing his collection of charitable cookbooks, Louis Szathmary points to the first as *A Poetical Cook-Book* by M. J. M. (Maria J. Moss), published in Philadelphia in 1864; Louis Szathmary, "The Szathmary Culinary Archives," *Books at Iowa* 42 (April 1985). Available from: http://www.lib.uiowa.edu/spec-coll/Bai/szathmary.htm (accessed January 1, 2006). Jan Longone, who donated her collection of cookbooks to the University of Michigan, apparently concurs; see Jan Longone, "Food for Thought: American Culinary History Center Opens," University of Michigan Press Service, November 10, 2004. Available from: http://www.umich.edu/news/index.html?Releases/2004/Nov04/r111004 (accessed September 1, 2011).

32 Arjun Appadurai, "How to Make a National Cuisine: Cookbooks in Contemporary India," *Comparative Studies in Society and History* 30:1 (1988): 3–24; Jeffrey Pilcher, "Recipes for *Patria*: Cuisine, Gender, and Nation in Nineteenth-Century Mexico," in Anne L. Bower (ed.) *Recipes for Reading: Community Cookbooks, Stories, Histories* (Amherst, MA: University of Massachusetts Press, 1997), pp. 200–15.

33 *Carolina Receipt Book*, p. 3.

34 It is worth noting that the *Carolina Housewife*, like its 1832 predecessor, appeared at a moment of rising Southern sectionalism: the onset of the US/Mexico War in 1846 encouraged Southern slave-owners' hopes for expansion into an area that soon became the Southwest of the United States.

35 *Charleston Mercury*, January 27, 1848.

36 On the revolutionary and Federalist political lives of Thomas and Charles Cotesworth Pinckney, see Marvin R. Zahniser, *Charles Cotesworth Pinckney, Founding Father* (Chapel Hill, NC: Institute of Early American History and Culture and University of North Carolina Press); Frances Leigh Williams, *A Founding Family: The Pinckneys of South Carolina* (New York: Harcourt Brace Jovanovich, 1978); Charles Cotesworth Pinckney, *Life of General Thomas Pinckney* (Boston, MA: Houghton, Mifflin, 1895).

37 Freehling, *Prelude to Civil War*, 254.

38 Maria Henrietta Pinckney, *The Quintessence of Long Speeches, Arranged as a Political Catechism, by a Lady, for her God-daughter* (Charleston, SC: A.E. Miller, 1830).

39 William Stinchcombe, *The XYZ Affair* (Westport, CT: Greenwood, 1980). Pinckney's refusal when solicited by Talleyrand for a bribe and a loan has been reported in various forms, including "no, no, not a sixpence."

40 *Proceedings of the Celebration of the 4th July, 1831, at Charleston, S.C. by the States*

FOOD,
CULTURE
SOCIETY

VOLUME 15

ISSUE 2

JUNE 2012

Rights and Free Trade Party (Charleston, SC: Archibald E. Miller, 1831) cited in Miller Maurie D. McInnis, *The Politics of Taste in Antebellum Charleston* (Chapel Hill, NC: University of North Carolina Press, 2005), p. 80.

41 See Rev. C.E. Chichester, *Historical Sketch of the Charleston Port Society, For Promoting the Gospel Among Seamen* (Charleston, SC: News and Courier Book Presses, 1885).

42 We focus on this case in some detail because Pinckney's interest in the seamen provides the only plausible textual link of Pinckney to the 1832 cookbook. And, as is turns out, it is not a very close or convincing linkage. Marginalia in the *Carolina Receipt Book* include a conventional dedication "To Mrs. W. Rh…." From "Eva Eberstang" along with more random signatures, including "Mary—," "Joanna Yates," "E.M. Burton," and—in several places—the single name "Joanna." We could find no local references to Eva Eberstang or E.M. Burton nor could we identify an individual named "Joanna Yates." Although we cannot be sure, Joanna Yates may however have been related in some way to William B. Yates. The Yates connection could, for example, explain the recipe for "Jennie Lind Pudding" glued to one of the front pages of the 1832 cookbook, for the Swedish singer Jennie Lind had contributed $500 to the Charlotte Port Society, Chichester, *Historical Sketch of the Charleston Port Society*, 15. William B. Yates was the son of Charleston cooper and businessman, Joseph Yates and Elizabeth Ann Saylor Yates, the daughter of a German immigrant, who in the 1820s wrote a letter to a northern Congressman, describing her abhorrence of slavery.

43 This group still existed in 1849, when its activities included care of the sick and destitute seamen in the sailors' home. Already in 1827, however, yet another "Ladies Association" formed in Charleston, also hoping to assist visiting sailors; in 1840 it became the Bethel Flag Society. A very useful webpage devoted to Southern benevolent charities provides lists and key information and bibliography about Charleston societies, along with their relevant publications, see: http://www.warwick.ac.uk/fac/arts/SouthernCharitiesProject/index.htm (accessed May 24, 2006). To confuse matters still further, one finds references to a "Dorcas Society for the Moral and Religious Improvement of the Children of Seamen," *The Rosebud*, December 5, 1832.

44 Chichester, *Historical Sketch of the Charleston Port Society*, p. 63.

45 See the brief history of the Seamen's home and church, available from: http://www.seamenschurchcharleston.org/archives/000004.php (accessed May 20, 2006).

46 A "Ladies Society" had founded a charity school already in 1805, and a Methodist Female Friend Association formed in 1810. The Catholic Sisters of Charity also began operating in Charleston in 1819.

47 Besides Bellows, *Benevolence among Slaveholders*, see Gail S. Murray, "Charity within the Bounds of Race and Class: Female Benevolence in the Old South," *South Carolina Historical Magazine* 96 (January 1995): 54–70.

48 Similarly, it is difficult to tell from these announcements what charitable cause benefited from the funds raised. The inmates at the Charleston Orphan asylum were feted with free admission and gifts on the last day of the fair but the annual celebration for this older charitable institution had already taken place later in the same year, *The Rosebud*, October 27, 1832. The Charleston Orphan Asylum was a long-standing object of interest and donations from the Pinckney family. Eliza Lucas Pinckney had donated the first building and her daughter Harriott Pinckney Horry had been one of the Lady Overseers of the orphanage. October, 1832, also saw the organization of a new female organization ("Ladies Fuel Society") which may also have benefited from the fair, see Kennedy, *Braided Lives*, pp.

135–6; *The Rosebud* October 20, 1832.

49 *Charleston Courier,* May 18, 1832.

50 This was the same newspaper that fifteen years later would publish announcements of the appearance of Sarah Rutledge's *Carolina Housewife.*

51 Maria Pinckney, "A Tyrant's Victims, a Tragedy, in Five Acts," "The Orphans," and "The Young Carolinians; or, Americans in Algiers" appeared in *Essays, Religious, Moral, Etc. By a Lady* (Charleston, SC: Archibald E. Miller, 1818). Miller's press also published the odes delivered at the funeral of Charles Cotesworth Pinckney's in 1825 and many of the reports on the works of benevolence associated with Charleston's elite Episcopalians. Already in 1827 the same press had reprinted one of the early salvos in the nullification crisis, written by one "Brutus" (Robert J. Turnbull).

52 Of course there was some overlap. For example, Nullifier Henry Laurens Pinckney published at least once with Burges, just as Samuel Gilman published one treatise with A.E. Miller.

53 *Unitarian Christianity free from objectionable extremes:—A sermon, preached at the dedication of the Unitarian Church, in Augusta, (Geo.) Dec. 27, 1827* (Charleston, SC: James R. Burges, 1828).

54 There is a surprisingly rich literature on both Samuel and Caroline Gilman. Daniel Walker Howe, "A Massachusetts Yankee in Senator Calhoun's Court: Samuel Gilman in South Carolina," *New England Quarterly* 44:2 (1971): 197–220; Daniel Walker Howe, "Samuel Gilman: Unitarian Minister and Public Man," *Proceedings of the Unitarian Historical Society* (1973–1975); Conrad Wright, "The Theological World of Samuel Gilman," *Proceedings of the Unitarian Historical Society* (1973–75); James W. Mathews, "A Yankee Southerner: The Aesthetic Flight of Samuel Gilman," in J. Lasley Dameron and James W. Mathews (eds) *No Fairer Land* (Troy, N.Y.: Whitson Publishers, 1986); and "The Doctrine of Contrasted Extremes," in *The Manichean Leitmotif*, ed. Arthur J. Graham (Los Angeles, CA: Image Analysts, 2000). Jan Bakker, "Another Dilemma of an Intellectual in the Old South: Caroline Gilman, the Peculiar Institution, and Greater Rights for Women in the Rose Magazines," *The Southern Literary Journal* 17:1 (1984): 15–25; and "Caroline Gilman and the Issue of Slavery in the Rose Magazines, 1832–1839," *Southern Studies* 24 (1985): 273–83. We have drawn particularly on the chronological account of Gilman's life presented as an appendix to Shauna Ann Thompson Bigham, "Entangled Commitments: The Life and Writings of Caroline Howard Gilman" (unpublished PhD dissertation, Purdue University, 2001).

55 See Gilman's letters in Mary Scott Saint-Amand, *A Balcony in Charleston* (Richmond: Garrett and Massie, 1941), pp. 16, 138.

56 Saint-Amand, *A Balcony in Charleston*, p. 19 contains a photograph of a page from her book of recipes and reprints recipes from Gilman, her daughters and granddaughters.

57 Besides *The Rosebud* (later *The Southern Rosebud* and *The Southern Rose*), see her *Recollections of a New England Housekeeper*, 1834; *Recollections of a Southern Matron*, 1838; and *Love's Progress*, 1840, *Poetry of Travelling in the United States*, 1838.

58 Caroline Gilman, "My Autobiography," in John S. Hart (ed.) *The Female Prose Writers of America, with Portraits, Biographical Notices, and Specimens of their Writings* (Philadelphia, PA: E.H. Butler, 1855), pp. 49–57.

59 Of the many works that focus on and interpret Caroline Gilman's literary works, see Janice Joan Thompson, "Caroline H. Gilman: Her Mind and Her Art" (unpublished PhD dissertation, University of North Carolina at Chapel Hill, 1975); Cindy Ann Stiles, "Windows

into Antebellum Charleston: Caroline Gilman and the *Southern Rose* Magazine" (unpublished PhD dissertation, University of South Carolina, 1994); Jane H. and William H. Pease, *Ladies, Women, and Wenches: Choice and Constraint in Antebellum Charleston and Boston* (Chapel Hill, NC: University of North Carolina Press, 1990); Elizabeth Moss, *Domestic Novelists in the Old South: Defenders of Southern Culture* (Baton Rouge, LA: Louisiana State University Press, 1992); Christine Macdonald, "Judging Jurisdictions: Geography and Race in Slave Law and Literature of the 1830s," *American Literature* 71:4 (1999): 625–56.

60 See Bigham, "Entangled Commitments," Chapter xx.

61 It is reprinted in Saint-Amand, *A Balcony in Charleston*, p. 28.

62 Saint-Amand, *A Balcony in Charleston*, pp. 25–27. In one of these letters, Gilman notes that Mr. Bee, her "nullifying agent" for *The Rosebud*, sent her a daily copy of the *Charleston Mercury*.

63 Wells, *The Origins of the Southern Middle Class*, pp. 36–7.

64 John Allen Macaulay, *Unitarianism in the Antebellum South* (Tuscaloosa, AL: University of Alabama, 2001).

65 Rutledge, *Carolina Housewife*, vi.

66 *Charleston Mercury*, January 27, 1848.

67 In Charleston, the "Pinckney Legend" refers specifically to Maria Henrietta Pinckney, *A Notice of the Pinckneys* (Charleston, SC: Evans and Cogswell, 1860). As the most experienced writer among Charles Cotesworth Pinckney's three daughters, she memorialized family stories about the early years of her father and uncle, and their parents, towards the end of her long life.

68 Rutledge, *Carolina Housewife*, p. 223.

69 Bellows, "Eliza Lucas Pinckney," p. 165. Apparently in imitation of her close friend Eliza Lucas Pinckney, Rebecca Motte also began a handwritten collection of recipes but these have not found their way into print.

70 The Gilmans' second daughter, Caroline (Caddy) Howard Gilman Glover Jervey (who was a widow from 1846 to 1864) both wrote novels and plays and stories for children and co-authored at least one work with Caroline Gilman. Clare Jervey (presumably the granddaughter of Caroline Gilman) published a study of the tombstones in St. Michael's Churchyard in Charleston; it was to Clare that Mary Scott St. Amand dedicated *A Balcony in Charleston* in 1941.

71 Pinckney, *A Notice of the Pinckneys*.

72 Pinckney, "The Young Carolinians."

73 Harriott Pinckney Holbrook, *Journal and Letters of Eliza Lucas*, Wormsloe Quartos, no. 3 (Wormsloe: George Wymberly Jones, 1850). This was a limited edition of only nineteen copies. Holbrook was the granddaughter of Harriott Pinckney Horry's daughter and Sarah Rutledge's cousin Frederick.

74 Harriott Horry Ravenel, *Eliza Pinckney* (New York: Charles Scribner's, 1896), Harriott Horry Ravenel family papers, 1694-ca. 1935. (1086.00) South Carolina Historical Society include Ravenel's poems, a story for children and a cookbook.

75 *Recipe Book of Eliza Lucas Pinckney, 1756*.

76 Stephanie E. Yuhl, *A Golden Haze of Memory: The Making of Historical Charleston* (Chapel Hill, NC: University of North Carolina Press, 2005).

77 Eliza Lucas Pinckney wrote for example, circa 1768, "Mary-Ann understands roasting poultry in the greatest perfection you ever saw … Caphne makes me a loaf of very nice

bread. You know I am no epicure but I am pleased they can do things so well … I shall keep young Ebba to do the drudgery part, fetch wood, and water and scour, and learn as much as she is capable of cooking and washing. Mary-Ann cooks, make my bed, and makes my punch. Daphne works and makes the bread old Ebba boils the cow's victuals, raises and fattens the poultry … I intend Daphne shall take her turn sometimes to cook that she may not forget what she learnt at Santee. Mary-Ann has pickled me some oysters very good, so I have sent you a little pot by the boat. Moses gets them at low water without a boat." Ravenel, *Eliza Pinckney*, p. 245. Pinckney's recipes provide additional evidence of elite women having learned from their African and African-American slaves: her recipe for boiling rice definitely described the distinctive Carolina technique that Karen Hess has attributed to African origins.

78 See, e.g. Maria Henrietta Pinckney's gloss on the family's relationships to the original namesake of the (then) childless Charles Pinckney, a man who became a leader of upland Jeffersonians, thus bringing him into sharp conflict with his Charleston "cousins" Thomas and Charles Coatesworth Pinckney, who were products of Justice Pinckney's late, second marriage, to Eliza Lucas Pinckney.

79 See "Letter to 'My dear Madam,'" 1785 where Edward Rutledge—Sarah Rutledge's father—reports to Eliza Lucas Pinckney on her son Charles Cotesworth Pinckney's duel in defense of family honor (after Harriott Horry Pinckney's son Daniel Huger Horry had changed his name to Charles Lucas Pinckney Horry—so repelled was he, apparently, by his own father's connections to the British and by the fines imposed on the Horry family, and his more patriotic mother, as a result).

80 Bellows, *Benevolence among Slaveholders*, 98–101. The text of Pinckney's 1822 pamphlet is available from: http://memory.loc.gov/cgi-bin/query/r?ammem/llst:@field%28DOCID +@lit%28gcmisclst0048div0%29%29 (accessed December 13, 2011).

81 The aforementioned Daniel Huger Horry—who was acknowledged as difficult even by his own mother, Harriott Pinckney Horry—subsequently moved to France, married there, and never returned.

82 Compare, for example, the treatment of the three women's benevolent societies discussed above in Murray, "Charity within the Bounds of Race and Class," which devoted only a line to the FCA, to the far more satisfying treatment in Cynthia Kennedy's *Braided Relations*, that offers a more balanced comparison of LBS and FCA. See Cynthia M. Kennedy, *Braided Relations, Entwined Lives: The Women of Charleston's Urban Slave Society* (Bloomington, IN: Indiana University Press, 2005).

83 R.W. Apple, Jr. "A Southern Star Rises in the Low Country," *New York Times*, March 15, 2006. The author refers to his wife as a descendant of Rutledges and Pinckneys. She may very well be that but what authority her roots lend to her author husband's culinary or historical authority is scarcely obvious, at least to those beyond the circle of Charleston worshipers of that particular circle of kin.

84 See the papers of Anna Wells Rutledge, South Carolina Historical Society.

FOOD,
CULTURE &
SOCIETY

VOLUME 15

ISSUE 2

JUNE 2012

FOOD,
CULTURE&
SOCIETY

VOLUME 15 | ISSUE 2 | JUNE 2012

El Gallo Pinto

AFRO-CARIBBEAN RICE AND BEANS CONQUER THE COSTA RICAN NATIONAL
CUISINE

Patricia Vega Jiménez

University of Costa Rica

Abstract

This paper examines the historical origins of gallo pinto (spotted rooster) to show how a plebeian dish of black beans and rice came to be embraced as a symbol of Costa Rican national identity. Beans have been a basic staple in Central America since pre-Hispanic times, but although Spaniards planted rice in the sixteenth century, it became a significant part of the diet only in the nineteenth century as a result of the transition from subsistence agriculture to coffee exports. The combination of rice and beans was introduced in the nineteenth century by Afro-Caribbean migrant railroad workers. Notwithstanding elite self-perception of Costa Rica as a white, European nation, economic necessity during the Great Depression helped gallo pinto gain middle class acceptance. This case illustrates both the importance of social and economic history in shaping cultural symbols and also the ways that lower-class foods can become central to national identities.

Keywords: national identity, migration, race, consumption

Introduction

As in the case of all national identities, Costa Ricans have invented a complex of symbols to distinguish themselves from other nations. Alongside the flag, emblem and national anthem, government decrees have established a national tree, bird and even a symbol of labor (the cart). While no comparable legislation has singled out a national dish, nevertheless, in the collective imaginary and in countless tourist restaurants, that category has been filled by *el gallo pinto* (the spotted rooster), a mix of rice and beans, generally black, which is served frequently in both public and private spaces.

Not surprisingly, a survey published in *La Nación*, the most widely read newspaper in the country, in January 2006, found that no less than 92 percent of

0.2752/175174412X13233545145228
ts available directly from the
ers. Photocopying permitted by
only © Association for the Study of
nd Society 2012

223

Costa Ricans "affirmed that one of the things that most identified 'being Tico' [a diminutive for 'Costa Rican'] is the taste for *gallo pinto*,"[1] even more than tamales or *arroz con pollo* (rice and chicken), common plates on the national table. This observation raises the immediate question: when did the custom of eating *gallo pinto* become a national standard in Costa Rica?

To assign a food the category of "national dish"—such as Germans and sausage, Chinese and rice, Italians and pasta, Japanese and sushi—is an unquestionable indication that foods are endowed with significant social, cultural, economic and historic meanings. In the words of Roland Barthes, food "is not only a collection of products that can be used for statistical or nutritional studies. It is also, and at the same time, a system of communication, a body of images, a protocol of usages, situations, and behavior."[2] Foods do not have an intrinsic significance; they are assigned by individuals, and therefore it is impossible to analyze changes in patterns of consumption without considering their social context. Foods and its methods of preparation are considered signs by those who participate in a process of interaction that signifies the act of eating; thus, they exist in a world of representation.

The distinction that has been conferred on the mixture of white rice and black beans as a component of national culinary culture among Costa Ricans has provoked a reaction in neighboring countries. Nicaraguans claim the dish as their own, use the same name, and have likewise elevated it to the rank of national dish. Indeed, rice and beans have become the common foundation of diets in various Latin American countries, including Cuba, Colombia, Ecuador, Honduras, in addition to Nicaragua and some regions of Mexico and Panama. The rituals and forms of preparing and serving them, and the times at which they are consumed, vary from one country to the next. Yet these countries have a common heritage. In all of them, frijoles derive from pre-Hispanic cultures, and were eaten accompanied by maize— in the form of tortillas or on the cob. Rice, by contrast, was carried to America in the early days of the Spanish conquest.

Regardless of where *gallo pinto* originated, its status as a national cuisine produced a tension between its place within the social hierarchy and the ideals of citizenship and equality. As Arnold Bauer has observed: "For food to have a socially integrative effect in a country [or community], there must be, if not a national cuisine, at least some dishes that make the consumer feel as if he or she is part of national culinary communion."[3] Given the accessibility—the presence and price— of rice and beans, it is possible that this dish arose from the kitchens of the popular sectors and over time, cultural conjunctures permitted it to spread to other classes. In general, the creations that signal national identity descend from the top to bottom on the social pyramid, helping those at the summit to maintain their position through artifices that exalt a sense of belonging and common identity. In the case of *gallo pinto*, the phenomenon was reversed, and a dish which constituted the principal plate of the popular sectors in the first three decades of the twentieth century was conveyed to those groups at the peak of the social pyramid, even as they had acquired other culinary habits that permitted them symbolically to maintain their social and gastronomic distinction.[4]

At the end of the nineteenth century, the national dish was considered to be the indigenous black bean, served dry, and generally accompanied by tortillas. This association was observed both by foreign travelers as well as in the first cookbook published in Costa Rica, by Juana Ramírez de Aragón.[5] Rice, by contrast, was still symbolically associated with foreign, particularly Spanish foods. Nevertheless, the transformation of the domestic agriculture from a subsistence base of corn and beans to an export economy founded on coffee over the course of the nineteenth century had made cheap imported rice an increasingly significant component of the diet for common Costa Ricans. Once a particular social group—in this case, proletarian migrants—had established *gallo pinto* as a folkloric symbol, it became available for appropriation as a national icon. A recent article by anthropologist Theresa Preston-Werner has situated *gallo pinto* in contemporary battles over historical memory in Costa Rica.[6] This paper, by contrast, seeks to document the dish's historical origins, particularly in the crucial symbolic displacement from beans alone to rice and beans, which took place in the national imaginary about 1930, when the economic crisis of the Great Depression produced changes at all levels, but particularly in the subsistence of the country.[7]

The sources for investigating this proposition are, first of all, the statistical yearbooks published by the National Institute of Statistics and Census, which contain data about population, imports and exports, referring to weight and value. Population censuses also provide information about the number of inhabitants, and particularly that of 1892, refer to data of import and export of goods. With these references it is possible to make an approximation of the consumption of rice and beans among Costa Ricans and to determine the manner in which they were eaten. In addition, chronicles written by foreign travelers add to this study by providing knowledge of everyday life. Commercial advertisements are equally useful for the information they provide about the sales of these goods in the national market.

The Historical Context of *Gallo Pinto*

To make *gallo pinto* requires precisely two ingredients: rice and beans. In contrast to frijoles, which had been domesticated in the Americas thousands of years earlier, rice was part of a basket of new cultivars that arrived in the sixteenth century. The spread of rice occurred gradually through a succession of colonial agricultural systems and led to changes in dietary patterns, creating a new universe of food habits with new social signifiers. The mestizo (a mixture of Spanish and Indian) populations—in Costa Rica in 1791 there were mulattos, free blacks, poor mestizos, Native Americans, and peninsular Spaniards—were the original carriers of this heterogeneous material culture, but subsequent migrants also contributed to the spread of rice.

In the early days of the Audiencia of Guatemala, of which Costa Rica was a provincial territory, rice held relatively minor significance for Spaniards compared with the Mediterranean staple wheat, which was planted almost immediately in all parts of the Costa Rican territory where the conquistadors settled beginning in 1561. Already in 1577, Governor Artieda informed the King that "here they have begun to plant wheat," although he commented timidly on the absence of mills, for

FOOD,
CULTURE &
SOCIETY

VOLUME 15

ISSUE 2

JUNE 2012

which reason he ordered the construction of one.[8] The consumption of wheat permitted Spaniards to differentiate themselves from the natives, whose diet was based on maize, potatoes and other tubers. As late as 1850, according to the observation of John Belly, those products were the foodstuffs of the indigenous population, and wheat, which was scarcely available, "was not consumed by the [native] community, which assigns it little importance."[9]

Indeed, maize constituted the staple and most extensively planted crop in the isthmus. It was harvested by indigenous communities as well as by Spanish haciendas dedicated to export crops. The quantity of frijoles grown was almost as important as that of maize. Those two were the principal sources of protein for the great majority of the people, although they were often accompanied by smaller amounts of meat and fish. Like maize, frijoles can be grown at different altitudes although not in humid climates because of a vulnerability to fungal diseases. None of the crops introduced by the Spaniards extended as widely as maize and frijoles. The production of wheat, for example, was restricted to cool and dry climates.

While the Spaniards were primarily concerned with assuring supplies of wheat, the indigenous people had neither economic nor cultural incentives to adopt rice, except in the *tierra caliente* (hot country), where maize fared relatively poorly. Its cultivation requires extensive and well-watered plains, competing in most areas with the native staple maize. Rice also required enormous manual labor, constraining production in a family-based agricultural system. In the Audiencia of Guatemala at the end of the colonial era, the cultivation of rice was confined to swampy valleys of Honduras, and the Pacific lowlands of San Salvador, Nicaragua and Costa Rica. In the exceptional cases of Veragua and Panama, rice was as common as maize.[10] In his historical outline (*Bosquejo Histórico*) of Costa Rica, the Guatemalan Felipe Molina affirmed that in 1835 maize and beans "were harvested in all parts and rice in great quantities."[11] Rice was also cultivated in the towns of Matina, Esparza, Cartago and Escazú.[12]

Spanish authorities issued general orders for the cultivation of rice but only as part of a diversified agricultural program intended to assure provisions during times of hunger in the colony. In 1789, the Lieutenant Governor de Esparza, complying with demands from the provincial governor to prevent or at least lessen shortages "that were experienced annually for lack of foods," required residents to plant "maize, cotton, plantains, and rice" or suffer "five pesos fine and ten days in jail."[13] As scarcity continued, a year later the governor specified more clearly that every citizen should have a field "in which they plant two parts of maize, one of rice, and five *matas* [an orchard of variable dimensions] of plantains."[14] Despite these measures, in 1804 there was again a shortage of maize, rice, frijoles, and vegetables in the Central Valley, and once again the solution was to increase planting.[15] Twenty years later, a drought provoked deficits of rice and beans in Alajuela, prompting renewed demands for increased planting. The decline of food supplies at the beginning of the nineteenth century resulted from various causes: primitive farming methods, the small scale of production, natural disasters—excessive rains, droughts, insects—and the inefficient work of smallholders.[16] The shortage of foodstuffs also was a result of excess exports of provisions and a decline in the area cultivated by farmers.

The insufficiency was resolved, partially, in the second half of the nineteenth century, with the importation of rice, beans and maize, a practice that continued to increase in the twentieth century. In a parallel fashion over the nineteenth century, the mestizo descendents of Europeans, Native Americans and Africans began to gain a taste for rice, without discarding either the tortilla or beans, but rather combined and mixed, to produce an alimentary regimen that was equally hybrid. Like few dishes, *gallo pinto* was the result and clear expression of the hybrid culture of Latin America.

Rice and Beans in the Market

Rice rose to become an important staple over the course of the nineteenth century as an offshoot of the introduction of an important export crop—coffee. Beginning in 1840, and growing more copious with each passing year, coffee came to be the principal product of Costa Rican agriculture, steadily displacing the cultivation of basic grains. After forty years, one observer noted that "coffee growers have substituted for the majority of those maize and bean farms."[17] In 1883, government authorities concurred on "the excessive decline of the coefficient of production in almost all cantons with respect to maize, rice, beans, and potatoes, the base of the population's subsistence."[18] Fundamental changes in the global economy made rice an economical import crop, and as Costa Ricans acquired a taste for the crop, domestic production began to grow because rice did not compete with coffee for valuable agricultural land. This section follows the development of rice and beans through the 1920s, noting the ways that price and accessibility of these grains provided incentives for consumption.

In 1825, the Englishman John Hale noted the price of products sold in the market plaza of San José, which was the Costa Rican capital's principal weekly activity and drew numerous buyers, sellers and observers. There, for the cost of half a real, one could purchase four pounds of beef (1.8 kg), an equal amount of sugar, sixteen eggs and two pounds of coffee (0.9 kg) and for twice that one could buy vegetables to satisfy two or three persons.[19] He mentioned neither rice nor beans, probably because they were planted with some frequency on small plots and obtained by way of barter or in small general stores (*pulperías*). Almost two decades later, however, in 1852, the German traveler Moritz Wagner observed that in the market plaza they sold rice "in open sacks" and measured it with small ceramic jars.[20] By the 1880s, rice also abounded in the markets of the principal head towns (*cabeceras*) such as Cartago, where the vendors set up in a park in front of the cathedral. Englishman John Belly likewise noted, while traveling from Alajuela to San José, multiple wagons "carrying sacks of rice, cacao, and coffee" heading to the market of Alajuela which met on Mondays.[21]

Meanwhile, in those same markets frijoles were sold by the bushel. From 1835 to 1852, their price multiplied four times, passing from 4 to 18 piastres a bushel. In the 1850s, the wages of an average worker oscillated between 15 and 18 pesos a month, so a bushel of beans represented then the totality of their income. According to Moritz Wagner "the daily consumption of this so popular national dish

FOOD,
CULTURE &
SOCIETY

VOLUME 15

ISSUE 2

JUNE 2012

[black beans] could be valued at half a pound per head, that is 75,000 pounds a day and 18,250,000 pounds per year for the entire population," supposing a population of more than 100,000 inhabitants.[22]

Yet Costa Rican production of rice and beans was increasingly unstable in the latter nineteenth century and did not meet local demand. In 1876, forty years after coffee began to expand in the national territory at the expense of basic grains for subsistence, the country had to import 182,709 pounds of rice (82,875 kg) and 19,493 pounds (8,842 kg) of frijoles. This also indicates an important demand for rice among the population that had incorporated the new grain alongside traditional beans and maize. Between 1883 and 1888, average rice consumption was 3 pounds (1.38 kg) per person and in the following five years it grew to 8.75 pounds (3.98 kg); between 1899 and 1903 it surpassed 12 pounds (5.5 kg) annually. By the end of the first decade of the twentieth century, rice was the leading import in the country, followed distantly by beer, cured hides, preserved foods, and iron for construction. Only with the outbreak of the First World War did rice imports begin to decline, resulting in serious dislocations for consumers who had become accustomed to the grain. The return of peace, and renewed demand for Costa Rican coffee, allowed rice and bean consumption again to climb, especially between 1924 and 1928, when it reached an average of 40 pounds (18 kg) annually for rice and another 35 pounds (16 kg) for beans.[23]

Advertisements[24] indicate the diverse sources of Costa Rican rice imports. Some retailers did not specify the origin of their merchandise, such as Gustavo A. D. Meinecke, who in 1858 simply publicized the sale of rice along with multiple foreign products, including wine, cognac, asparagus, mushrooms, patés, mustard, sardines, sugar and candied fruit.[25] By contrast, Eugenio Lamicq, proprietor of the French Grocery (Almacen), proudly advertised the finest rice in the world from China and the Carolinas.[26] Meanwhile, the Hotel Roma advertised Italian rice for wholesale or retail, although it did not specify whether it served risotto in the cafe.[27] While these products did not carry a brand name, the merchants revealed these exotic origins as an indication of the virtues of the rice, an antecedent to the brand that would later symbolize the particularities of the good or service.

Rice arrived in the Costa Rican market from different countries, including Germany, Belgium, Spain, Italy, United States, France, United Kingdom, El Salvador, Guatemala, Panama, and China. Although the largest amount came from Germany until 1914, after that point, the United States became the principal supplier to Costa Rica.[28] This was no longer Carolina Gold, but rather industrial rice from Texas, or even re-exports from the Orient. Already in 1874, traveler Helmuth Polakowski claimed that "the rice imported to Costa Rica almost always comes from China and Japan by way of California; national rice production is small and the product is good, but in most cases it is impure due to the lack of good sorting machines."[29] A decade later, his countryman, Carl Schwalbe, had the same opinion:

in Costa Rica, rice (Oryza sativa) is grown in excellent quality, but it is not sufficient for consumption. Rice cultivated in the country is more expensive than imports from China and Japan. Imports cost approximately 27 marks [54 pesos], while domestic product, 30 marks the metric quintal [60 pounds]. This important cereal grows very well up to 1,000 meters.[30]

Price also changed according to the province where it was sold. For example, in 1883 and 1884, domestic rice in San José fluctuated between 5 and 8 centavos per kilogram, but in other provinces it rose to 10 and even in Puntarenas to 15 centavos. Foreign rice was fixed at exactly the same price as domestic. Nevertheless, a package in San José could arrive at 1 peso but in Limón it exceeded 1.25 pesos and in Liberia even 3 pesos. In 1890, rice, considered by the authorities to be one of the articles of prime necessity, was taxed at 20 centavos per kilogram, while beans were taxed at 15 centavos. In this year, salaries oscillated between 2 and 3 pesos daily for trades such as carpenters, cobblers, bricklayers and tailors; peons who worked on the railroad and road building, made 1.5 to 2 pesos daily; meanwhile farm workers were paid 1.25 to 1.5 pesos daily. Thus, around the turn of the twentieth century, both rice and beans were within reach of the majority of the population based on price.[31]

During the First World War, however, rice and beans, like other articles of prime necessity, became expensive, both through higher import costs and the speculation of local merchants. In 1915, for example, retail merchants made 935 percent profit on the sale of imported beans, a considerable sum that decidedly affected the consumer. The excessive inflation of prices for beans and rice obliged the government to search for solutions to avoid the growing threat of social conflict. For this reason, President Alfredo González Flores signed a decree that would ban exports of "beans, maize, rice, lard, and white and raw sugar" without previous authorization from the Ministry of Finance, and could "concede or deny authorization according to the quantity of those goods in the country."[32] These rising prices also had the unfortunate effect of forcing consumers to rely more exclusively on these basic staples, reducing variety in the national diet.

Migrants and the Consumption of Rice and Beans

Although rice had been cultivated in Costa Rica since the sixteenth century, it was not considered a basic product in daily diets until late in the nineteenth century. At mid-century, workers building the first railroads in the eastern part of the country, for example, received copious quantities of beans, maize and sugar, sporadically meat, and only occasionally rice. Their basic diet consisted of beans, tortillas and sweetened water (*aguadulce*) or sweetened coffee, as was typical of most Costa Ricans. Rice entered the Atlantic zone of the country after 1870 when three groups of migrants arrived to work on the construction of railroads: Afro-Caribbeans, Chinese and Italians. By examining consumption patterns among these ethnic groups, it is possible to explain the growing presence of rice and beans in the Costa Rican Caribbean, as well as coastal Nicaragua.

Table 1, which depicts the quantities of rice and beans consumed by railroad workers, permits some conclusions about how these items fit in their consumption patterns. For the Chinese, rice is a dietary essential, while for Italians, particularly in the north, it is an important complement. In the work camps with a majority of

FOOD,
CULTURE &
SOCIETY

VOLUME 15

ISSUE 2

JUNE 2012

Table 1: Food distribution among employees of the Costa Rican Railroad Company (1873–1888)

UFCO peons (150) April 12 to May 6, 1873	Chinese (653) April 12 to May 6, 1873	Italians (700) Daily 1888
2,055 lb meat (932 kg)	3,300 lb rice (1497 kg)	3 oz sugar (85 g)
2,891 lb potato (1311 kg)	1,532 lb potato (695 kg)	1.5 oz coffee (43 kg)
1,665 lb bread (755 kg)	394 lb bread or crackers (179 kg)	8 bread rolls
727 lb rice (330 kg)	300 lb salt cod (136 kg)	8 oz rice or beans (227 g)
139 lb beans (63 kg)	140 lb coffee (64 kg)	8 oz meat (227 g)
549 lb sugar (249 kg)	2 barrels lard	lard and salt
475 lb crackers (215 kg)		
120 lb salt cod (54 kg)		
102 lb coffee (46 kg)		
17 lb onions (8 kg)		
10 lb tea (5 kg)		

Sources: Jeffrey Casey Gaspar, "El ferrocarril al atlántico en Costa Rica, 1871–1874," *Anuario de Estudios Centroamericanos* 2 (1976): 321; ANCR, Serie Fomento, No. 1577, f. 191; *El Ferrocarril* (San José), September 14, 1872.
Metric conversions rounded to nearest whole unit.

Chinese workers, for example, "they had a giant caldron or sauce pan to boil the rice for their consumption."[33] The bulk of their diet consisted of rice, supplemented by potatoes, salt cod and coffee. Meanwhile, Italian workers on the Costa Rican railroad received either rice or beans (eight ounces daily) but not both ingredients, as either a risotto or minestrone soup would provide the *primi* or traditional first course of an Italian meal. The *segundi* or second course consisted of eight ounces of meat according to company records. Clearly the assignment of rations had a direct relationship with the workers' customary foods.

As the chart shows, only among black peons of the United Fruit Company was the combination of both grains widely eaten, with an average of about 93 ounces of rice and 20 ounces of beans daily per person. A popular dish in the Caribbean combines rice, beans and coconut milk. If one eliminates this final ingredient and substitutes a hot chili for sweet pepper, the result is *gallo pinto*. Thus, it is possible that the custom of *gallo pinto* derives from this typical Afro-Caribbean food. The majority of Afro-Caribbean workers came from Jamaica and nearby islands. All were descendents of slaves, a good part of them sugar workers. Although the arrival of blacks on the Caribbean coasts of Central America dates to the end of the seventeenth century, the first Jamaican migration to Costa Rica occurred in 1872 to work in the construction of the railroad line from the Central Valley to the Atlantic "and from there followed a constant influx as the banana plantations covered the province of Limón."[34]

The mixture of rice and beans is frequent in West Africa, but accompanied with animal protein—beef or fish—just as rice and beans are served in Limón, a province on the Caribbean coast. The name with which the plate is called is a derivation of "rice and peas," referring to the mixture of rice and *arvejas de Angola* (Angola pea or Congo pea) on the island of Martinique. In Cuba:

> precisely the alimentation of the plantations—that boils down to rice, beans, jerky or salt cod, and "*vianda*" (note that similarity with the basic diet of the present-day Cuban)—owes its influence to white rice and stew [of beans] have in the east the highest consumption, while less *congrí* (a dish better known, until not long ago, as "Moors and Christians" that, certainly, is prepared the same with pinto beans rather than black) and also the rice with meat, above all during daily meals.[35]

The word *congrí* is of French Haitian origin, incorporated into Cuban culture at the end of the eighteenth century by way of the massive migration of Haitians fleeing the consequences of revolution. Afro-Caribbeans reserved rice and beans for festive days, growing diverse varieties of beans in their family gardens.[36]

Railroad companies elsewhere in Latin America likewise provisioned workers, particularly Afro-Caribbeans, with rice and beans. In Colombia, in 1882, when they began work on the railroad from Puerto Wilches:

> the ration for workers contracted in the Atlantic Coast was composed as follows: "Breakfast, at 5:30 a.m. Coffee with cracker or some equivalent. Brunch, at 10 a.m. Rice, meat, beans, cornbread, and brown sugar in sufficient quantities. Dinner, at 5 p.m. Rice, meat, beans, lard, cornbread, and brown sugar. They were also supplied plantain, yucca, and other vegetables."[37]

FOOD,
CULTURE &
SOCIETY

VOLUME 15

ISSUE 2

JUNE 2012

Rice and beans, although not mixed, were present in the camps of Costa Rican workers on the Atlantic railroad. In 1876 and 1878, when the state assumed control of some of these camps, the diet fell under the following pattern:

In the morning, a cup of black coffee with rum or brandy, at the brunch hour (*almuerzo*), beans with lard, rice, and plantains; at midday or the main meal, a little soup, enough for one man, with meat or rice varied and plantains, and at night for dinner, black coffee and crackers.[38]

Rice and beans also was a part of the diet for railroad engineers and the foremen and mechanics of trackmen. The former were served, in glass jars, first-class rice along with stews, cheese, fine rum, ham, oysters and lobster, among other taste delights. The latter accompanied their rice with pickled vegetables, fresh or salt meat, and tea, coffee, rum and sweets.

With the dawn of the twentieth century and the massive proletarian migrations to the banana zone, the diet was simplified to the extreme. Beginning in the 1930s, company workers had *gallo pinto* as their principal dish, which they received for breakfast, lunch and dinner. Carlos Luis Fallas recalled that an ostentatious breakfast among the banana plantations consisted of "the famous *burra*: a plate of oats that was added to the accustomed plate, a mountain of rice and beans mixed together and toasted called '*gallo pinto*' and the parboiled bananas. Then a cup of black coffee without sugar."[39] The daily menu nevertheless consisted of "a heap of rice and beans, four bananas and a bit of brown sugar."[40]

Most striking is that in the 1930s, the name *gallo pinto* was already familiar to those working for the banana companies. At this point it had established a close contact with other ethnic groups, particularly Afro-Caribbeans, who reproduced their culinary customs in Costa Rica. It is clear that the name was created by this group of men who longed for the taste of *gallo*. Among those living in the Central Valley, *gallo* was frequently associated with the black and white spotted rooster commonly seen in cockfights. Although there is no direct archival link in this case, aficionados of cockfights (even although the sport is banned today) consider the *gallo pinto*, or rooster with black and white colors in its plumage, to be the best fighter. It therefore is reasonable to suppose that these workers believed that the mixture of rice and beans inside a tortilla was the most satisfying of all foods that could be put in a tortilla.

That *gallo pinto* was a derivation of the African American rice and beans makes it unsurprising that the symbolic association positioned the plate as food of the poor or peasant subsistence. The mobility of material culture permits fashions and customs, particularly for foods, to filter from the elite to the base of society and vice versa. The symbolic associations of these goods can be used and renegotiated in order to sublimate differences in lifestyle that distinguish social relations. What motivates this phenomenon is the prestige and the process of imitation. Clearly, the preferences in matters of consumption in general and in styles of life, carry discriminatory judgments that simultaneously identify and make classifiable for others the particular judgment of taste of distinct social groups. In this way, *gallo pinto* differentiates rich from poor, slaves from whites, and workers from bosses.

Yet *gallo pinto* could have been created in the Central Valley because of the simple availability of the products and the Iberian heritage of mixing peas with rice, now frequently substituted with frijoles. The combination of colors and tastes make consumption more interesting, while at the same time providing complementary nutrients. Besides, rice is always combined with other products, generally meat or sweet, and so it is no surprise to mix it with frijoles, as a way of transforming a monotonous meal comprising tortillas and beans—in the form of *gallos*, a popular term for the wrapping of diverse foods in a maize tortilla—as a new dish. The flavors supplement and round out the diet, giving it a variable character.

Dietary patterns are a cultural phenomenon and the culture should be understood not only as a product but also as an act of production, not only socially constructed but also constitutive of society.[41] The presence of rice in great quantities that excess production in Asia brought to the world, was re-exported to Latin American countries by European powers and by the United States, placing at their disposition a cheap and well-known product, in such a manner that favored a change in the dietary patterns of a population whose access to economic subsistence was becoming more precarious due to war and depression in the early decades of the twentieth century. The arrival of migrant workers cemented this pattern, but it did so not from the Chinese presence but rather from Afro-Caribbeans, whose hybrid culture contributed both to the consumption and symbolization of *gallo pinto*.

One final conundrum remains: if one pays attention to the Costa Rican national discourse on race in the early twentieth century, it is notable that politicians and intellectuals had imagined Costa Rica as a white country, not an Indian, black or mestizo one. Why, therefore, did the Costa Rican national discourse identify its imagined community with Europe racially but not in terms of food, for example, by using rice as evidence that Costa Rica was as white as Spain.[42] The answer to this conundrum may lie in the fact that national cuisines develop from the ground up, unlike many other symbols of national identity imposed from the top down. To demonstrate this point, it is therefore necessary to examine the domestic consumption of rice more closely.

Rice and Beans at Home

In 1903, Juana Ramírez Carrera de Aragón published the first Costa Rican cookbook, and despite the collection of more than 800 recipes, it did not include *gallo pinto*. Rather, the work unified diverse dishes based on rice, such as *arroz a la valenciana*, fried rice, rice pudding, rice with milk, etc., and just as many based on frijoles—white, with sugar or sweets, with ham, in soup, and specifically black beans, dried, were identified as the "national dish."[43] Note that Señora de Aragón did not refer to *gallo pinto* at this time, a revealing omission. Her cookbook provides an overview of nineteenth-century consumption habits of Costa Rica's middle classes, who considered rice an important celebratory dish. Nevertheless, it still held foreign associations—the prestige of imported Spanish luxury goods—despite the growing levels of popular consumption. Only at a time of economic crisis in the 1930s, when Afro-Caribbean migrants at the bottom of the social hierarchy had

FOOD,
CULTURE&
SOCIETY

VOLUME 15

ISSUE 2

JUNE 2012

combined the grain with the indigenous beans to form a nutritionally balanced dish, did the fusion become recognized as the national cuisine.

Rice was mixed with other ingredients, sweets, beef or pork, both in public spaces and in private, and was considered a dish for special occasions. For example, at wedding celebrations, such as the following example from 1838, it was usual in families of sufficient economic means to thank the guests with:

> sacks of rice, jugs of milk [besides the indispensable bride's cake, rice in aromas and *achiote*, a flavorful, bright red seed], egg yolk candies, candied coconut, *rosquetes* and *enlustrados* (donut-shaped pastries), *corazones atravesados* (pierced hearts), and candy flowers of exquisite filigree; big cups of angel's hair, milk rolls, sweet and savory empanadas of meat, cheese, goat's cheese, and blackberries; round sweets (*alfajores*) of pineapple with ginger; fine china cups and artistic gourds with soft drinks, *tistes* and *pinoles* (toasted cornmeal drinks) and chocolate, spiked eggnog that inspires happiness and delicious *mistelas* (sweet Muscat liquors).[44]

For Christmas carols (*posadas*) and other public gatherings where foods were sold, white or mixed rice was never missing. In 1841, while traveling to Puntarenas, the English explorer John Lloyd Stephens stopped in Montes del Aguacate, in the Hacienda of Aranjuez, where he received as food: "'tortillas,' rice cooked with bacon, served in a shell, and salt that Nicolás brought me in the palm of his hand."[45] The frequency of "rice with pork" is such that it was considered a common dish together with frijoles, tortillas, "soup of field greens, hominy, *ajiaco* (spicy Cuban soup), fries, tender meatballs, stuffed meat, pork cracklings with yucca, *mondongos* (stewed tripe)."[46] In 1870, a wedding festival had as the main dish for the guests, "rice with pork, ground beans, more little tortillas that for their whiteness and delicacies resembled communion wafers, and fine coffee."[47] They then served mixed rice and beans separately, a custom that remained decades later, and rice was not only customary in the midday meal or at night, but also formed part of breakfast, according to the description of the Prussian Carl Hoffmann in 1855, accepting from a wealthy family "a genuinely national breakfast ... roasted chicken and beef, boiled and fried eggs, maize tortillas which were never absent and beans, rice with *achiote*, grilled plantains, and diverse sweets."[48]

Foreigners, in particular Europeans, accustomed to rice, carried this practice to areas where it was not yet established. At the end of the nineteenth century, Karl Sapper, a countryman of Hoffmann, in his travel through the Nicoya Peninsula, carried with him rice, tea and meat to feed himself on the road.[49] This habit of frugal breakfast was not always maintained in the twentieth century and the midday meal was the most prodigious. In 1905, recalled José Basilio Acuña:

> in the homes they breakfasted ... bread with butter and coffee. The brunch was abundant; one could never lack for beefsteak, vegetables, rice, chopped meat, cakes, empanadas, beans, tortillas, and bread ... In addition, they ate dinner at eight with chocolate, beans, tortillas with cheese, and *bocadillos* (mouthfuls).[50]

There were two special moments during the year when the diet changed: Holy Week and Christmas. In the latter proliferated tamales, *chicha* (corn beer) and other sweets; in the former, by contrast, presumed to be a fast, according to the requirements of the Catholic Church, with the absolute absence of pork, beef, and chicken. As a result, a common daily round consisted of:

> in the morning, a small breakfast; a cup of bread and rice, a bean or hard boiled egg tamal, a piece of *tonto*, and sweetened water; in the afternoon, at three, once again sweetened water and a piece of bread or two rolls of roasted cornmeal (*bizcocho totoposte*) or a small goat's cheese empanada. [51]

Funerals were also a space for sociability, and the food was very important; in the collective imagination there was a wish to thank the attendees who accompanied the mourning families with special foods that were prepared only on this occasion. Among the dishes were served, as in the novenas of the death of Arrieta in the novel by Carlos Luis Fallas, *Mi Madrina* (My Mother-in-law), "the brunch ... the most succulent mouthfuls: great spoonfuls of *humeantes* (tamales), dense and deliciously fried; fat thighs and tender breasts of chicken; stuffed loin; potato and meat *picadillo* (minced meat), *rojo* (red sauce) with *achiote* (seed) and pepper; rice cakes; grapefruit honey; coffee with bizcochos and sweet rolls kneaded especially by doña María Arrieta."[52]

Even in 1874, rice and beans were not present together in the form of *gallo pinto* according to the observations of the German Helmuth Polakowski. According to him, at that time, "the principal dish was black beans, fried plantain, and a mixture of rice, red pepper, and scallops, whose dough was colored bright red with *achiote*" in such a manner that the rice was not served boiled alone, but rather mixed with the meat, following the custom inherited from Spain.[53]

What is certain is that for restaurants in the capital, rice was not important, or at least they did not promote it among the dishes that they served. In April 1903, the Italian Gilberto Cavalinni, invited the audience of an opera to go to his restaurant, where he offered them "eggs, fish, veal and pork cutlets, beans, beefsteak, chicken, lamb in *salmis*, the same grilled, fried catfish, cheese, sabayon, English pudding, coffee, tea, and chocolate."[54] By contrast, in the improvised food stands, designated for the popular sectors, rice was present, although not necessarily mixed with beans but rather boiled, or at least it was encountered that way by Eugene Cunningham, a French traveler who visited Costa Rica in 1919. He explained that:

> outside of the market plaza, running the length of nearby streets, native women still had restaurants like those of Mexico, but cleaner, much cleaner! In those small stands they prepared and ate the same plantains—the big brother of the banana—cooked, fried, and grilled; bananas, oranges, pineapples, and coconuts; chicken, *tortillas* and cooked rice, white cheese and strange sweets. [55]

FOOD,
CULTURE&
SOCIETY

VOLUME 15

ISSUE 2

JUNE 2012

About 1900, Joaquín García Monge referred to a moderate brunch received at home with a peasant family. At nine in the morning, they were offered "two *arepas*

(Venezuelan round corn pancakes), a lardy egg, rice, beans, and a sweetened chocolate,"[56] but there was no mention of the mixing both grains, which leads one to suppose that in those times they still were not accustomed to *gallo pinto*. In 1915, rice and beans, together with sugar water, constituted the basic foods to satisfy families in the lowest position on the social pyramid. Luisa González recalls that in her family, all "had to stoop hard to work day and night, if necessary. Only thus could we have assurance of rice, beans, and *aguadulce* every day."[57] In March 1914, *La Prensa Libre* (The Free Press), which took the initiative in publishing fortnightly prices of staple foods, lamented the rapid rise in the price of beans leading to a "disequilibrium for the budgets of the poor classes, as is known, they make use of these [frijoles] and maize as the principal base of a frugal table."[58]

It is possible, nevertheless, that at this time, especially from 1920, with the return to the Central Valley of those who worked in the Atlantic, the combination of rice and beans increasingly came to be considered—like maize—a staple food in Costa Rica. As discussed, rice and beans passed from being a dish of the popular classes to become the "national dish" of *gallo pinto*. This illustrates how goods can be used to renegotiate social relations with the goal of sublimating the differences in lifestyle between the rich and poor as well as between different ethnic groups.

Conclusion

Rice and beans, mixed or separate, are served frequently in the majority of Costa Rican homes. Having them in the pantry signifies the ability to feed the family, particularly for those of scarce resources. To offer guests a dish of rice and beans in Costa Rica fulfills the basic norms of courtesy and hospitality. If one can add meat or other condiments, then the banquet is complete, and the host appears even more gracious.

Rice and beans have in them an affective signification: they are a means to validate existing social relations. Moreover, they are disposable goods, which is a basic requisite for facilitating consumption. Diverse historical processes favored the emergence of *gallo pinto* as a national dish, placing it in the pantheon of national symbols. Certainly, goods that are consumed in a determined region have to be available, but dietary preferences are constructed according to social and cultural rules. Forms of preparation, methods of eating, times of consumption, utensils for eating, and the company in which foods are shared are all indicators of social relations.

Tastes and dietary patterns are dynamic and changing, depending not just on availability but also the transformations of cultures and societies. The combination of rice and beans is a new dietary pattern that appeared at the end of the nineteenth century but was cemented in the decade of the 1930s. This pattern did not displace but rather added to tortillas and beans. Diverse factors, such as climate, war, economy, politics and even diplomacy, combined to change the diet. Massive planting of coffee in Costa Rica, for example, affected the cultivation of traditional products, including maize and beans, while the excess cultivation of rice in diverse parts of the world subject to colonial powers favored the purchase of legumes by dependent monoculture economies. With the growing presence of rice in Costa Rica, the basic products for the creation of *gallo pinto* were present—what was missing was the recipe. The presence of diverse ethnic groups along the Atlantic coast offered different methods of preparing rice as well as beans, favoring the confection of a hybrid dish.

Gallo pinto was born as a cheap and nutritive dish that supplied the peons of the United Fruit Company, who may well have baptized the dish. This new dish—with a particular name—was converted into a reference of identity for a group of workers forging their daily subsistence. Rice and beans mixed and fried in lard, their taste, the company with which they were consumed and the schedule, were conducive to the construction of a sense of belonging and sharing related to an alimentary pattern. United Fruit Company workers then returned home with the recipe, along with the identifying references. The symbolic meaning of the dish then changed, as happens with signals of identity that are evolving and dynamic.

The appropriation of the new dish by the middle classes resulted from a growth in the demand for rice and beans. Although beans had long been a centerpiece of the Costa Rican table, rice consumption became widespread during the second half of the nineteenth century, and imports peaked during moments of crisis. In the early decades of the twentieth century, during the dislocations of world war and depression, the nutritionally sound and inexpensive combination became an obligatory presence on rural and urban tables. At such a time, the proletarian dish, with its colorful symbolism, secured an anchor in the collective imagination, eventually leading to its recognition as a "national dish." This category, obviously a modern introduction, grew in importance over the course of the twentieth century, in large part from the value it added in selling the image of a country, both to foreigners and to Costa Ricans themselves. Now even transnational corporations like McDonald's offer *gallo pinto*, incorporating it into the morning menu. Once tourist restaurants had proclaimed it as a national dish, the trajectory of *gallo pinto* was complete.

Acknowledgment

The author is grateful for the assistance of Natalia Rodríguez and Marta Palacios. An earlier version of this paper was presented as "*El Gallo Pinto* and Costa Rica's National Cuisine," at the Conference on Latin American History, Atlanta, GA, USA, January 6, 2007.

FOOD,
CULTURE &
SOCIETY

VOLUME 15

ISSUE 2

JUNE 2012

Patricia Vega Jiménez earned a PhD in history and has done postgraduate studies in communication sciences. She writes on the history of communication, consumption and labor markets. She heads the research committee at the University of Costa Rica's School of Collective Communication Sciences. In addition, she is a researcher and editorial board director at the Center for Latin American Identity, and Culture and Assistant Dean in the Faculty of Social Sciences, also at the University of Costa Rica. School of Communication Sciences, University of Costa Rica, Sede "Rodrigo Facio Brenes" Montes de Oca, San José 2060, Costa Rica (patricia.vega@ucr.ac.cr).

Notes

1 *La Nación*, January 9, 2006, p. 2.

2 Roland Barthes, "Toward a Psychosociology of Contemporary Food Consumption," in Carole Counihan and Penny Van Esterik (eds) *Food and Culture. A Reader* (London: Routledge, 1997), p. 21.

3 Arnold J. Bauer, *Goods, Power, History: Latin America's Material Culture* (Cambridge: Cambridge University Press, 2001), p. 198.

4 A similar phenomenon has been observed in the case of the Mexican taco, which arose from the popular classes to become a source of national identity. See Jeffrey M. Pilcher, "¡Tacos, joven! Cosmopolitismo proletario y la cocina nacional mexicana," *Dimensión Antropológica* 13:37 (2006): 87–125.

5 Juana R. de Aragón, *La cocina costarricense* (San José: Editorial de la Universidad de Costa Rica, 2003 [1903]). For two works on the theme of food and society in Costa Rica, see Marjorie Ross González, *Entre el comal y la olla: Fundamentos de la gastronomía costarricense* (San José: Editorial Universidad Estatal a Distancia, 2001); Patricia Vega Jiménez, "Alimentos e identidades: Trabajadores de las bananeras costarricenses, 1934," *Ciencias Sociales* 98 (2002): 99–110.

6 Theresa Preston-Werner, "*Gallo Pinto*: Tradition, Memory, and Identity in Costa Rican Foodways," *Journal of American Folklore* 122 (2009): 11–27.

7 Simultaneously in the United States, the deprivations of war and the Depression led to the granting of "cultural citizenship" to cheap and nutritious foreign foods such as spaghetti and hotdogs. See Donna R. Gabaccia, *We Are What We Eat: Ethnic Food and the Making of Americans* (Cambridge, MA: Harvard University Press, 1998), pp. 122–48.

8 Yamileth González, *Continuidad y cambio en la historia agraria de Costa Rica* (San José: Editorial Costa Rica, 1985), p. 20. On the introduction of wheat in 1561, see Carlos Meléndez, *Costa Rica: Tierra y poblamiento en la colonia* (San José: Editorial Costa Rica, 1978), p. 109.

9 Miguel Angel Quesada Pacheco, *Entre silladas y rejoyas. Viajeros por Costa Rica de 1850 a 1950* (San José: Editorial Tecnológica de Costa Rice, 2001), p. 38.

10 Carolyn Hall and Héctor Pérez, *Historical Atlas of Central America* (Norman, OK: University of Oklahoma Press, 2003), p. 155.

11 Felipe Molina, "Bosquejo Histórico de la República de Costa Rica" (Alajuela: Museo Histórico Cultural Juan Santamaría, 2001).

12 Archivo Nacional de Costa Rica (ANCR), Fondo Judicial, No. 17318, 1837, f. 1; Fondo Municipal, No. 12372, 1820, f. 1.

13 ANCR, Fondo Colonial, No. 845-CO. 1789, f. 1.

14 ANCR, Fondo Colonial, No. 845-CO. 1790, f. 1.

15 ANCR, Serie Cartago, No. 1138, 1804, f. 1.

16 Carolyn Hall, *El café y el desarrollo histórico-geográfico de Costa Rica* (San José: Editorial Costa Rica, 1976), p. 29.

17 Ibid., 82.

18 Departamento Nacional de Estadística de Costa Rica, *Resúmenes estadísticos (1883–1893)* (San José: Tipografía Nacional, 1884), p. 5.

19 Ricardo Fernández Guardia, *Costa Rica en el siglo XIX* (San José: Educam 1982), p. 21.

20 Moritz Wagner and Carl Schelzer, *La República de Costa Rica en Centro América* (San José: Biblioteca Yorusti, 1944), p. 99.

21 Elías Zeledón, *Viajes por la República de Costa Rica*, 2 vols. (San José: Editorial de la Dirección de publicaciones Museo Nacional de Costa Rica, 1997), Vol. 1, p. 77; Jesús Mata Gamboa, *Monografía de Cartago* (San José: Editorial Tecnológica de Costa Rica, 1999), p. 101.

22 Wagner and Schelzer, *La República de Costa Rica*, p. 199.

23 ANCR, Fondo Estadística y Censos, No. 935, f. 6. For an analysis of these trends, see Emmanuel Barrantes, Hilda Bonilla, and Olga Ramírez, *Las subsistencias en una coyuntura de crisis, Costa Rica 1914–1920* (Memorial del Seminario de Graduación para optar al grado de Licenciatura en Historia, Universidad de Costa Rica, 2002), p. 124.

24 The advertisements used for this paper were taken from newspapers published in Costa Rica between 1850 and 1930.

25 *Crónica de Costa Rica*, November 13, 1859, p. 4.

26 *El Heraldo. Diario del Comercio*, January 14, 1898, p. 4.

27 Ibid., March 16, 1887, p. 1.

28 Departamento General de Estadísticas y Censos, *Anuario Estadístico* (1907–1919).

29 Quesada Pacheco, *Entre silladas y rejoyas*, p. 200.

30 Ibid., p. 312.

31 Departamento General de Estadísticas y Censos, *Anuario Estadístico* (1890, 1907–1922).

32 Barrentes, Bonilla, and Ramírez, *Las subsistencias en una coyuntura*, pp. 267, 289.

33 Carmen Murillo, *Identidades de hierro y humo: La construcción del ferrocarril al Atlántico, 1870–1890* (San José: Editorial Porvenir, 1995), p. 96.

34 Victor Hugo Acuña, "Clases subalternas y movimientos socials en Centro América (1870–1930)," in Víctor Hugo Acuña (ed.) *Las repúblicas agroexportadoras (1870–1945)*, vol. 4 of Edelberto Torres-Rivas (ed.) *Historia general de Centroamérica*, 6 vols. (Madrid: Sociedad Estatal Quinto Centenario-FLACSO, 1993), p. 266.

35 Niurka Núñez González and Estrella Gonález Noriega, "Diferencias regionales en las comidas tradicionales de la población rural de Cuba," Available from: http://www.bvs.sld. cu/revistas/ali/vol9_2_ali01295.htm (accessed September 1, 2011).

36 Carlos Meléndez and Duncan Quince, *El negro en Costa Rica* (San José: Editorial Costa Rica, 1976), p. 112.

37 Victor Manuel Patiño, "Historia de la cultura material en la América Equinoccial," Vol. 1 "Alimentación y alimentos." Available from: http://www.lablaa.org/blaavirtual/letra-h/historia/partpr4.htm (accessed September 1, 2011).

38 Murillo, "Identidades de hierro y humo," p. 99.

39 Carlos Luis Fallas, *Mamita Yunai* (San José: Editorial Costa Rica, 1998), p. 111.

40 Ibid., p. 142.

41 Sidney Mintz, *Sweetness and Power: The Place of Sugar in Modern History* (New York: Viking Penguin, 1985), p. 41.

42 Víctor Hugo Acuña, "La invención de la diferencia costarricense, 1810–1870," *Revista de Historia* (Costa Rica), p. 45 (January to June 2002): 191–228; Carlos Sandoval García, *Threatening Others: Nicaraguans and the Formation of National Identities in Costa Rica* (Athens, OH: Ohio University Press, 2004); Ronald Soto, "Desaparecidos de la nación: los indígenas en la construcción de la identidad nacional costarricense 1851–1924," *Revista de Ciencias Sociales* (Costa Rica) 82 (December 1998): 31–53; Iván Molina Jiménez, *Costarricense por dicha: identidad nacional y cambio cultural en Costa Rica durante los siglos XIX y XX* (San José: Editorial de la Universidad de Costa Rica, 2002); Steven Palmer, "Racismo Intelectual en Costa Rica y Guatemala, 1870–1920," *Mesoamérica* (Guatemala)

FOOD,
CULTURE &
SOCIETY

VOLUME 15

ISSUE 2

JUNE 2012

17:31 (1996): 99–121; Ronald Harpelle, "Racism and Nationalism in the Creation of Costa Rica's Pacific Coast Banana Enclave," *The Americas* 56:3 (2000): 29–51.

43 De Aragón, *La cocina costarricense*, p. 26.

44 Gonzalo Chacón Trejos, *Tradiciones costarricenses* (San José: Editorial Costa Rica, n.d.), p. 8.

45 Fernández Guardia, *Costa Rica en el siglo XIX*, p. 88.

46 Chacón Trejos, *Tradiciones costarricenses*, p. 52.

47 Macabeo Vargas, *¡Oh tiempos aquellos! Atañerías* (San José: Imprenta Borrasé, 1952), p. 7.

48 Zeledón, *Viajes por la República de Costa Rica*, Vol. 2, p. 178.

49 Ibid., p. 52.

50 Lilia Ramos, *Júbilo y pena del recuerdo* (San José: Editorial Costa Rica, 1965), p. 272.

51 Adela Ferreto, *Crónicas de un tiempo* (San José: Editorial Costa Rica, 1978), p. 250.

52 Carlos Luis Fallas, *Mi Madrina* (San José: Editorial Costa Rica, 1972), p. 23.

53 Quesada Pacheco, *Entre silladas y rejoyas*, p. 253.

54 *El Entreacto*, April 14, 1903, p. 1.

55 Quesdada Pacheco, *Entre silladas y rejoyas*, p. 665.

56 Joaquín Monge García, *El Moto* (San José: Edice, 1968), p. 46.

57 Luisa González, *A ras del suelo* (San José: Editorial Costa Rica, 1994).

58 *La Prensa Libre*, March 7, 1914, p. 1.

FOOD, CULTURE & SOCIETY

VOLUME 15 | ISSUE 2 | JUNE 2012

Mirrors in the Kitchen

THE *NEW CUBAN WOMAN* COOKS REVOLUTIONARILY

Marisela Fleites-Lear

Green River Community College

Abstract

This paper examines the complex relationship between gender politics, food, cooking and the ideology of the Cuban revolution by analyzing the cooking section of the important women's magazine Mujeres, *and three foundational cookbooks that established an inter-textual dialogue of omissions and additions, symbolizing both the transformations that occurred on the island with the revolution and the divisions brought about by the Cuban diaspora. At the center of the analysis are the writings of Nitza Villapol, the Cuban food guru that have continued to dominate Cuban cuisine on both sides of the strait of Florida. The paper therefore looks at different editions of her main cookbook, from both the island as well as Miami, as an instrument to understand on the one hand, elements in the redefinition of women within the revolution, and on the other, the way in which cooking as a part of popular culture is fictionalized in response to ideological changes.*

Keywords: gender politics, Cuban revolution, cookbooks, Nitza Villapol

Introduction

"Cook revolutionarily" is the title of an early but crucial article by Ada Oramas, published in the Cuban magazine *Vanidades* (Vanities) on August 15, 1961. One of the first steps of the US economic embargo, which began in 1960, was to suspend the supply of pork lard for cooking. The new Cuban government organized an assembly of cooks and prominent revolutionaries to analyze how this crisis could be resolved, taking into account that Cubans are "a courageous people who are not frightened to boil instead of fry" (Oramas 1961: 26). As part of this effort, the "revolutionary" *Vanidades* published a "popular menu" that was proposed in the assembly along with recipes "so that the lady of the house familiarize herself with the manner in which the central dish of each popular menu must be prepared, and thus ... the Cuban woman not only responds to the

2752/175174412X13233545145264
available directly from the
rs. Photocopying permitted by
nly © Association for the Study of
Society 2012

brutal imperialistic attack, but also produces meals more fitted to our climate" (Oramas 1961:27–8).

Forty-four years later, in the central act to celebrate International Women's Day on March 8, 2005, before an assembly of hundreds of delegates from the Federation of Cuban Women (FMC), Commander-in-Chief Fidel Castro personally announced to the gathered women the sale of rice cookers at subsidized prices to facilitate the preparation of this national staple, among other steps destined to save electricity during the so-called "special period in time of peace" (Castro 2005).[1] As in 1961, women's presence in the kitchen is still a key part of the state's interpellation of the Cuban people's response to shortages.

The preceding examples serve to introduce the controversial discursive path taken by the state and its ideologues in post-1959 Cuba, a path that moves from "cooking revolutionarily" to the promise by the country's president to distribute rice cookers to Cuban women. By showing the relations between cooking, food, gender and politics, I argue that the "revolutionary cook" is an essential yet paradoxical element of the "new Cuban woman" discourse that was cooked up in the "soup of signs"[2] developed within the Cuban revolutionary process as presented by its official ideology. My analysis will be guided by a close reading of the popular women's magazine *Vanidades* (renamed *Mujeres* (Women) in November 1961), as well as of the speeches by revolutionary leaders and of the most important cookbooks published in Cuba since the 1950s that have guided the culinary ups and downs of Cuban families. The objective is to strain from these texts the implicit meanings that function as signposts for everyday life, the strategies that are used to appeal to readers and the connoted values and common myths that the texts simultaneously affirm and challenge. In clarifying this rich linguistic broth, I give attention to the performative character of language, to the notion that all discourse is a social action that uses signs to persuade, intimidate, convince, in summary, to affect social performance. Moreover, I will foreground the texts of one person who was transformed into a symbol, the epitome of the "revolutionary cook," Nitza Villapol—a woman deeply honored but at the same time vilified in the popular Cuban imaginary on both shores of the strait of Florida.

In 1960, the Cuban revolutionary government, and more directly its Commander Fidel, created the FMC to embrace all Cuban women, thus eliminating all political and social organizations for women that existed before 1959. The goal was to organize women for participation in revolutionary tasks. The accomplishments by Cuban women under the leadership of the FMC are undisputable, as I have discussed elsewhere.[3] As soon as the FMC was formed, it nationalized the influential magazine *Vanidades* in August 1960 because it was perceived as representing the "American way of life." *Vanidades* had been the leading Cuban magazine for women since it was established by Josefina Mosquera in 1937. Its last director, Herminia del Portal, emigrated from Cuba to New York in 1960 (where she created a new edition of *Vanidades*, with a continental character, later sold to Televisa). After taking over the publication, the FMC continued publishing *Vanidades* with the same name (identified in this paper as "the revolutionary *Vanidades*") from September 1960 until October 1961, when it was replaced by *Mujeres* (November

1961 to the present), as a self-proclaimed non-feminist women's journal, that has functioned ever since as the official voice of the FMC, and therefore, of the Cuban government and the Cuban Communist Party with respect to women and the family.[4] The latter justifies focusing on these publications for the analysis of the relation between gender, food and politics within the Cuban revolution, given their enormous importance in shaping Cubans' ideas in this area, particularly as around 84 percent of Cuban women are members of the FMC and for the last 50 years, *Mujeres* has been either the only or one of two allowed publications for women on the island.

For our analysis, it is important also to keep in mind that a metonymic association between woman, fertility and nourishment—with its sensual, sexual, and political connotations—has been traditionally part of the witty, musical, poetic and political Cuban imaginary, which, for complex and historical reasons, concedes a preferential place to food.[5] Think about the lyrics of songs and popular sayings in Cuba with phrases like "*quimbombo que resbala pa'la yuca seca*" (slimy okra for the dry yucca); "*agua pa' la olla que se quema el pollo*" (water for the pot, the chicken is burning); "*los tamalitos de Olga*" (Olga's little tamales); "*el que siembra su maiz, que recoja su pilon*" (he who plants corn, may he pick up his mortar); "*si me pides el pesca'o te lo doy*" (if you ask me for fish I will give it to you); "*si cocinas como caminas…*" (if you cook like you walk…) These phrases express and reinforce ideas and stereotypes that inform everything from law and politics to carnival processions, even after the 1959 revolution. In particular, they have contributed to enshrine the "revolutionary cook" as part of the ideal of a "new Cuban woman" within a cultural tradition that bestows a preferential place upon food and that in politics assumed the motto "to feed the people" as a central task of revolutionary Cuba.[6]

"Who Does the Cooking in Socialism? Feeding the New Revolutionary Generations, a Frontline Task…"

The historically changing conceptualization of the "Cuban woman," who was called to transform the kitchen into a defensive bastion of the socialist revolution, was articulated in the pages of *Mujeres*, particularly in the cartoons and the sections dedicated to recipes and nutritional advice, and in the works of *la cocinera mayor* (the leading cook), Nitza Villapol. I propose here a chronology of three distinct codifications of the relationship between women and the kitchen within Cuban revolutionary ideology, as expressed in *Mujeres*. The first, which I identify with the exhortation: "cook revolutionarily," extended from 1959 to 1987; the second, from 1988 to 1999, was represented by the expression: "invite him smoothly into your kitchen"; the third, beginning in 2000, assumed the imperative: "start sharing: you and him into the kitchen." This periodization reveals a textual movement toward more "feminist" positions—long overdue—in the response to the question "who cooks in socialism?"[7] I will try to demonstrate the changing and contradictory manner in which the magazine *Mujeres* has answered this question—an answer that by the new millennium had adopted explicit gender analysis, and in doing so, began to challenge the official discourse of the historical (mostly masculine) leaders of the revolution. The greatest example of these divergent discursive and ideological

FOOD,
CULTURE &
SOCIETY

VOLUME 15

ISSUE 2

JUNE 2012

243

paths is that while women managed in 2003 to get the Cuban parliament to approve a law allowing either paid maternity or paternity leave, in 2005, the Cuban leader Fidel Castro still assigned cooking appliances to women (as explained above).

The economic crisis of the lard blockade of 1960 brought women to the forefront of revolutionary ideology, and the aforementioned 1961 article exhorting Cuban women to cook in a revolutionary way strongly proposed that in doing so they should follow government directions and orientations. The majority of the recipes that were offered in this early time period sought to instruct domestic cooks (assuming them to be the woman of the house, not a servant) in how to substitute ingredients and cooking techniques for products that were lacking, and how to use new ones, even if they did not correspond with Cuban tastes or traditions. Little by little, vegetables (the majority not traditional in the Cuban diet, like eggplants, turnips, celery and beets), pasta, and non-traditional beans (carita, gandul, soy) were given preference, because they were the products most available in the market. As a result, the range of domestic culinary possibilities expanded. Recipes were selected by the FMC according to their usefulness for cooking with what was available. I group the recommendations from *Mujeres* under different strategies that have remained as a constant throughout the fifty-year history of this publication: "substitution," "learning to utilize new products from our socialist brothers," "saving," "varying the menu with what is available and with Cuban products that are not traditionally used" and "maintaining beauty in spite of stress." The most illustrative example of the last strategy, and the one from which this paper's title derives, appeared in *Mujeres* in March 1967 in the article "Hang a mirror in the kitchen" (*Mujeres* 1967: 111), that advises women to put two mirrors in the kitchen to look at themselves periodically while cooking and to correct the facial expression of stress that produces wrinkles. It suggests that women should smile in front of the mirror and loosen the lips as a beauty treatment while they cook, to make this unavoidable task entertaining.

Because of the constant scarcity of food throughout the history of the revolution, as well as the oversight of government censors, this authoritarian "orienting" element is constant throughout all three periods. *Mujeres* is similar to the majority of traditional female-targeted magazines around the world with the difference that in Cuba the editorial orientations respond to an ideology and to strategies at the level of the state, and they are taken on as jobs with a function not only at the domestic level but also at the general socio-political level. The magazine never discussed the "resistance" strategies developed by the population, such as using the government provided "soy *picadillo*" (a substitute for traditional chopped meat) as birdfeed instead of as a protein complement, or resorting to the black market in all its versions, as these non-official strategies do not conform to ideological mandates. It is no wonder then that in the 1990s, the Cuban government was reluctant to allow radio stations to play the popular NG La Banda song "Picadillo de soya," whose lyrics put in evidence this resistance to state mandated food policies (NG La Banda 1995).

Instead, *Mujeres* encouraged adapting Cuban culinary taste to available food, as demonstrated in a July 1969 interview with Nitza Villapol, in which she explained the difference between her function as a culinary educator before and after the revolution. Before, she said, her television program served to orient the consumer following the demands of capitalist companies; post-revolution, the objective became to educate people and to get women to see the work of the kitchen not just as something routine, but as an activity on which the health of the people depends (*Mujeres* 1969: 96). In this way a new discourse on domestic duty was established, one that conceded to it a new value: its social function, its contribution to the wellbeing of society, and its relation to political life.[8] But at the same time, domestic work was devalued as "enslaving" (Castro 1981 [1966]), following the ideas established by Marx, Engels and Lenin, reformulated by Che Guevara in his famous "Socialism and Man in Cuba."[9] This is a paradox latent in all official discourses on the subject but not dealt with critically in the official media.

An interesting example of cooking as a revolutionary task formulated by the government and implemented by *Mujeres* and the FMC is the aforementioned issue of saving oil. Since the government decreed in 1960 that all cooking oil be saved and reused, the magazine has repeatedly insisted on that point. In 1974, Nitza Villapol explicitly connected the Cuban habit of consuming fried food to the relationship of economic dependence on the United States before 1959. She stated that the Cuban predilection for fried food arose, in part, because "during the years of the pseudo-republic our country was an easy market for the excess of lard from the Yankee porcine industry" (Villapol 1974:62). She retakes this idea in her 1980 edition of *Cocina al minuto*:

> These [Yankees], knowing the value of pork meat as a source of protein of high quality containing vitamin B-1, sold to Cuba—an almost illiterate people and therefore largely unknowing about these nutrition issues—and to its rulers—in turn uninterested in the public health—a good part of the pork fat that they did not consume. Therefore, without knowing it, the Cubans helped to enable their exploiters to eat pork. (Villapol 1980: 10)

Journalist Silvia Bota summarizes this political and ideological connection of the revolutionary kitchen: "In a socialist society, when the food is prepared it is a fundamental response to the satisfaction of the nutritional needs of the people" (Bota 1986: 41). Lastly, since 1990, reports appear constantly about the mobilization of women for agricultural labor in order to resolve the economic and political crisis, and to strengthen the family and the children's patriotic spirit. There is no doubt that producing, conserving and cooking the food is conceived as a political act, a revolutionary task for "the feminine masses."[10]

Mujeres began to question the exclusive association of woman and cooking around 1988. It was in February of this year that the magazine suggested to women for the first time the possibility of inviting their male partner to enter the kitchen: "Prepare them [the provided cooking recipes] together; after tasting them, he might consider that it would be nice to enter the kitchen again…" (*Mujeres* 1988: 25), downplaying the explicit association of cooking as a women's revolutionary task typical of the first 29 years of the revolution.[11] These subtle changes do not

FOOD,
CULTURE &
SOCIETY

VOLUME 15
ISSUE 2
JUNE 2012

immediately abandon the primary assumption of the kitchen as a woman's duty. For example, in April 1990 a recently married female reader wrote to Silvia Bota, the writer of *Mujeres'* section *Mil Ideas* (A Thousand Ideas). She was desperate because she did not know how to make bean soup (*potajes*) and her husband was "a bean soup man." The magazine offered recipes for making beans "for her and other girls that might be in the same situation" (Bota 1990: 36). Of course, the magazine did not dare respond with the suggestion that both husband and wife should learn, or that she should give her husband this task, but neither did it imply that this is part of the woman's revolutionary duty.

Nonetheless, women remained central to government food planning through the creation, toward the end of 1991, of "Women's Houses" (*Casas de la mujer*), which offer workshops mostly related to domestic labor, particularly food preparation. These *casas* have great potential to help women with different problems and finding a space for support, but they do not depart from the traditional association of women with domesticity and stereotypes of "femininity" that elsewhere the magazine has said to criticize. For example, in the first issue of 1992, *Mujeres* reviewed some of the activities and workshops offered by the *casas*, among them: "education for family economy and the special period, food elaboration, home esthetics, rational use of space in the home, making the most of scraps in the transformation of the wardrobe, television or radio soap opera debates, book discussion and ethics of romantic relationships." To these were added others less traditional like "problems with living with someone else, arrangement of electro-domestic objects, plumbing, and carpentry" (*Mujeres* 1992: 11). Elements like these give evidence of the internal contradictory nature of the discourse about women's equality in the ideologues of the Cuban revolution due to the lack of a critical conceptual analysis and framework.

Given the urgency of the nutritional crisis starting in 1990, due to the fall of the Soviet Union which initiated the economic crisis—officially known as the "special period in time of peace"—women resorted to unofficial mechanisms—above all in relations between women, with neighbors and family members—to share and interchange products through the gray or black market. In fact, many women began to sell food they had grown and/or cooked illegally, either as street vendors, "under the table" at their workplaces, or out of their private homes. Nevertheless, these activities at a basic level of family and neighborhood initiative did not go so far as to acquire a stable and official character and, of course, they are not mentioned in the press. For example, in 1990 a news item appeared in *Mujeres* about the subversive use in Chile of traditional women's activities like cooking. The magazine described the example of the Chilean woman who cooked an egg in the eternal flame of the monument dedicated to commemorate Pinochet's coup d'état. In this case, one can see some sort of social vindication of the casserole in Latin America "not as a symbol of subordination, but as a path to liberation" (*Mujeres* 1990: 40). The fact that the magazine published this article the year when the deep Cuban crisis began could be interpreted in two opposite ways: as a reaffirmation of the cook's revolutionary potential following the line established in the first stage of the "social function of the kitchen," or as a "trick" to inform Cuban women about the subversive potential and the possibilities for provoking a change while using this very traditional role. The ideological danger of the second interpretation explains why the subject of food becomes central within the analyses of the Maximum Leader, who insists on providing the "communal pot" personally as the embodiment of the state. It is interesting to note that in 2005, for the first time, there were peaceful protest marches in Cuba in which the wives, mothers and grandmothers of dissidents incarcerated in Cuba participated. These "Ladies in White" received, in October of that year, the "Sajarov" Award of the European Parliament, for their efforts in the field of human rights. It is not a coincidence that Fidel begun then to give preferential attention in his televised interventions to issues related to the kitchen, not only to cooking appliances, but to recipes about how to prepare chocolate milk for breakfast, how to use the new pure coffee that was being distributed to the population, and the like.

"You and Him to the Kitchen," the title of the recipe section in the December 2000 issue of *Mujeres*, announced the new discursive code of the third period, reinforced in the following years with repeated images and articles about the participation of fathers in domestic tasks, including the kitchen, reflecting the subtle changes in the magazine that started in 1986 and that were increasingly demanded by women like the journalist Mirta Rodríguez Calderón (1989, 1994). Nevertheless, the magazine recognized that in spite of all the effort, the kitchen continued to be "the almost exclusive kingdom for women" (Campo Nodal 2002: 46). From 2001 to 2005, in almost all the issues, the recipe sections were dedicated to the results of the Community Food Conservation Project, initiated by a married couple in Havana, and thus the association "kitchen-food-marriage-family" was established. This formed part of a general plan to re-strengthen the heterosexual and stable family. In fact, from March 1990 until 1996 the magazine acquired the subtitle "Family and Society," denominating itself "The Cuban family magazine," strengthening the association between woman and family. The aforementioned food project divulged information about ways to conserve meats and vegetables, and about the nutritional value of traditional national products, with recipes for their preparation that included a "return to the seed," the vindication of aboriginal or very antique uses for products like yucca, which can be used as a substitute for wheat flour.

The question then becomes whether this discursive change in the magazine has had any effect in transferring political power to women.[12] One example will suffice to suggest an answer: the most powerful leader of the Cuban revolution, who from the beginning of the revolutionary process understood the need for the support of women, and who is officially considered "the best ideologue and spokesperson for women,"[13] chose to commemorate International Women's Day in 2005 by announcing a series of steps intended to facilitate domestic work. Fidel announced the sale of rice cookers and pressure cookers and asked for approval for this from the women summoned to the event. These appliances became the subject of multiple public speeches by the Commander, who sought to resolve with a stroke the problems of hunger and energy. Why were the cooking appliances announced to women? In the dominant ideology, the revolutionary cook persists, despite the

FOOD,
CULTURE &
SOCIETY

VOLUME 15

ISSUE 2

JUNE 2012

newly vigorous efforts of *Mujeres* and of some academic institutions to argue for gender equality.

The revolutionary government has maintained this view in part because of the persistent myth that under socialism, machines and social institutions will resolve domestic problems. An essay written by a leading communist intellectual, Blas Roca Calderío, first published in the prominent newspaper *Hoy* and reprinted in *Mujeres* in May 1964, prefigured Fidel's "rice cooker discourse." In it, Roca Calderío responded to a very sincere letter from Antonio on the subject of "women's emancipation" in which he asked: "So then who attends to the home, to the kitchen and to the children in communism?" The ideologue Roca Calderío explained: in capitalism, when equality is spoken of it is understood in a limited way, only as political and civil equality. In socialism, these demands become reality when women are massively incorporated into production, education, government, and the military. But this is not enough to reach pure equality because one obstacle persists: the slavery of the home, domestic work, and children. The liberation from such slavery commences with socialism and will be fully reached in communism. As the organization of society advances, women are freed from their burdens. How? Well, through use of appliances and social institutions: cafeterias, restaurants, and packaged food. All that will be left will be adding condiments and warming them up, which "will only take a few minutes in the electric pot or skillet" (Roca Calderío 1964: 77). Thus, the kitchen will be "a social job that will not enslave anyone. The kitchen in the house will be like recreation for a day of rest, like an opportunity to show the culinary faculties of women … or men." Women will then be, in pure equality, "the dignified companions of men." Roca Calderío recognized that due to the still-existing underdevelopment "in the beginning the incorporation of all women in social life was not possible" (Roca Calderío 1964: 77).[14]

The state therefore claimed from the beginning the ability to solve domestic problems without questioning the patriarchal structure of Cuban society. This reveals the mythological nature of the official ideology, by simplifying and purifying things, it bestows a natural and eternal justification, and a clarity that does not demand an explanation but only an affirmation of the "facts." Like almost all myths,[15] the rice cooker offers us an explanation of the world, with characters that are not human (cafeterias, electric gadgets), existing in a "proto world"[16] (the primitive community of communism), with a plot that expresses the conflict between two worlds (capitalism, socialism). They thus have a functional character, performative of attitudes that evoke the presence of something mysterious, counterposing good and evil. This meta-language conjures the technological solution to the drama of domesticity. Hoping for better times, the revolutionary woman will keep cooking.

The Revolutionary Cook, the *Ideologization* of "*Ajiaco*" and the *Tamalization* of Oats: Homage to Nitza Villapol

Born in New York in 1923 to exiled Cuban parents, and named after a Russian river, Villapol summarizes the geographic, political and metaphoric triangle that has determined the fate—and diet—of Cuba for the last hundred years. Nitza Villapol,

Cuba's version of Julia Child, with her cooking books and television cooking show, serves as a perfect example of the pervasive association of women with cooking within Cuba's revolutionary ideology, as well as an example of how the revolution entered the kitchen in Cuba's households, while maintaining the traditional social role of women attached to the stoves. Villapol's transformation from the typical cook à l'américaine, advertising the cooking wares and food products of big and small capitalist Cuban and US companies, to the self-proclaimed revolutionary cook serving the new society and working to educate the "new Cuban women" in how to cook for the "New Man," personalizes the periodization and connections examined in the previous section of this paper. In fact, between 1968 and 1987, Nitza Villapol was in charge of Mujeres' cooking section, and most of the cooking recipes published by the magazine before and after those years were taken from her cooking books and her television program. From the pages of the magazine, of her books and the television screen she was crucial in the implementation of the strategies devised by the socialist state in relation to cooking and for the development of a politicized Cuban domesticity.

Moreover, her major work continues to dominate Cuban homes on both shores of the "Sea of Lentils,"[17] and in this sense she is also a symbol of the diaspora and rupture of Cuban society. When Cuban families emigrated, they took with them treasured copies, used thousands of times, of her already legendary book Cocina al Minuto (Cook in a Minute, 1956). They also permitted Cubamerica to republish this work in Miami. Because it was unauthorized, this edition omitted the author and date of publication, perhaps as some form of punishment for the woman who for so many years taught them to eat and cook, but who then defended a revolution that contradicted their ardently desired "American way."[18] Equally revisionist was the new Cuban edition of this book, published in 1980. Despite having the same title and being for the most part a reissue of the earlier volume, the revolutionary edition does not even mention the existence of the one published in 1956, nor does it recognize the participation of the co-author of the previous book, Martha Martínez.[19] These different editions of Cocina al Minuto began an inter-textual dialogue of omissions and additions that have fueled the bonfires of two seemingly antagonistic worlds.

I propose to read comparatively the 1956 and 1980 Cuban editions of Cocina al Minuto, not only to verify the introduced changes, that in the end serve to connote the symbol of the new revolutionary cook propagated by Mujeres, but also to examine the textual strategies and values of politicized domesticity in revolutionary Cuba.[20] In this sense, I argue that Cocina al Minuto goes from being a commercial cookbook (1956) to being a community cookbook (1980), because the objective of the 1980 edition was to recreate and adapt cooking to a common social cause. As such, it has "a story to tell"—it is a form of "public participation," a form of activism in defense of a cause and, in a way, it is "collecting funds" (Bower 1997: 3–6) by teaching ways to save not only food but other resources like energy and time. Both texts share certain values that obviously formed part of the author's progressive ideology from before 1959, like the defense of cubanidad (national identity)[21] and the objective of improving the nutritional habits of the Cuban population.

FOOD,
CULTURE &
SOCIETY

VOLUME 15

ISSUE 2

JUNE 2012

Yet the books differ in that the edition of 1980 has an explicit defense of the new master narrative, which determined the Cuban revolutionary ideology and in particular a celebration of Cuba's African roots that is absent from the commercial 1956 edition. The "revolutionary" *Cocina al Minuto* transmits a sense of duty and historical perspective when it directly connects food and kitchen with political and social aspects at the national and international levels. This is why its conceptualization as a community cookbook is valid, because here the context takes precedence over individual history and voices, and because we can find a plot that tells a dramatic social story: that of the revolutionary cook, who is presented as an authority but also as a collective voice, in search of nourishing the revolutionary family with grace, variation, and a strong sense of nutritional values. It is a domestic plot that is presented as integrated into the general work of the radical transformation of Cuban society. If the "integration" plot (Bower 1997: 38) in 1956 looked for women's integration and acceptance into society as good planners of menus and of the domestic economy[22] and as guarantors of the family's good nutrition, the plot of 1980 looked for integration and acceptance of the kitchen as an instrument of the victorious revolutionary society to reach new levels of nutritional development, as part of the logic of the national history. This is why the narrative voice changes: in 1956 it is the individual directly addressing women in the style established by the American way of life (like those of Julia Child), maintaining a sense of intimacy, of being in the "feminine world." In the second, the intimacy is lost; the narrative authority is presented as the spokesperson of a community directed toward an audience that is not now defined by its sex, but by its insertion into the process of the construction of socialism. The voice and the public assumed abandon the personal relationship to present themselves as agents of social change, recognizing themselves as the results of a process of transculturation and as actors in the battle against the imperialist blockade and for a new society.

In the cooking sections directed by Villapol in *Mujeres* (including the cartoons), in the television program that reached Cuban homes on the island for forty-four years, in the interviews with her, even in the one done by the *Miami Herald* (Whitefield 1991), she constantly refers to and maintains a dialogue with the Mother, the Cuban woman, the revolutionary cook. These connections were clear in a 1981 interview with Marilys Suárez, a reporter for *Mujeres*, one year after the first "revolutionary" edition of *Cocina al Minuto* appeared. The journalist assures her that for "the feminine masses" Villapol "has been a challenge and an incentive … throughout these years of the hard economic blockade with her easy recipes … by teaching us to replace certain products with others and to give them maximum usage." To which Villapol responds: "Women are not as tied to the kitchen as they were in the past, which should not mean that we lose our tastes, our peculiarities … we should save our native cooking and adapt it to the times we live in" (Suárez 1981: 20–1). Not only do the reporter and Villapol assume that the person who cooks and who listens and reads Villapol is the Cuban woman, but also Villapol assigns her another revolutionary task: the rescue of culinary traditions.

The 1980 edition does not explicitly assume a female reader. In fact, it is obvious that Villapol makes an effort to remove gender references from her text: the 1956 edition initiates her introduction with a cartoon of a female cook worried about what to prepare for each day of the week (Villapol and Martínez 1956: 7); she refers to the "lady of the house that will equip her kitchen for the first time" (Villapol and Martínez 1956: 17); she explains that "our grandmothers made recipes with 'little bits' and 'pinches' …but they needed to have great experience … The modern woman does not need that big competency …the modern lady of the house uses cups and measuring spoons." All of this is transformed in the 1980 edition. Nowhere does it mention either the "lady of the house" or the "modern woman," and the cartoons disappear completely. The phrase referring to grandmothers is reformulated as "old books provided recipes using 'little bits' and 'pinches'" (Villapol 1980: 26) and the rest of the text remains neutral, using nouns and pronouns like "people," "you," "some," "one" and even when referring to herself as an author she uses a synecdoche, substituting the singular for the plural. The loss of the narrative intimacy is evident in the disappearance, in the 1980 edition, of the public assumed to be the "lady of the house."

There can be multiple reasons for this androgynous voice. Perhaps Villapol was moving herself beyond her time and space, assuming a shared kitchen and a reading public of both sexes. But this contradicts her other texts, television programs and interviews where she explicitly talks to women, assuming they are the cooks. I think it is partly a strategy for presenting her work as a community cookbook, in which, in the words of Anne Bower, a community authorship is assumed (Bower 1997: 8). In this case, Villapol is recognizing herself as a compiler of a written and oral tradition, the result of a social history of transculturation, with an explicit social function: that of contributing to the "satisfaction of one of the daily growing needs of our society"[23] (Villapol 1980: 14). On the other hand, with the disappearance of the more intimate tone, Villapol is trying to confer to the text a more scientific, more academic character, like the narrative strategy of the colonial Mexican author, Sor Juana Inez de la Cruz, who uses references to Aristotle and science in the kitchen as a means of being taken seriously by male authorities in her "Answer to Sor Filotea de la Cruz" justifying women's education (Ludmer 1985). This is why Villapol's introduction insists that cooking is a form of art that applies "an understanding of science and methodology, physics, chemistry, and basics of mathematics, besides a deep understanding of the characteristics of each food and ingredient" (Villapol 1980: 13). The 1980 work is preceded by a quote from Friedrich Engels that appears as an epigraph after the title page: "traditions play tricks on the minds of men," establishing in advance the seriousness and the analytical tradition of the text within the dialectic materialism. She confesses that her aspiration is ambitious: "to obtain something more than a list of recipes." In fact, Villapol considered herself an educator, and she inserted her work as part of the educative effort of the revolution (Suárez 1981: 21). Indeed, she received her diploma from the University of Havana as a doctor in pedagogy in 1948, and she worked as a Spanish and English teacher for some years.

Another of the big differences between the two editions of *Cocina al Minuto* is precisely the treatment of traditions, in particular Villapol's effort to emphasize the African roots of Cuban cooking. With it the new political meaning of the kitchen and

FOOD,
CULTURE &
SOCIETY

VOLUME 15

ISSUE 2

JUNE 2012

the cook in socialist Cuba is reinforced: in conferring a dominant role to African roots, she contributes to the effort to eliminate racial discrimination and to revalue the Afro-Cuban contributions to the culture officially denied by history before 1959. She manages this in two ways: through a historical introduction to the 1980 text, based on the investigations she made earlier for her contribution to the anthology *Africa in Latin America*,[24] and in dedicating a special chapter to *ajiaco* (Cuban soup). Paradoxically, in her television show, Villapol contributed to maintaining some of the persistent Cuban racism and stereotypes associated with black women in Cuba. There was always a black female assistant with a white apron who never spoke and who is not mentioned in either the cookbooks or *Mujeres*. This assistant, Margot, was interviewed on Cuban television in December of 2005. The interviewer and Margot herself never questioned her relegation to a silent black presence subordinated to the all white dominant master. Instead, they celebrated and exalted the never-questioned role played by Villapol in keeping women in the kitchen.

In the 1980 *Cocina al Minuto*, Villapol explains that "the fundamental influence in our nutritional culture comes from the African continent" (Villapol 1980: 8), because the Spanish contributions came principally from the south—a region shaped by Arab influence—so that in reality Hispanic cooking can be considered part of the African inheritance. Here Villapol joins a national effort to revalue "the black" that reached the point of considering a taste for what was Spanish to be "bourgeois." Of course, the word "Africa" does not appear at all in the 1956 edition. It cannot be a coincidence that in the 1980 edition the Spanish dishes typically consumed in Cuba were eliminated; among soups and stews alone she dropped gazpacho, *cocido*, Catalan *escudilla*, Aragonian *potaje*, and Canary Island soup. So, the revolutionary cook, as Villapol solicited from the pages of *Mujeres*, should contribute from her kitchen to the rescue of traditions, but obviously, to a selective rescue that not only adapts to what is available, but also redefines the national identity and grants primacy to what had up until then been discriminated against.

It is for this reason that *ajiaco* goes from being just another soup (Villapol and Martínez 1956: 36) to obtaining the dignity of an independent chapter. Villapol was obviously influenced by the work of Fernando Ortiz, whom she quotes in the introduction of the 1980 edition of her book. A renowned anthropologist, Ortiz coined the term "Afro Cuban" and used precisely the example of *ajiaco* to explain his novel concept of "transculturation" in his *Cuban Counterpoint of Sugar and Tobacco* (Ortiz 1963). Villapol has proposed that cooking became truly Cuban when garbanzos were removed from the *ajiaco*, because until then:

> that broth, which combined varied dry and fresh meats, had not been more than the encounter between the Spanish *cocido* and the island roots. The difference was accentuated when the domestic servant—black or Chinese—took charge of the white kitchen. (Bianchi Ross 2002: 4)

Not only does the Afro-Cuban dish *ascend* to the category of a chapter, it also serves as a conclusion for the text in 1980.

Following the methodology of Colleen Cotter (in Bower 1997), I analyze the language used in the same recipe in different cookbooks in order to expose the strategies and values behind the list of ingredients. In the 1956 edition, not only is *ajiaco* just another recipe in the soup section, but it does not have an explanatory historical introduction, nor is it presented as the national soup. On the other hand, in 1980 the introduction explains its origin as an African soup, the name of which comes from the original use of the hot pepper,[25] saying that it constitutes the dish that characterizes Cuba in the same way that minestrone symbolizes Italy and borscht symbolizes Ukraine (Villapol 1980: 319). It is curious that at least since 1959, *ajiaco* is not eaten regularly in Cuba, especially in the Western part. In fact, for example, at neighborhood parties of the Revolution Defense Committees, what is normally made is a *caldosa*, another kind of stew similar to the *ajiaco*. Again, I think that Villapol is interested in following Fernando Ortiz and emphasizing what is African.

Between the two editions of the book the ingredients also change a little due to growing shortages: in the 1980 edition, *ñame* (yam) disappears (the most difficult root to obtain at the time), the quantity of beef is reduced from one pound (454 g) to half a pound (223 g), the product brand names disappear (in the 1956 version *El Liro* chicken, *Libby's* tomato sauce, and *La Lechera* milk are recommended), alternatives are offered (oil or butter; onion or leek; cornballs or not), and the quantity of garlic is reduced. This "ideologization of the *ajiaco*" demonstrates the intersection of language, social relations and gender in each publication of *Cocina al Minuto*. In the 1956 publication, race, discrimination and national history are not discussed, because the reader is assumed to be the "traditional woman" of the period (the middle class bourgeois woman who consumes brand-named products). The 1980 publication, for all intents, is directed toward the "new Cuban woman," who is supposed not only to be more educated, but also taking an active part in the political and cultural transformation of society, and who has to do more cooking from scratch, paradoxically reversing the techno-optimism of the earlier decades. This ideologization of *ajiaco* is even more obvious if we compare Villapol's 1980 work with that of a Cuban author who emigrated to the United States and who belongs to a family of the Cuban rural aristocracy. I am referring to Mary Urrutia, for whom *ajiaco* is a "peasant stew." She not only includes Spanish olive oil and cumin in the ingredients, but also, to legitimize it as "Cuban Creole," she cites a dubious letter written by a Spanish colonist supposedly in the 1500s (Urrutia Randelman and Schwartz 1992: 104–5). Urrutia addresses a Cuban emigrant community that is mostly looking to reaffirm its white Spanish roots, and that dreams of recovering an "idyllic past" BC (Before Castro). Her *ajiaco* recipe is included in the chapter where she describes life on her Catalan uncle's tobacco farm, where around 800 people lived and worked, all seemingly happy to receive education, to be well-treated by their owners, and to receive part of the profits.

The ideologization of *ajiaco* contributes to the affirmation of the national identity and unity through the previously weakest link in the social chain: the Afro-Cubans. Metonymically, *ajiaco* invokes what is black, what belongs only to Cuba, what is unique, what is national—not what is bourgeois, not what is Yankee. From there

FOOD,
CULTURE &
SOCIETY

VOLUME 15

ISSUE 2

JUNE 2012

centrality is conferred to it. This nationalizing effort is also appreciable in another element that differentiates the two volumes: the minimization of English terms in the 1980 edition, leaving only those words that are so rooted in the Cuban culinary dialect that to eliminate them would have created communication problems, such as *catsup*, *Spam*, *Royal* (baking powder) and *cake*. The 1980 edition also omits a number of things, such as the glossary of high-quality American cuts of meat that previously included the names in English (Villapol and Martínez 1956: 87), the section dedicated to *rosbif*, and recipes like *Trader Vic's*, lobster *à la Newburg* and *à la Thermidor*, *Mornay* crab, chicken *à la King*, and *Boston Cream Pie*.[26] Not only do the names in English almost disappear, but also other "foreign" recipes like *jambalaya*, *gnocchies*, Puerto Rican *asopao*, *Madeira* sauce, *Veloute*, fish *à la Lusitana*, among many more. The recipes that remain are the most "creole," those that are most common on the lower and middle class Cuban table, and those that can be made with what is available. As such, there are multiple recipes with spam and with *macarela*—products from socialist countries that go unmentioned in the 1956 edition but subsequently became subsistence foods for revolutionary Cuba. In essence, Villapol's revolutionary cooking is cooking of what is possible: the simplest and the most creole; the cooking that uses "what's there."

There is no better example to illustrate this than the treatment that Villapol gives to oats, what I call "the tamalization of oats," a great example of the strategy of substitution and the strategy that required women to use new products coming from the socialist Eastern Bloc, analyzed in the first section of this paper. One of the differences between the two editions with which I am working is the organization of some chapters. In the 1956 version, there are no actual chapters, but unnumbered sections dedicated to specific food groups. The 1980 version is divided by chapters that in some cases redistribute the original food groupings. In 1956 there is no section devoted to cereals, but there are twenty-five pages with "rice and pasta" recipes. In 1980, the first recipe chapter is titled "cereals" and is dedicated to explanations and recipes about rice, wheat, oats and corn, to which it dedicates forty-three pages. After informing the reader about the etymology of the word "cereal," its connection to antiquity, and the new ways in which it appears with industrialization, Villapol explains in the introduction to the chapter the relation between a basic cereal and the culture of each region. She analyzes why corn is the most consumed cereal in Latin America and for which historical reasons rice and wheat are the most consumed in the Caribbean. Her historical explanation of oats is reduced to saying that it was practically unknown in Cuba until the "pseudo-republican period, fundamentally in minority sectors of the population that consumed products imported from the United States of North America" (Villapol 1980: 32) in the form of Quaker. This obviously explains the absence of any mention of oats in the 1956 edition, but not the existence of fourteen recipes using them in the 1980 edition, including one for "oats with salt and garlic" (Villapol 1980: 49), and another for *Avena en cazuela* ("stewed oats") which is prepared in the same way as the traditional Cuban recipe of *Tamal en cazuela* ("stewed corn tamale"), with ingredients like dry wine, tomato paste, oil or lard, and the traditional Cuban *sofrito* (chopped onion and garlic fried in oil) (Villapol 1980: 50). This *tamalization* of oats makes it creole, by connecting Russian oats with one of the most traditional Cuban dishes originally made with corn. With inventions such as these, Villapol is contributing to paying the "eternal debt of gratitude to the people of the Soviet Union and other countries of the socialist community that in the most difficult moments extended a friendly hand" (Villapol 1980: 10). Oats came, along with wheat, from the USSR, and Cubans did not know what to do with them. In fact, "Russian oats" were incorporated into the popular dialect to make fun of things "Soviet," with the characteristic Cuban survival humor. Villapol, conscious of the nutritional value of this cereal, does what is expected of the revolutionary cook: substitutes (wheat flour for oats), saves (meat, in adding oats to "stretch it out") (Villapol 1980: 51), learns to use whatever comes from the socialist countries, varies the menu (oats not only for cereal, but as a main dish with garlic and onions, or fried, or blended, or in tamales).

From the pages of *Mujeres* and in her "revolutionary" *Cocina al Minuto*, Villapol was the educator who took on the mission of teaching the *new Cuban woman* to implement the strategies to defeat, from the kitchen, the US embargo; to strengthen, from the kitchen, the healthy and well-nourished "new man"; and to adapt, from the kitchen, to the presence of the "new socialist brothers." With this, in a way, Villapol converted the kitchen into another "internationalist mission" and at the same time, in a trench for the rescue of Cuban national identity and the defense of the new revolutionary society.

I have tried to demonstrate that the ideology of Cuba's leadership and the official voice of the FMC have symbolically fused women, domestic work and the revolution. Nevertheless, the language of gender equality began to be used, at least in *Mujeres* and in the FMC's propaganda work since 1975, when, on other levels, laws and regulations were established that recognize the legal, economic and political equality of Cuban women. The absence of an open discussion with different theoretical and political approximations on the subject of domesticity; the absolute rejection of feminism and the dogmatic defense of a paternalistic and utopian vision like the one formulated by Blas Roca and still maintained by Castro, and the lack of a thorough discussion about the patriarchal nature of Cuban society, have contributed to keeping women "making stews" and using "rice cookers." Nitza Villapol, in summarizing the values connoted in these messages, became the epitome of the revolutionary cook in presenting her role as a female cook as a contribution to the revolutionary process and to the selective rescue of traditions that legitimized the established status quo.

The obvious change perceived in *Mujeres* in recent years (in opening to other possibilities of critical analysis) has allowed the magazine to carefully and without open confrontation, question anew domesticity and the ideological myths with which the leadership of the country has been working. Unfortunately, the magazine has now an extremely limited impact at the social level as few Cubans have access to it since the crisis of the 1990s.[27] In any case, it is trying to reopen the question of domesticity and to break the association between woman and kitchen—although it seems like it is doing this by placing the responsibility fundamentally on women, asking them to be the ones inviting men into the kitchen. Everything appears to

FOOD,
CULTURE &
SOCIETY

VOLUME 15

ISSUE 2

JUNE 2012

indicate that we are witnessing the beginnings of a challenge to the official discourse that continues to assign rice cookers to the FMC, in the tradition established in 1959 of the patriarch deciding who cooks, with what, and for whom.

Acknowledgment

I am indebted to Marena Lear for her translation of the first manuscript of this paper, to Jeff Pilcher for editing it, and to the very useful suggestions of the anonymous readers of the present version.

Marisela Fleites-Lear teaches Spanish and Literature at Green River Community College. She has a PhD in Romance languages and literature from the University of Washington and an ABD in philosophy from the University of Havana. Her research and publications examine the construction of images of Cuban women from the perspectives of literary, gender and cultural studies. Green River Community College, 12401 SE 320th Street, Auburn, WA 98092, USA (mfleites@greenriver.edu).

Notes

1   This period, 1990–2007, was characterized by a severe economic crisis with political consequences due to the collapse of the Socialist Bloc, Cuba's main trading partner and political support.

2   Expression taken from Benítez Rojo (1998: 16).

3   In "Women, Family and the Cuban Revolution" (Fleites-Lear 2001), I identified six paradoxes related to the situation of women within the revolutionary process: (1) while women gained the freedom to join the social process of the revolution, this same freedom doubled or tripled their workload given the persistence patriarchal nature of Cuban society; (2) while women gained sexual freedom, their relationships became more unstable; (3) women gained freedom to participate in the political system on one hand, but on the other, met continual barriers to creating their own organizations outside the system; (4) the younger generation, women who grew up with the revolution, gained new freedom and opportunities while women in middle age—their mothers and older sisters—felt somehow left behind; (5) in spite of all the educational work and laws to achieve women's equality, sexist language and images are still pervasive, even in Communist Party rhetoric; (6) some of the significant gains for women within the revolution, particularly in the area of employment, were jeopardized by the economic crisis of the 1990s, as evidenced in the resurgence of prostitution and sex tourism.

4   Fleites-Lear (2008) offers an analysis of the complex relationship between the Cuban women movement after 1959 and feminist ideologies.

5   Although the analysis of these historical reasons is beyond the scope of the present work, one can suggest looking at Spanish and African traditions in the creation of a food-centered culture in Cuba, as well as to the anxieties created by food scarcity after 1959. Whoever participates in an informal gathering of Cuban friends and families can testify to the fact that one of the main topics of conversation (if not the main) is food (rather than money or politics).

6   From the scarce academic works on the subject, *No Free Lunch* (Benjamin *et al.* 1989) and

Entre frijoles, papas y ají (Padilla Dieste 2002) are two texts that analyze with great detail and serious documentation the different aspects, achievements, and problems of the food policies developed by the revolution. These texts complement each other analytically and chronologically, given that the first ends in 1984 and the second examines the period that begins in 1990 and goes until 2000, in other words, the so-called "special period in a time of peace."

7   This question was originally posed by a member of the Revolutionary Armed Forces (FAR) in 1964 to an ideologue of Cuban socialism in the newspaper *Hoy* and was subsequently reprinted in *Mujeres*. I will analyze this text at the end of this section, due to its evident connection with the year 2005 at the level of the official discourse of the heads of the country.

8   This could have borne great theoretical fruits in Cuba had it been threaded into the discussions that were being held inside "occidental Marxism" and feminism about women and domestic work

9   Fleites-Lear (2008) offers an in-depth discussion of Cuba's leadership ideas about domestic work as "enslaving," not appropriate for the political avant-garde, as a necessary evil to be done by women.

10 "Feminine masses," a common sign within the revolutionary political discourse (see for example *Mujeres* 1975: 3). I cannot avoid associating it with the use of *masa* (dough) in Spanish cooking terminology.

11 This move toward a subtle critique of dominant official views should be understood as part of a general trend of those years. In 1986, the news about the Glasnost initiated by Mikhail Gorbachev to promote a liberalization policy in the public discussions about historical and political problems was reaching Cuba. Repercussions in Cuba came quickly. For example, Soviet publications like the magazines *Sputnik* and *News from Moscow*, were read very little before but began to sell on the black market at higher prices because they became so coveted after 1986. In Cuba, organizations like the Union de Jóvenes Comunistas (Young Communists Union) and the trade unions called for the freedom to critique policy. This lasted until 1989, when the sale of these publications was suspended (see *Granma* 1989).

12 We should not forget that as of 2006, at the highest level of the leadership of the Communist Party there were only two women out of the 27 members of the Politburo, where all the main decisions are taken. The first woman to enter the Politburo was Vilma Espín, and only in 1981.

13 This phrase was used by Ramón Machado Ventura, a member of the Communist Party Politburo in his speech to commemorate the forty-fifth anniversary of the establishment of the Federation of Cuban Women (Machado 2005: 7).

14 This is the closest thing to a theoretical formulation by Cuban revolutionary leaders on the question of women's equality. Due to ideological orthodoxy, the rich debate about domestic work that was going on in the 1960s within non-Soviet Marxist thought, above all since the publication of Betty Friedman's *The Feminine Mystique*, was never publicized in Cuba. In fact, the Cuban university magazine *Critical Thought* was closed when it began to take up some of the theoretical debates of the "Marxist left."

15 I follow the characterization summarized by Mary Magoulick (n.d.).

16 It is with good reason that Blas Roca Calderío refers to the primitive community as the original locus in which feminine domestic work was done "for society, not for an individual entity. That is why her work and equal position in that primitive society are appreciated"

FOOD,
CULTURE &
SOCIETY

VOLUME 15

ISSUE 2

JUNE 2012

(Roca Calderío 1964: 77).

17 This is the name given to the Caribbean Sea by the French geographer Guillaume le Testu, in 1556, in the first map in which the Caribbean appears (Benitez Rojo 1999: 7).

18 Other notable differences between this and the 1956 edition are: (1) the adverts within the text disappear—there are only two on the covers but now they are of two Miami companies; (2) the cartoons that begin each chapter are different from the original's; (3) although the text of the introduction is the same word for word, what it does not include is the conversion table for measurements, nor the suggestion for a menu for two weeks, nor the section "How to equip your kitchen"; (4) lastly, it only has six pages for the index, arranged alphabetically by recipe, as opposed to the 15 pages in the original because the index was reorganized to eliminate repetitions (for example, in the original "avocado croquettes" appear twice: by croquettes and by avocado).

19 Martha Martinez was in charge of the recipe section in *Mujeres* until she was replaced by Villapol in December of 1968. Martha then disappeared from the public scene given that she had apparently emigrated to the United States.

20 I recognize here the methodological value for my analysis of the texts contained in the anthology edited by Anne L. Bower, *Recipes for Reading. Community Cookbooks, Stories, Histories* (Bower 1997) as well as those included in Janet Floyd and Laurel Forster's edited volume *The Recipe Reader: Narratives-Contexts-Traditions* (Floyd and Forster 2003) . I also want to recognize the work that inspired me to think of the connections between socio-political history and cooking and that in fact revolutionized my own kitchen, Jeffrey Pilcher's *Que vivan los tamales* (Pilcher 1998).

21 This is evident in the case of the 1956 edition, in her giving preference for commercial advertisements to Cuban products, for example: "Tide is made in Cuba by Cuban workers" (p. 35), "Nescafe made in Cuba … Cuban coffee!" (p. 37) "Hatuey, the great Cuban beer" (p. 43), "Bacardi, healthy, tasty, and Cuban" (p. 109), "Doña Delicias, the first Cuban mayonnaise!" (p. 73).

22 For example, in her section "How to equip your kitchen," she explains the necessity of adapting to the household budget and she provides three lists of things to buy depending on the money one has at one's disposal. This, of course, disappears from the 1980 edition.

23 Here she is obviously paraphrasing the famous Marxist statement that defines socialism's goals.

24 Compiled by Manuel Moreno Fraginals (1977). Villapol was in charge of the chapter titled: "African Nutritional Habits in Latin America."

25 A use that is lost in the Cuban version, but Villapol does not mention this in order to avoid emphasizing the difference with the African soup, and to avoid having to recognize the presence of Spanish influence, which has little taste for "hot" food.

26 These are written in English in the original like the names that follow here.

27 As explained in the introduction, *Mujeres* replaced the "revolutionary" *Vanidades* in 1960. It appeared originally as a bi-monthly magazine but in 1962 it became a monthly publication, available not only in kiosks all over the country (including a "rural" special edition from 1969 until 1973), and by individual subscription, but also distributed to its members by the FMC. In fact, most of the study circles that were part of the FMC neighborhood meetings for many years were organized around the discussion of articles that appeared in the magazine. But with the economic crisis in 1990, the publication became irregular, and given the scarcity of paper in this period, it was not published at all from 1993 until 1997. From 1997 until 2000 it appeared only in tabloid format. Since 2001

it is published only four times a year, although is is very hard to find. It is also available as a weekly online magazine (obviously geared to an international audience, as Cubans do not have regular access to the internet).

References

Benítez Rojo, Antonio. 1998. *La isla que se repite*. Barcelona: Editorial Casiopea.

Benítez Rojo, Antonio. 1999. *El mar de las lentejas*. Barcelona: Editorial Casiopea.

Benjamin, M, Collins, J. and Scott, M. 1989. *No Free Lunch. Food & Revolution in Cuba Today*. San Francisco, CA: Food First.

Bianchi Ross, Ciro. 2002. Nitza Villapol. La mujer que escribía de cocina. Available from: http://www.lajiribilla.co.cu/2002/n57_junio/memoria.html (accessed January 7, 2012).

Bota, Silvia.1986. Platos típicos regionals.*Mujeres* (April): 41

Bota, Silvia. 1990. ¡No sé hacer potajes! *Mujeres* (April): 36.

Bower, Anne L. (ed.) 1997 *Recipes for Reading: Community Cookbooks, Stories, Histories*. Amherst, MA: University Press of Massachusetts.

Campo Nodal, Idaida. 2002. La cocina es para quien la ame. *Mujeres* (February): 46–7.

Castro, Fidel. 1981 [1966] Discurso pronunciado el primero de diciembre de 1966 en la clausura de la quinta plenaria nacional de la FMC en Santa Clara. In Elizabeth Stone (ed.) *Women and the Cuban Revolution: Speeches & Documents by Fidel Castro, Vilma Espín & Others*. New York: Pathfinder Press, pp. 48–54.

Castro, Fidel. 2005. Discurso pronunciado el 8 de marzo de 2005. Available from: www.cubaminrex.cu/Archivo/Presidente/2005/FC_080305.htm (accessed June 26, 2006).

Cubamerica. 1970. *Cocina al minuto; selecciones de recetas favoritas*. Miami: Ediciones Cubamerica.

Fleites-Lear, Marisela. 2001. Women, Family and the Cuban Revolution. In Irving L. Horowits and Jaime Suchilicki (eds) *Cuban Communism*. New Brunswick, NJ and London: Transaction Publishers, pp. 344–72.

Fleites-Lear, Marisela. 2008. ¡Mi cielo, alcánzame las botas!: Feminismos, Mujeres y el "Hombre Nuevo" dentro de la revolución cubana. *JILAR- Journal of Iberian and Latin American Research* 14(1): 49–77.

Floyd, Janet and Forster, Laurel (eds). 2003. *The Recipe Reader: Narratives-Contexts-Traditions*. Aldershot: Ashgate.

Granma. 1989. Una decisión inaplazable, consecuente con nuestros principios. *Granma* (4 August), p. 2.

Ludmer, Josefina, 1985. Tretas del débil. In Patricia E. González and Eliana Ortega (eds) *La sartén por el mango.*. Río Piedras, P.R.: Huracán, pp. 47–54.

Machado Ventura, Ramón.2005. Fieles a la tradición mambisa y rebelde. *Mujeres* 3: 6–7.

Magoulick, M. n.d. What is Myth? Available from: http://www.faculty.de.gcsu.edu/~mmagouli/defmyth.htm (accessed 26 July, 2009).

Moreno Fraginals, M. (ed.) 1977. *África en América Latina*. México, D.F.: Siglo XXI.

Mujeres. 1967. Cuelgue un espejo en la cocina. *Mujeres* (March): 111.

Mujeres. 1969. Entrevista [Interview with Nitza Villapol]. *Mujeres* (July): 96.

Mujeres. 1975. Masas Femeninas. *Mujeres* (January): 3.

Mujeres. 1988. Para saborear el día de los enamorados. *Mujeres* (February): 25.

Mujeres. 1990. La cacerola: Todo un símbolo. *Mujeres* (April): 40.

FOOD,
CULTURE&
SOCIETY

VOLUME 15

ISSUE 2

JUNE 2012

259

Mujeres. 1992. La casa de la mujer. *Mujeres* (January-March): 11.

NG La Banda. 1995. *La cachimba*. Havana: Caribe Productions Inc.

Oramas, Ada. 1961. Cocine revolucionariamente. *Vanidades* (15 August): 26–9.

Ortiz, Fernando. 1963. *Contrapunteo cubano del azúcar y el tabaco*. Havana: Consejo Nacional de Cultura.

Padilla Dieste, Cristina. 2002. *Entre frijoles, papa y ají. La distribución de alimentos en Cuba*. Guadalajara: Universidad de Guadalajara.

Pilcher, Jeffrey M. 1998. *¡Que vivan los tamales! Food and the Making of Mexican Identity*. Albuquerque, NM: University of New Mexico Press.

Roca Calderío, Blas.¿Quién atiende al hogar, a la cocina y a los niños en el comunismo? *Mujeres* (May): 76–7.

Rodríguez Calderón, Mirta. 1989. *Dígame usted*. Havana: Editorial Pablo de la Torriente.

Rodríguez Calderón, Mirta. 1994. Estereotipos sexistas: Póngase usted a pensar. *Bohemia* (13 May): 3–6.

Suárez, Marilys. 1981. La Nitza que no conocemos. *Mujeres* (January): 20–1.

Urrutia Randelman, Mary and Schwartz, Joan. 1992. *Memories of a Cuban Kitchen*. New York: Wiley Publishing, Inc.

Villapol, Nitza. 1974. Cocinemos. *Mujeres* (July): 64.

Villapol, Nitza. c. 1979. *Cocina criolla*. Mexico, D.F.: Ediciones Zócalo, S.A.

Villapol, Nitza. 1980. *Cocina al minuto*. Santiago de Cuba: Editorial Oriente.

Villapol, Nitza, 1993.*Cocina cubana*. Havana: Editorial Científico-Técnica.

Villapol, Nitza, 1999. *Desde su cocina*. Havana: Editorial Científico-Técnica.

Villapol, Nitza and Martínez, Martha. 1956. *Cocina al minuto*. Havana: Talleres Roger A. Queralt-Artes Gráficas.

Whitefield, Mimi. 1991. Cuban Cooking Guru Copes with Food Rations, Shortages. *Miami Herald* (December 29), 1A.

FOOD, CULTURE & SOCIETY

VOLUME 15 | ISSUE 2 | JUNE 2012

Nostalgia for Origins in a Fast Food Culture

TEACHING WITH THE FOOD MEMORIES OF CAROLINA COLLEGE WOMEN

Corrie Norman

Independent scholar

Abstract

This paper describes an active learning exercise encouraging student researchers to analyze food-related memories in a religious studies classroom. Inspired by the interactive methods of Deborah Lupton, students were asked to record a personal narrative about food and then to examine the writings of their classmates. In particular, they looked for cosmologies, or origin stories that orient people between the sacred and the profane, like the apple in the Garden of Eden. Student researchers perceptively discussed how food mediated family relationships, generational conflicts, and insecurities about dietary change. Their narratives often contrasted the sacred time of home-cooked holiday meals with the profane commercial world of fast food. The paper concludes with a poignant student poem capturing visceral memories of food, culture, and society in the modern-day South.

Keywords: religion, pedagogy, memory, cosmology

Her favorite was her grandmother's turkey and dressing ... The first bite is like heaven in her mouth. The tender juicy turkey accompanied by the dressing is a perfect combo. She eats until she is full. This Thanksgiving was one that she'll remember forever.

Her mother said, "You will not leave the table until you have eaten them." She tried to force another spoonful; she spit it back out. She couldn't do it. Grits was then deemed as the food that would kill her and until this day she believes that.

Because of their time overseas, they almost always make meals from scratch ... This is a tradition they have never lost.

These quotations come from three of the approximately two hundred food memories collected from college students by their peers in my course, "Food, Meaning, and the Sacred." Students who took the course had an ample menu. We feasted on the words of M. F. K. Fisher. We struggled to digest the theoretical structures of Mary Douglas and Claude Lévi-Strauss.[1] Technically, this was a course in religious studies. Thus, we ruminated on food as a medium for human expression about meaning and identity. We savored what is considered holy in several religious traditions and cultures. With historians of religion, we sniffed out the aroma of the sacred, often in times and spaces usually considered profane.[2] Why, we have been at table with practically everybody from Jesus and the Buddha to Tony Bourdain and Iron Chef.[3] But we especially savored what women and the study of gender brought to the table, particularly appropriate in our women's college setting.[4] We were fed heartily by novelists Anita Desai and Laura Esquivel, essayist Sallie Tisdale, environmental activist Vendanta Shiva, and raconteur *par excellence* Vertamae Grosvenor.[5] There was good food and good company all around.

Perhaps the most satisfying courses of this feast were those shared with the people closest to us. Communing over food helped us get to know neighbors we may not have noticed before and to become better acquainted with those we see practically every day. Students developed profiles on foodways in religious communities in the Carolinas, focusing particularly on new Muslim, Hindu and Buddhist communities. They also studied their own religious communities, all Christian, at table.[6] As a last course, students studied themselves and how they make meaning with food through memory. We tasted the familiar in "foreign" foods and discovered some unexpected exotic flavors as we chewed over our own daily fare. When asked to tell stories about themselves and food, we discovered both new immigrants and native Southerners told about struggles with cherished traditions and social realities.

"Write a food memory," I asked the students in the course, "about an event, episode, or action in third person with as much detail as possible." I suggested that they think of key images, sounds or tastes. Otherwise, they were on their own. In turn, each student collected and analyzed at least six memories from her peers.[7] We also gathered information on the class, race, age, family, hometown and religious heritage of participants in this project. It was a very homogeneous group of Southern women primarily from South Carolina, in their early twenties, overwhelmingly middle class, white, and evangelical Protestant.

The format for this experiment is not original. It is based on a study Australian sociologist Deborah Lupton conducted with thirty-five of her own students some years ago.[8] Lupton was primarily interested in using memory to determine how food symbolism might be a predictor of students' developing food preferences.[9] Lupton also pointed to something else that memories of food might reveal. According to her, "Food serves … symbolically to … construct a cosmology."[10]

This term is a familiar one in religious studies. A cosmology is a particular type of myth or sacred story. A well-known example is the Genesis story of creation. In that story, as in all cosmologies, people discover how their world began and how they came to be. In other words, they learn something basic about their origin that serves to give them orientation, a means by which to understand and articulate who they are and why they are here. The "here" is important. Most cosmologies are located in a particular place, like the Garden of Eden. And often, food, a food source, or a meal, is at the center of that sacred space. The Tree of Knowledge is a fruit tree, after all, and the acts of eating and sharing a piece of fruit come to provide the orientation for much of human experience. The sacrality of original time is also central here, as one must return to how it was in the beginning in order to regain meaning and order. People still try to recover that paradisal time before the Fall.

Especially when identity is threatened from without or within, the need to return to the sacred may manifest itself in a desire, often unconscious, to revive one's mythology. Scholar Mircea Eliade called this "nostalgia for origins."[11] It can be expressed vividly in memories that recall sacred time, place and activity, even in ordinary meals. Original activity is often memorialized in ritual repetition, even when, like eating the apple, the original acts might not have turned out to be such a good thing. In these cases, myths might get a new overlay, with new symbolic elements that nevertheless somehow remind of the old ones. Another meal, a Passover or a Communion perhaps, might gradually develop to redo (or undo) the original in new ritualized forms. In particularly chaotic situations, the new elements may be especially dramatic, illustrating the tension between what ought to be or have been and what is: between myth and reality. Again, both Passover and Communion are sacrificial meals that involve redemptive suffering and death. The new application reveals the distance and the congruity between the mythic time and present reality. To use a food analogy, people take leftovers—usually elements of old stories that model "the way it was" (or should be)—stir them together and reheat them when they are hungry for meaning. The student memories collected by my class are excellent examples of such complex meaning-making that express the desire for origins or attempts at "re-enchantment" through food. Being asked to recall a "food memory" was like coming to a commercial pause—it prompted them to rummage through the refrigerator looking for something, as Lévi-Strauss put it, "good to think."[12]

What the students cooked up is a rather complex stew of mythic ingredients savoring of evangelical Christianity and Southern culture, strongly seasoned with the sanctity of family and traditional women's roles. Newer ingredients from the food industry, media, advertising and evolving lifestyles lend piquancy, contrasting notes, and even sometimes a bitter edge to the mix. The work of cooking up food memories for my students is primarily a task of blending their taste for old-fashioned Southern home-cooking with flavors of the present fast food culture. Prompted by the three memories from which the quotations at the beginning of the paper were taken, I will discuss the key ingredients of my students' attempts to come to terms with the sacred and the profane through food.

Grandmother's Thanksgiving Dressing and Sacred Time

It was Thanksgiving Day and all the family had gathered at her grandmother's house. The sound of clashing pots and pans, running water, and the women

FOOD,
CULTURE &
SOCIETY

VOLUME 15

ISSUE 2

JUNE 2012

singing joyously as they prepared the Thanksgiving feast filled the air. Her favorite was her grandmother's turkey and dressing. The aroma of chopped onion, dressing, and the fresh turkey lured her into the kitchen, just to be chased out by her grandmother. Hours later, the feast is done. The small children come in from outside and assemble at the children's table. Her grandmother says grace over the meal, and along with the other women, begins to serve ... She is finally served with lots of her grandmother's delicious turkey and dressing. The first bite is like heaven in her mouth. The tender juicy turkey accompanied by the dressing is a perfect combo. She eats until she is full. This Thanksgiving was one that she'll remember forever.

Although it took a long time for the national Thanksgiving holiday to take hold in the South, for this student and most of her peers, the traditional Southern Thanksgiving meal with turkey and cornbread dressing is now the "perfect" meal.[13] It is the holiday mentioned the most, by far, in the food memories. Thanksgiving is hardly a national holiday for my students, however. It is a family feast with a variety of traditional foods. They associate these foods vaguely with the "Old" South with more mythic sincerity than historical accuracy. (Macaroni and cheese hardly seems to qualify as a Southern dish, but my students believe it is. Nor is the often-mentioned sweet-potato casserole with marshmallows an ancient recipe.) The word "plenty" usually appears with emphasis in descriptions of the menu. Thanksgiving means an abundant meal consumed among extended family and drawn out over time.

Student comments about family Thankgivings often focus on time and imbue it with sacred qualities.[14] They talk about its permanence. As this student puts it, "she'll remember [it] forever." Other students focus on what the family "always" has or the way it is "always" done. Even the anticipation experienced through the "eternal" time of preparation and waiting heightens the rewards of finally getting to eat favorite foods. This eternal time is not ordinary or linear. It can be recovered in memory or memorial acts, but it is also unique. As one student puts it, Thanksgiving "is the *only time* my family can get together."

At the center of this memory, even more than the dressing, is its maker, the grandmother. She is the one who makes the sacred time of family feasts happen. Grandmothers are "ritual experts" as student researcher Joy Ann Lane surmised. The memory at the beginning of this section reads as a kind of worship service with grandmother acting as a high priest whose ministrations evoke the sacred: "All the family gathered at grandmother's house," begins this student. She describes the scene in terms of transition from ordinary reality to the sacred, as she hears "the sound of clashing pots and pans, running water, and the women of the family singing joyously at they prepared the Thanksgiving feast." The smell of turkey and dressing "lured her into the kitchen" and she tries to jump ahead in the ritual by entering the inner sanctum to sneak a bite, "just to be chased out by her grandmother." "Hours later," she says, "the feast is done" and the children are "called in from outside and assemble themselves" at their table. The student describes this meal as a ritual religious meal. Her model is the Christian Communion and her description is uncannily similar to a Catholic Eucharist, a bit surprising coming from a low-church

Protestant. Her grandmother prepares the food and the table, "says grace over the meal," and then the other women serve the family, much as a priest might consecrate the ritual elements and deacons distribute them. When it comes her turn to receive "her grandmother's delicious turkey and dressing," she experiences what might be likened to "the real presence" of the holy. "The first bite," she says, "is like heaven in her mouth." Following the paradigmatic role of Communion as memorial, this student sums up her grandmother's Thanksgiving in the phrase, "she'll remember [it] forever."

Over 30 percent of the memories center on grandmothers and express a profound nostalgia for their food and presence. Nostalgia for grandmother's table is not new nor is it uniquely Southern. Students in my course read about grandmothers and food in a number of cultures. They also live in a culture that has produced a plethora of nostalgic writing on grandmothers and food, particularly of late.[15] As historian Rebecca Sharpless explains, grandmother's food has become even more significant as fears of the demise of Southern culture and foodways have arisen:

> Some Southern cultural historians argue that the distinctiveness of Southern culture is dying … The same might be argued for Southern food, suffocating under the weight of national chain restaurants. Certainly, most Southern women do not cook as their grandmothers did—at least not most of the time … But at holiday time … Southerners return to their roots … Such cooking is fraught with memory, nostalgia, and emotion.[16]

Their grandmother's food inaugurates a different time and place for students. While most talk about holidays or summer visits to their grandmother's house, there is the sense that her food has the ability to turn even everyday (profane) existence into something sacred. A student who lived with her grandparents as a child recalls "normal" mealtimes:

> [Dinner] was always at the table, all together. There would be no other distractions, but the ticking … and chime of the grandfather clock. Each meal included all food groups. It gave her a sense of togetherness to sit with the family and eat, sitting back from the busy world.

Looking back on those dinners from her busy life as a college student now, this student projects an image of sacred time and space out of "the busy (profane) world" that is cooked up in her grandmother's meals. Even the "ancestral" clock seems to tick away to a different kind of special time brought about by grandmother's ministrations.

Students assume that grandmothers initiate these sacred times by two means quite familiar to scholars of religion: secret knowledge and sacrifice. Students repeatedly emphasize, often in great detail recalled from early childhood observation, the extensive labor that grandmothers expend in preparing food. Their labor is described in terms of the amount of time it takes and the infinite amount of love it communicates. One student's interpretation of her

FOOD,
CULTURE &
SOCIETY

VOLUME 15

ISSUE 2

JUNE 2012

grandmother's meal speaks for many: "Even though it took her a long time to complete, the grandma enjoyed doing it because it made her feel like she was taking care of her family."

Another student explains the source of the Christmas cookies that the women in her family used to get together to bake. Expressing both grandma's sacrifice and secret knowledge, she relates, "These (cookie) recipes are guarded with a lock in her grandma's cupboard. Only grandma really knows them, and until she dies, no one else will." Here, as traditionally, female power is bound to women's sacrifice. Only by grandmother's death do other women in the family get the knowledge to make the special cookies; but this is a power that will be associated thereafter with her passing.

Student researcher Heather Barclay's analysis focused on a number of memories about students realizing that their grandmothers would die one day. There is an almost visceral dread of losing this special person, her food, and the special times only she can perfectly create in these stories. Students cope with this in a variety of ways. Amy was confronted with her grandmother's mortality one recent Thanksgiving when "she saw her grandmother sitting in a chair" rather than cooking. Looking up, her grandmother, "in a weak voice … said, 'Just can't cook it all this year.'" Amy's grandmother did make the most important dish, her dressing, which Amy had "never imagined there would be a Thanksgiving without." Amy coped with the anxiety of potential loss by making "sure to get an extra helping of dressing" that year.

Foods associated with grandmother come to embody her and, in a sense, make her eternal. As Heather notes, these foods are most often described as "perfect." For one student, great-grandmother's pie evokes her presence. Recreating it is the responsibility of subsequent generations of women in the family. She says that she "just recently mastered the art before I left for college." At Thanksgiving, the student continues, "we all hold hands and go around the table and tell one thing we are thankful for. My grandmother then cuts each of us a piece of pie and we are each reminded of our great-grandmother and the tradition she passed on to our family." This ritual commemoration re-incorporates the family through sharing great-grandmother's presence in the pie. "The taste of the pie," she says, "reminds me of my great-grandmother and the love her family has for one another." In an expression of nostalgia for the original she says, "As good as it is, it isn't nearly as good as when my great-grandmother made it." When great-grandmother died, some of the flavor of the pie was lost as well. Its absence in the present commemoration especially "reminds her of her great-grandmother."

Much of the nostalgia for grandmother's food does not focus on communal rites, however. Rather, it reveals a longing for the special, individual care that grandmothers bestow on young children. In many memories, grandmothers prepare favorite foods for each grandchild. One student's reflection on a Low-country tradition illustrates this emphasis on the individual child. "When I was little," she begins, "my grandmother would feed me this dish made of white rice and black-eyed peas mixed together. I really liked it a lot. I'd get platefuls of it. I had no clue what it was." The memory centers on the day she intuited the need to know more about this special dish: "So one day I went to grandma and asked her what it was.

She told me it was Hoppin' John." Thinking the lesson over, the girl asked her grandmother to make some, only to have her grandmother refuse, "because Hoppin' John was a dish cooked only for New Year's Day." As student researcher Stephanie Barron interprets, "The girl at first enjoys … the dish solely for its taste, but comes to comprehend (something of) its cultural significance." The student immediately returns, however, to personal meaning. "This little girl couldn't quite get the name right," she remembers, "calling the dish 'Hoppy John.' And I still call it 'Hoppy John,'" she concludes, "to make my grandmother smile." For the student, it is not the cultural heritage or holiday tradition but rather the bond between grandmother and granddaughter, memorialized in a new name that makes this food, so symbolic of Low-country history and identity, one of her personal favorites.

Mother's Cold Grits and Profane Time

> She was sitting at the breakfast table about an hour before the bus. She never liked grits but this morning she had put off eating them so long they were cold … The cold grainy taste appalled her. Her mother was still home from work and came out of the bedroom in her robe. She gave the little girl a sour look because the grits had been given about a half hour before. Her mother said, "You will not leave the table until you have eaten them." She tried to force another spoonful; she spit it back out. She couldn't do it. Grits was then deemed as the food that would kill her and until this day she believes that.

Just as the national (and theological) significance of Thanksgiving is sublimated under the familial for my students, and culturally significant dishes like Hoppin' John can become primarily personal favorites symbolic of special intimate relationships, so Southern food or any food can become profane to these Southern students if served by the wrong person in the wrong time. The wrong person in these food memories is usually the hurried and hassled mother.

In the memory above, a student evokes a time-starved world of working mothers and children who have to eat around bus and work schedules, symbolized in the "cold grits" she rejects. Fifteen percent of the students focus on particular foods, most of them negatively. Traditional Southern foods are the most reviled. While in grandmother's hands they can be nurturing sacramental fare in sacred time, in mother's they represent moralistic control in fleeting time. Being "Southern" alone does not make a food sacred for these Southern students. How it is given to them in time by the females who feed them—that is, what it tells them about their identity in relation to their female models—is the primary factor.[17]

Many students recall when mothers forced them to "stay at table" and "hurry up and eat" foods they disliked at the same time. Several "to this day I won't eat that" stories are about being forced to eat traditional Southern foods. As this student put it, "Grits was then deemed the food that would kill the little girl and until this day she believes that." Another recalls eating "nasty (butter) beans and (yellow) squash while holding her nose and hoping not to gag." "To this day," she continues, "she doesn't eat beans or squash because of that terrible memory." Another says,

FOOD,
CULTURE
SOCIETY

VOLUME 15

ISSUE 2

JUNE 2012

267

"As far as cornbread goes, I eat Jiffy cake like they make in the North," after being forced regularly by her mother to eat cornbread and pinto beans growing up.

The rejection of convenience foods in the memories parallels the rejection of traditional foods forced by time-crunched moms. One students tells of "dinnertime in the autumn of 1995" when "both the mother and father of the family worked late." A "quick meal of Hamburger Helper" was dinner. Saying that the children ate the meal despite not liking it, she goes on to say she got sick at the table. "Because of this, her mother made her go to bed early with no snack." "To this day," the student says, "she won't eat Hamburger Helper." As student researcher Carolyn Bone interprets, this student's "myth" of what family nurture should be was transgressed when her parents devoted their time to work rather than making food. Her disgust was further compounded by being "punished" by her mother and being refused nourishment a second time: no bedtime snack. Carolyn continues, "her reaction to the meal may indicate that she has nostalgia for a time when her mother had the time to prepare a quality meal for her family." Nausea, Carolyn concludes, indicates "not only physical disgust with the food, but also a psychological disgust with her current family situation."

About 12 percent of the students focus on their mothers in the memories. What appear mostly are stories that reveal the difference in the mythic roles assigned to mothers and grandmothers expressed by relating time (and sometimes place) to food quality. The majority of students who wrote about their families' food habits express dissatisfaction with the lack of home cooking "from scratch"; their complaints are targeted at mothers who do not cook, do not cook well, or who take shortcuts of convenience or fast foods. Mother's labor in the kitchen is almost never mentioned positively. Indeed, when mothers try to cook "a real meal," they wind up the butt of family jokes or their daughters' disdain. One student relates how her mother's attempts at cooking often resulted in dishes that got "flushed down the toilet." Many students' stories of moms' kitchen misadventures poke fun at their lack of nurture through food as well as their culinary inabilities. "The funniest memory" one student recalls is a Sunday dinner when "mom really didn't want to cook … She made vegetable burritos with hot-dogs as a side item, just closing her eyes and reaching into the fridge, picking out whatever." The children survived the meal through their own culinary creativity, converting the hot dogs into "burrito dogs." It was hardly grandma's Sunday dinner.

Another student shows clearly that the failure of her mother to revive a sacred time is related to being in a time in which sacred events must accommodate other schedules. Her mother tried to prepare "the traditional Thanksgiving meal," but the family did not have it at the traditional noontime. Because of her "brother's flight home from school," they waited until evening. Among the foods were some commemorative dishes including "granny's rolls." In the margin, she writes, "They were good but not quite the same as when Granny made them." That marginal comment and what followed it reflect the contrast between her granny's perfect Thanksgiving and her mother's imperfect one. Instead of a comment about the memorable meal, she summarizes, "After dinner, the children help put leftovers in Tupperware." Mother's is never quite as good as grandmother's. Mother's timing was off, the rolls were not perfect; and everything wound up "plastic." The key difference between foods in mother's hands and grandmother's may be more about the perception of a loss of the sacred time students felt at grandmother's table than about the foods themselves.

The mythic quality of grandmother and mother memories is even more apparent as one recognizes the distance between historical reality and mythical thinking here. Sharpless and the Southern women writers who have mourned the passing of grandmothers' cooking are mature women whose own grandmothers are deceased. Many if not most had lived in a time and in contexts in which much of the Southern diet was still composed of regional or local foods and cooked from scratch according to traditional methods passed down through families and communities. My students, who were born in the early 1980s, express a similar nostalgia for grandmothers who are still living and had microwave ovens in their kitchens and shopped in supermarkets with access to convenience foods when their grandchildren were small. No doubt many of those grandmothers worked or still work outside the home and do not spend all day cooking for their grandchildren.[18] Only a few of the students tell stories that indicate that they ate on a daily basis with grandmothers. Most tell stories of special sacred times such as Sunday dinners or Thanksgivings. Grandmothers' slowly-prepared, home-cooked abundant meals loom larger and seem both more "ancient" and more frequent in the memories of students than they probably were in reality, especially in contrast to the perceived lack of time and homemade food in their experience of their mothers.

According to my students' stories, grandmothers live in a paradisal world where women cook wonderful meals at home and nurture grandchildren. Their mothers live after the fast food Fall and may even be blamed for it. They are, however, their mothers' daughters. They too live in a fast food world where women labor outside the home.

Another thing mothers and daughters share is ambivalence about spending time cooking. A few students proudly relate how grandmothers passed secret family recipes to them, but they do so soberly, expressing a keen awareness of the passing of grandmother and her time and the sacrifice of their own time and labor it would take for them to try to recreate it. Some say they would like to revive the old family meals that their grandmothers used to make, "if only I knew how." Fewer than 10 percent of the memories, however, involve students as cooks. Most often, students follow their mothers rather than their grandmothers in the kitchen.

One student's story is typical. Her mother called from work to ask her to "put cans of peas and corn in the microwave for dinner." Saying that she "had to leave her position at the piano reluctantly," she did exactly as her mother asked and went back to her music—until the boom: "The cans were black and the microwave always made a funny noise after that." She was not a total failure: "The peas and corn were nice and cooked just right." With both humor and disgust, the memories reveal a reality in which women make do with little time and culinary skill and simply are relieved to have provided something edible. Clearly, the sharp contrast in the ways that mothers, grandmothers, and their "times" are remembered by these young women through food gives us a glimpse into the

FOOD,
CULTURE &
SOCIETY

VOLUME 15

ISSUE 2

JUNE 2012

challenges that confront them as they seek their own identities as women in their time to come.

Understanding the meeting of reality and myth helps a few students revive their mothers as cooks and nurturers and models to follow. This usually occurs with situations in which the family's myth has been challenged by a catastrophic event. One student says that "Mom used to always make cookies, cupcakes, and cakes for (her siblings) during school events or just because she wanted to." But by the time she came along, mom was different. "All my childhood," she laments, "I had heard these stories and it upset me to the point of tears. My mother never did any of this for me (other than box-mix cakes for my birthday)." At age fifteen, she finally asked her mother "why she never was a grade-mother for me." "All she ever wanted to do," her mother explained, "was to be a mother and a homemaker." She tried to live out her dream despite an abusive marriage. After her husband left the family, "anytime that something would go wrong, like a cracked cake, it would just destroy her." Finally, the student relates, "She got to the point where she could not take the emotional pain and stress involved and had to quit baking in order to save her sanity." This student came to understand that as her mother's life changed, so did the way she related to old mythic roles and symbols. Then she was able to see her relationship to her mother differently. It was not that her mother did not love her as much as her siblings; she just came along after the cracked cake and the broken myth. Thus she is able to redeem her mother: "It was through her creativeness with what little she had to work with, that she was able to feed us and teach us."

Fried Chicken and Re-Enchantment in a Fast Food Culture

> Her father always (grows) vegetables in his garden. Many family rituals revolved around mealtime. Special care always went into the selection of ingredients and their cooking. Because of their time overseas, they almost always make meals from scratch … This is a tradition they have never lost.

This student describes her family's abnormal life in the South. Hers is one of only three memories in which a male provides food. In contrast to thrown-together meals of other families, "special care always goes into the selection of ingredients and their cooking" in this one. As she explains, "Because of their time overseas, they almost always make meals from scratch …" Her family comes from another time and place, an enchanted world of homemade food that originates in father's garden. Her sense of difference is verified by a profound absence in the other memories. A sense of Southern foodways and their basis in the land is almost completely non-existent, even though several of the students who wrote memories come from families with rural heritage.

All that is left of a land-based Southern culture is a feeling of nostalgia for the time that grandmothers cooked "Southern" foods. Even when students describe those meals, however, they resort to the language of the fast food culture they inhabit. In the memory about grandmother's Thanksgiving, the student said, "The first bite is like heaven in (my) mouth. The *tender, juicy* turkey accompanied by the dressing is *a perfect combo*." The description is a metaphor built on sacred symbolism with the "tender, juicy … perfect combo" of fast food advertising. "Perfectly seasoned" green beans do not come from granny's garden in another student's memory, nor is she talking about slow-cooking with pork. Seasoning to her is commercial marketing's "secret blend of spices."

Even though they resort to the *lingua franca* of contemporary foodways to describe traditional home-cooking, fast food itself is not "good to think" with for most of the young women who described meaningful meals. While traditional and fast foods alike are rejected by students when associated with a lack of nurturing time, no student expresses nostalgic family memories involving fast food meals. Only one student relates an attempt at making a happy, family memory in a fast food restaurant: her first trip to McDonald's at age three when she gagged, ironically, on her Happy Meal. Most often, fast food is part of dismal, mundane reality, as in one student's description of getting sick after having to "gulp down" fast food at work. Fast food memories usually have a dark side. They are sometimes about transgressive, late-night "pig outs" with college friends that end with everyone feeling sick or guilty. Indeed, a few students who "admit" their fondness for fast food use the words "addiction" or "temptation" to describe their relationship to the food. Fast food, indeed, is the food of "The Fall" for these students. Their world, for the most part, has lost the enchantment they desire to relive in grandmother's meals.

Some students can still find meaning and pleasure in a fast food world in ways other than vomiting or nostalgia for the old days. Holly says her "mother and father have absolutely no cooking abilities. They live off frozen entrées and microwavable food at their house." So at age ten, she and her sister took matters into their own hands. As Holly tells it, "They bought some mashed potato mix and even bought a measuring cup." Measuring incorrectly the first time, they created a "watery mess," but eventually after using the entire box they had "white, flaky, mashed potatoes." Proudly she comments, "They were even better than the mashed potatoes at Ryan's Steak House … (The girls) felt like chefs!" They taught the entire family how to make instant potatoes and now they are "a regular dish." This student still understands the mythic "real" dish (white and flaky and mediated here through the new mythos of the family steak house). Even though they cannot cook, her family can revive the mythic family meal through a simple communal act of rehydrating. She ends, "We may not know how to fix lasagna or chocolate cake, but we can handle the mashed potatoes."

Holly's list of "real" foods points to another way in which my Southern students are making meaning with food these days. Steakhouse mashed potatoes, Southern comfort foods, and even chocolate cake are competing with foods of a mythos that hearkens back not only to another time but also another place strongly associated with leisurely family meals. A student approvingly describes a single-dish meal her mother recently prepared for her homecoming from college. The wonderful aroma of the dish caused the home kitchen to smell "like a nice Italian restaurant." Another described a recent birthday meal with her family at "her favorite Italian restaurant back home." "As the food came, the smell of garlic and other spices spread across

FOOD,
CULTURE &
SOCIETY

VOLUME 15

ISSUE 2

JUNE 2012

their table. Everyone ended up sampling a tiny piece of almost everyone else's dinner." She recalls with pleasure the "smiles, laughter, and hugs" in the atmosphere of "dim lighting and Frank Sinatra." It seems that Southern hospitality is being replaced with "hospitaliano."[19]

That the quintessential Southern food fried chicken is discussed in only three memories might be sign of its loss of mythic power. It may have gone from being the gospel bird of Sunday dinners to something bagged on every street corner; however, it can still carry a range of meanings. Student memories reveal a complex confrontation of reality and myth in the ways they think of this Southern staple. In one memory, a student vomits in the middle of the SAT after "gobbling down" a fast food fried chicken and biscuit because she had been told to eat a "good breakfast with protein" before the exam. As student researcher Ashley Kirstein explains, the fast food fried chicken taught the student a lesson about preparing properly for major events. The sense this memory gives of the student's mistake is that not only did she try to substitute a fast food for a real ("good") breakfast, but that fast food chicken is not "real" protein or, real fried chicken and eating it, as Ashley says, caused "revolting consequences."

Another memory about fried chicken, however, reveals how a food profaned can become re-enchanted, even in a paper bucket. "Chicken was once a favorite" of a student and her sister, "especially when it was prepared with tender love by the wrinkled hands of their grandmother." The girls' attitude changed to "distaste" when the family situation changed from one where "daddy was home playing" to when "mother was the only one at home anymore." But mother was not at home much either. She had to take on several jobs in the father's absence. One was at a local gas station. The job paid the bills and provided a "never-ending supply of fried chicken" which her mother brought home "in a bucket." As the free, leftover, gas station chicken became a regular meal in financially-troubled times, the girls and their mother came to hate it: "It was a constant reminder of how difficult life had become." In retrospect, with that time behind them, "chicken from the gas station became less and less a symbol of sadness." Looking back now, mother and daughters "think of fried chicken and how strong, perseverant, and close to one another they became through their ordeal." Here, expressed through multiple meanings of fried chicken, mother's work and the solidarity of shared sacrifice in this family become as precious as "grandmother's wrinkled hands." And, fried chicken becomes re-enchanted, once again symbolic of a sacred time.

Analyzing that fried chicken memory prompted student researcher Sarah Jane Nicholas to reflect on nostalgia for origins and fast food culture, not in her own family, but in Southern society. As she states, "Fried chicken has come up again and again in my own realizations about food. It stands for a variety of conflicting meanings: poverty, Southern traditions, picnics, grandmothers; obesity. This has caused me to seek out the conflicts that (food symbols) contain." Sarah Jane is a poet; and poets, like religious people, often are better at evoking complex perceptions of time, space, and reality through foodways than scholars. Here, Sarah Jane stirs up in a poem the complex aroma of nostalgia in the fast lane that she experienced on a drive through Savannah. Food, for Sarah Jane, reveals the realities of class and race in the contemporary South and the profanity in its sacred mythology. Yet it hints at the possibility for re-enchantment in the constantly reforming play of myth and memory that human beings undertake. Dark meat and white scallops on opposite ends of the street will not tell the whole story.

A History of Savannah, by Sarah Jane Nicholas

Savannah smells like searing flesh
Choice sirloin of the few.
The smell is hot as the August summer sun,
Filling my nostrils and my mind.
The acrid stench pervades River Street
But the fibers of the inner blocks
Still run red with blood and cheap, sour wine.
Riding in a burgundy Suburban,
I roll my back-seat window down
As the blast of heat from Abercorn
Mixes with the cool comfort of leather seats.
My heart is silent while we glide past
Cast iron rails and balconies that give a glimpse
Of plush interiors, guided tours of gardens
And molded fountains fed with the purest, richest, and most heroic
Bloodlines in the South.
A park bench in a square off Bull St.
Cradles a homeless man, darkened with life and poverty.
He grasps a pencil stub barely long enough to hold
And writes a different story.
Two lounging boys with matching afros
Guard the Bull St. General Store,
Staring me down and challenging the illusion.
We reach the houses struck by war and left to rot
Now crying flakes of paint and
Split into duplexes, whose shriveled gardens and fountains long gone
Hold reflected images of poor and hungry—
An obese Negro woman sheltering six children on
The crumbling cement steps
Eats French fries out of a bag from McDonalds.
The children's eyes follow me
Their expressions are blank
Do they hate me? Is there envy, greed, or jealousy
That eats at them?
Does the woman knitting at the bus stop
Think about the poverty that controls her callused knuckles?
The tourists seem oblivious to the smell
That is eating me alive.

FOOD,
CULTURE &
SOCIETY

VOLUME 15

ISSUE 2

JUNE 2012

They stand by, Mother and Father with
Triplets dressed alike in Baby Gap
That squeal with simple delight at the
Fancy bubble machine outside the River St. toy store.
The idyllic waterfront numbs their minds as they snap pictures
Of a historical façade built here just for them
They feed off ten-dollar appetizers and the grill fans
Disguise the scent that now sticks to my sweaty skin.
This city is not real, and the history that we read was created
To feed our pale, wanton sensibilities
Snow crab, whitefish, scallops
While four blocks away a Church's chicken advertises dark meat,
12 pc. for 6.99.
Two brothers play on the sidewalk in front of it,
Their creamy mixed faces framed by beaded dreadlocks.
The younger follows in every footstep of the elder,
Hopping over cracks and jumping to touch tree branches.
They hold hands, laughing and creating a history all their own.
For a moment, I forget the smell.

Corrie Norman earned her theology doctorate from Harvard University. Her academic publications include books and essays on religion and culture in the United States and Italy, including several essays on food. Having taught for many years in liberal arts colleges in the South, she now teaches occasionally at the University of Wisconsin at Madison, where she is involved in several food-related organizations and community projects. 3722 Odana Road, Madison, WI 53711, USA (corrienorman1959@yahoo.com).

Notes

1 Students in the course read excerpts from works of the great American food writer M.F.K Fisher, and anthropologists Mary Douglas and Claude Lévi-Strauss in Carole Counihan and Penny Van Esterik (eds) *Food and Culture: A Reader* (New York: Routledge, 1997), pp. 1, 28–54.

2 For an overview of the study of religion and food and a more complete bibliography, see Corrie Norman, "Religion and Food," *The Encyclopedia of Food and Culture*, Solomon Katz (ed.) (New York: Schribners, 2003) Vol. 3, pp. 171–6. Discussion of the sacred here reflects basic notions in religious methodology but references the work of historian of religion, Mircea Eliade, especially, *The Sacred and the Profane: The Nature of Religion*, William R. Trask, trans. (London: Harcourt, Brace, and Jovanovich, 1959). Eliade's theories are undeniably influential in the field but have been criticized by scholars such as Jonathan Z. Smith in *To Take Place: Toward Theory in Ritual* (Chicago, IL: University of Chicago Press, 1987). More recently, other scholars have revisited Eliade's approach more positively. See for example, David Carrasco, *City of Sacrifice: The Aztec Empire and the Role of Violence in Civilization* (Boston, MA: Beacon Press, 1999). As this is an paper primarily about students and a pedagogical experience with food rather than an attempt at comprehensive

critical analysis, it is especially appropriate to reference a text that the student researchers read and used in their own analysis. They would understand the references; they also understand that no analysis is complete.

3   Anthony Bourdain is an "anti-celebrity" chef, novelist, and author of two culinary memoirs, including *A Cook's Tour: In Search of the Perfect Meal* (New York: Bloomsbury, 2001), read by my students.

4   There is a large body of literature on gender and food, most of it focusing on women's agency or constructions of the female through food. See especially the introduction in Carole M. Counihan and Stephen L. Kaplan (eds) *Food and Gender: Identity and Power* (Newark, NJ: Harwood Academic Press, 1998) for an overview of types of women's agency and constructions of gender that are covered in studies of women and food cross-culturally. On women and food in the United States, see the essays in Part IV of Carole M. Counihan (ed.), *Food in the USA* (New York: Routledge, 2002); and the works of Sherrie A. Inness, including *Dinner Roles: American Women and Culinary Culture* (Iowa City, IA: University of Iowa Press, 2001). Several recent histories of food in the United States focus largely on women's roles. Among them are Barbara Haber, *From Hardtack to Home Fries: An Uncommon History of American Cooks and Meals* (New York: Free Press, Simon and Schuster, 2002); Laura Schenone, *A Thousand Years Over a Hot Stove: A History of American Women Told through Food, Recipes, and Remembrances* (New York: W.W. Norton, 2003); and Laura Shapiro, *Something from the Oven: Reinventing Dinner in 1950s America* (New York: Viking, 2004).

5   Anita Desai, *Feasting/Fasting* (New York: Mariner Books, 2000); Laura Esquivel, *Like Water for Chocolate*, trans. Carol and Thomas Christensen (New York: Anchor Books, 1992); Sallie Tisdale, *The Best Thing I Ever Tasted* (New York: Riverhead Books, 2000); Vandana Shiva, *Tomorrow's Biodiversity* (London: Thames and Hudson, 2000); Verta Mae Grosvenor, *Vibration Cooking: Travel Notes of a Geechee Girl* (New York: Doubleday, 1970).

6   Student research was supported with funding from The Pluralism Project, Harvard University. A website developed for the project which contains student profiles of communities can be found at http://pluralism.org/affiliates/norman/index.php (accessed September 1, 2011).

7   Student researchers obtained written permission to use memories in subsequent research presentations and publications from the participants. Participants were given the option of remaining anonymous and first names have been used here only when explicitly permitted. I read and analyzed all the food memories and use student analysis of memories here only where it advances my own arguments. When I use the analysis of a student researcher, I credit the student by name, with her permission, in the body of the paper. I would like to thank all the students who participated in the course and the project, and especially Sarah Jane Nicholas who gave permission to use her poem at the end of the essay.

8   Deborah Lupton, "Food, Memory, and Meaning: The Symbolic and Social Nature of Food Events," *The Sociology Review* 42 (1994): 664–83. There is also a wide literature on the "food voice" as a research strategy and pedagogical tool. See, for example, the essays in the special section of *Food, Culture & Society* 7:2 (2004).

9   Lupton, "Food, Memory, and Meaning," pp. 667–8.

10 Ibid., p. 666.

11 Eliade, *The Sacred and the Profane*, p. 92.

12 Now an axiom in food scholarship, "good to think" originated in Lévi-Strauss, *Totemism*

FOOD,
CULTURE &
SOCIETY

VOLUME 15

ISSUE 2

JUNE 2012

(Boston, MA: Beacon Press, 1963), p. 20.

13 On Thanksgiving observance in the South, see Charles R. Wilson, *Baptized in Blood: The Religion of the Lost Cause* (Athens, GA: University of Georgia Press, 1980), 176. On meanings of Thanksgiving, see Janet Siskind, "The Invention of Thanksgiving: A Ritual of American Nationality," in Counihan, *Food in the USA*, pp. 41–58.

14 Eliade, *The Sacred and the Profane*, Chapter 2, focuses on sacred time, characterizing it as cyclical and recoverable in memorial acts or rites, and therefore eternal in a religious worldview.

15 For example, see Ellen Perry Berkeley, *At Grandmother's Table* (Minneapolis, MN: Fairview Press, 2000). Food writer and scholar Jessica B. Harris remembers Grandma Harris "who brought the South North" in her gardening and cooking in *The Welcome Table* (New York: Simon and Schuster, 1995), p. 32. Caterer Kathy Starr recalls cooking with her Mississippi grandmother in the late 1950s when she was a small child. Her grandmother owned cafés, until "fast food became popular" and people no longer "found the time to eat and visit the cafés." Kathy Starr, "The Soul of Southern Cooking," in *Cornbread Nation I: The Best of Southern Food Writing* (ed.) John Egerton (Chapel Hill, NC: University of North Carolina Press, 2000), 111–15. See also, Kathy Starr, *The Soul of Southern Cooking* (Oxford: University of Mississippi Press, 1989).

16 Rebecca Sharpless, "Traditional Southern Cooking— Not Gone with the Wind," *Phi Kappa Phi Forum*, The Food Issue (Summer 2002), p. 12.

17 Sociologists of religion in recent decades have documented a similar personalization of religion in the United States. See Robert Bellah, *Habits of the Heart* (Berkeley, CA: University of California Press, 1986); Wade Clark Roof, *A Generation of Seekers* (San Francisco, CA: Harper Collins, 1993); and Robert Wuthnow, *After Heaven: Spirituality in America since the 1950s* (Berkeley, CA: University of California Press, 1998). In future research, I will examine the connections between the privatizing of religion and the development of food as a medium of spiritual expression in contemporary American gourmet culture.

18 Tisdale, *The Best Thing I Ever Tasted*, discusses the phenomena of projecting an "ancient" culinary past on more recent generation and the power of myth over memory. On the development of foodways in modern America and the emergence of convenience and fast foods, see Harvey Levenstein, *Paradox of Plenty: A Social History of Eating in Modern America* (New York: Oxford University Press, 1993), especially Chapter 7, and also Shapiro, *Something from the Oven* and Schenone, *A Thousand Years Over a Hot Stove*. On Southern foodways, see John Egerton, *Southern Food: At Home, on the Road, in History* (Chapel Hill, NC: University of North Carolina Press, 1993).

19 "Hospitaliano" is a pseudo-Italian word used in advertising for The Olive Garden, a national restaurant chain with an Italian theme.

FOOD, CULTURE & SOCIETY

VOLUME 15 | ISSUE 2 | JUNE 2012

Moral Economies of Food in Cuba

Marisa Wilson
University of the West Indies

Abstract

The way people produce, exchange and consume food in Cuba is underwritten by cultural and political economic rules as well as economic self-interest. These "rules" are not just formed from the top down, but also from the bottom up, though, as I will explain in this paper, norms established by what I call the national moral economy often give cultural form to local practices of food provisioning. Despite extreme scarcities in the early 1990s and continuing difficulties obtaining food in the present dual economy, Cubans often frame farming and household provisioning in terms of the national moral economy. The latter is, in turn, structured by values that have developed in Cuba over time such as asceticism and hard work.

Keywords: moral economies, values, commodities, entitlements, consumption, provisioning

Introduction

In this paper I focus on the contrast between food as a commodity that can be valued in terms of price or exchange value, and food as an entitlement (Sen 1981), which cannot. Ideas and values about what can and cannot be commoditized, when, for example, "community membership supersedes price as a basis of entitlement" (Thompson 1993 [1971]: 338, footnote 2), are what Edward Palmer Thompson called moral economies. Moral economies hinge on historical and cultural patterns formed when political economic models of state or market meet local schemes of value, and vice versa.

The association between economic processes and the creation of value is especially clear in regards to food, which, given its centrality to social life, has long been a subject of anthropological analysis. Audrey Richards, the first anthropologist to engage in a detailed ethnographic study of food and culture, understood the special characteristics of food in its commodity form:

[F]ood stands in a different category from the ordinary commodities of economic exchange. It is an insistent human want, occurring regularly at short intervals, and shared by the whole community alike ... [I]t is the mechanism by which food-getting habits are formed in the structure of each different culture that we have to analyze. (Richards 1932: 14–15)

While anthropologists have long associated food habits with other cultural forms, they have also found that social uses of food do not always reflect unidirectional flows of value from one domain of life to another. In continuing the sociological project initiated by Mauss (1954 [1925]) and rekindled by Polanyi (2001 [1944]) and his followers, in this paper I attempt to re-link embedded aspects of society with the more limited domains delineated by political economic models. I do so by considering the way dominant ideas are consolidated in Cuban history, the "residual" (Dumont 1980 [1966]: 38–9) forms of which shape everyday practices.

The paper is split into three parts. In the first I review the anthropological literature on food provisioning and economic or other value(s), situating Cuba within this theoretical setting. In the second part, I continue along these lines, drawing from historical contexts of value-formation in Cuba to outline the contours and contradictions of its national moral economy. In the final part, I use ethnographic examples to show how the national moral economy in Cuba shapes the production, exchange and consumption of foodstuffs on the ground (the local moral economy of provisioning). I use qualitative evidence from Tuta, a rural village in Cuba (which I have renamed, along with its inhabitants) where I conducted ethnographic fieldwork for fifteen months from 2005 to 2007, returning for another month during the summer of 2011.

Provisioning Processes and Value-formation in Changing Economies

Studies in economic anthropology have largely involved just one economic step in the "provisioning path" (Fine and Leopold 1993), e.g. consumption. This narrowing of focus has, however, often led the anthropologist to base analysis on assumptions embedded in his or her own value system. For instance, Marcel Mauss's (1954 [1925]) exclusive interest in exchange stemmed, in part, from his ties to the French Marxist tradition. As Marilyn Strathern (1999: 139) notes, Mauss's interest in exchange was the product of his situated position as a revolutionary socialist and the manager of a consumer cooperative in France. As did Maurice Bloch a decade earlier (Bloch 1989: 176), Strathern refers to the central idea of exchange in anthropology as arising from Mauss's political concern about the alienation of property in capitalism (Strathern 1999: 139).

More recently, and in a similar vein, much attention in anthropology has been given to non-market, localized aspects of consumption (e.g. Friedman 1994; Weiss 1996; Miller 1994, 2001), which have again tended to overshadow wider symbolic and material *processes* of provisioning such as the intentions and values of producers. Susan Narotsky (2005) has asserted that studies which focus entirely on the consumer end disregard the "complex ways that power and interest can shape a provisioning chain" (Narotsky 2005: 81). Over fifteen years ago, sociologists Ben Fine and Ellen Leopold made a similar point, insisting that consumption of any commodity is "contingent upon, if not determined by, the production, distribution and circulation of *value*" (Fine and Leopold 1993: 255; emphasis added).

The anthropology of consumption has too often ignored important work on the history and political economy of commodity flows (e.g. Mintz 1985; Watts 1999), as well as anthropologies and geographies of value and money,[1] key analytical tools for deciphering how, when and *what kinds of* valuations historically emerge and change in particular places. Cultural perspectives on the biographies of commodities (Appadurai 1986; Kopytoff 1986; Cook 2004) start with the commodity, a form of value that is historical rather than given. Similar studies such as *The Dialectics of Shopping* (Miller 2001) openly disregard more profound political economic and cultural processes of value-formation, which occur before the commodity reaches the megastore, or even before the megastore itself became a requisite for the "good" London housewife. Indeed, while Miller's consideration of "our labor of love" in shopping (Miller 2001: 53) follows the Maussian tradition of revealing the "universal" (Miller 2001: 53) link between persons and objects, he deliberately (Miller 2001: 2) leaves out wider historical and political economic issues that relate people to commodities, which may have clarified how norms of the market have come to define London shoppers as *persons* in the first place. Such blind spots in analyses allow the market to creep in through the back door: "exchange creates value rather than people," and the fetishism of commodities becomes a methodological principle (Gregory 1997: 44).

Following critical approaches to value in economic anthropology, in this paper I argue that local rules for provisioning in Cuba are related to historical determinations of appropriate economic action, some of which stem from a wider community (e.g. the nation state), some from the market. Finding oneself in the protected position of a tourist, a visitor to Cuba rarely has the opportunity to understand the bigger picture in which *both* state and market are embedded. Fortunately, the boundaries which separate tourist and Cuban, market and state spheres (Bohannan 1955, 1959) of economic activity were partially lifted for me during the fieldwork period. The visa I obtained was not that for an academic visitor, nor was it a tourist visa. Instead, I was entitled to a family visa, officially and locally legitimated by a fictitious kinship relationship with my Cuban "parents"—friends I had known since my first visit in 2002 and who had decided that this would be the best way for me to gain official approval to stay in their "humble" household.

Being accepted (to some extent) as a legitimate insider in an area relatively isolated from obvious contrasts between Cuban and tourist provisioning spheres (as opposed to those witnessed daily by Habaneros), I discovered a world in which economic action was far from a direct reflection of rules embedded in Cuban communism and other either/or scenarios (Shanin 1990: 86–91) that separate commodities from entitlements or state from market forms of provisioning.

FOOD,
CULTURE &
SOCIETY

VOLUME 15

ISSUE 2

JUNE 2012

State and Market in Cuba: The Historical Formation of the National Moral Economy

Historical representations of Cuban society, such as the national "fight" (*lucha*) to re-gain "our" land and its products from mercenary power-holders and the Guevarian vision of the "New Men" of socialism who secure collective "needs" through work effort (see below), have, in part, been reactions to the self-interested idea of "man" as depicted in the market model. In the post-1959 period, such historical formations became linked to a socialist version of "morality as asceticism" (Dumont 1977: 76), according to which inalienable goods for all, such as basic alimentary necessities, were officially valued over superfluous commodities and profits. According to such moral rules set by the Cuban state, which I call the national moral economy, provisioning at the local level must coincide with the "General Welfare" (Myrdal 1953: 16) of the community, a premise not unlike that of the market model, as I argue elsewhere (Wilson, in press). In the communist model, however, all property (e.g. food produced by individual farmers) that satisfies the general welfare of the collective is treated as *social* property rather than individual property, and thus should be redistributed from the national center to individual citizens in accordance with their work effort and state-defined needs. Below I show that geopolitical conditions and iconographic representations of José Martí and Ernesto "Che" Guevara not only worked to establish borders around post-1959 Cuba as a national community, but opened the way to cultural assessments of value, which are, as I show in the succeeding sections, still reflected in everyday provisioning practices.

Like other plantation-based societies in the Caribbean, Cuba emerged from colonialism as a bipolar society, with both affinity and aversion to metropolitan capital, commodities and values. A strong counter-hegemonic system surfaced in late nineteenth and twentieth-century Cuba to resist US domination. During and after the War of Independence (1895–98; callously or ignorantly called the Spanish-American War by some), the landowning classes were replaced by businessmen, merchants and other groups tied to the sugar industry, as Cuba became increasingly dominated by US interests. The other part of late nineteenth and early twentieth-century Cuban society was comprised of petty traders, service workers and "reconstituted" peasants (Mintz 1961: 31–4; e.g. *colonos* or sugar-cane sharecroppers). In the second half of the nineteenth century, many of the latter had moved to rural areas, especially to the coffee and pasture lands of the east, returning to their farms when Spanish General Weyler's ruthless reconcentration campaign to relocate rural settlements finally ended after the War of Independence. Yet independence it was not, and the resulting "stillbirth" (Guerra 2005: 3) of the republic led to heightened divisions between a large section of the population under the puppet strings of US policies and personalities, and another section united if only in their resistance to dominance by outsiders.

Polarities between Cuba as a *place* for Cubans and Cuba as an economic *space* that could be bought and sold, had been evident since the second half of the 19th century when the impersonal "factory central system" (Mintz 1956: 337) superseded the paternalist plantation model. The bifurcation of Cuban society continued into the twentieth century, characterized by a rent-seeking and largely corrupt political and economic elite dependent on the "benevolent" hand of the United States, on the one hand, and a heterogeneous group of counter-hegemonic forces, on the other. Indeed, according to Lilian Guerra, Cuba's national "creation myth" (Guerra 2005: 7) is symbolized by the mythical figure of José Martí, whose writings were based on a moral contrast between the dependency and greed of individuals, and autonomy and justice of the nation and of Latin America as a whole. The influential writings of Martí, the Cuban poet and hero who was killed in the War of Independence, perpetuated the idea that the Cuban nation was united in its "defense" against outside economic interests, a depiction that extended to race as well as class: "A Cuban is more than white, more than mulatto, more than black ... In the daily life of defense, loyalty, brotherhood, and attack, at the side of every white man there has always been a Negro" (Martí 1977: 29).

In the twentieth century, moralistic writings by Cuban social scientists largely focused on national polarities between internal and external economies, or between the upper and middle classes who mainly resided in Havana (though many owned land in the countryside) and the poorer rural classes in most other areas of Cuba. In Cuban historiography, for example, the contrast was depicted as that between "nation" and "plantation" (Martinez-Alier 1977: 125) in the nineteenth century, or between *conciencia* (conscience) and *existencia* (existence) (Martí 1959) in the twentieth. Such binarism became a key tool for Cuban nationalism. It was used by Fidel Castro and his confidant, Ernesto "Che" Guevara, to defend the communist cause and, more recently, by Raul Castro's government to give cultural shape to political calls for national food sovereignty (Wilson, in press).

Like Martí, Guevara was able to incorporate nearly all the political and cultural codes that had characterized Cuba as a nation with a "definable tradition of political dissent" (Kapcia 1997: 25–6). And, like earlier Cuban intellectuals, Guevara and his followers adopted a kind of "revolutionary ethics," which challenged the "economic rationality" (Silverman 1971: 3) of the United States and Cuban elites. Guevara's calls for moral over material incentives in what Ernest Mandel called the Great Debate of 1963–5 (Silverman 1971: 1) not only upset more market-based plans for the Cuban economy, but were also continuous with a certain kind of Cuban nationalism that developed from the time of José Martí. In line with Martí's writings, Guevara's model for society called for men and women to become "cultured" through values such as hard work and self-sacrifice rather than via increased access to metropolitan commodities. In the process, they were seen as becoming "New Men" of socialism:

FOOD,
CULTURE
SOCIETY

VOLUME 15

ISSUE 2

JUNE 2012

It is not a question of how many kilograms of meat are eaten or how many pretty imported things can be bought with present wages. It is rather that the individual feels greater fulfillment [in work], that he has greater inner wealth and many more responsibilities in our country, the individual knows that the glorious period in which it has fallen to him to live is one of sacrifice. (Guevara 1971: 352)

The most influential model of the Cuban economy in the post-1959 period was based on a subordination of individual desires for collective entitlements, such as centralized food distribution. Indeed, in the post-1959 period, historical values initiated by Martí became linked to a kind of "morality as asceticism" (Dumont 1977: 79), according to which inalienable goods for all, such as basic alimentary necessities, became officially valued over superfluous commodities and profits. From the early 1960s to the early 1990s, this value system evolved in conjunction with a centralized economy, which aligned work effort with peso salaries, which could, in turn, buy a limited selection of basic foodstuffs. As this system depended on the internal control of goods as well as money, pesos (valued on par with the US dollar) worked as tokens used to buy state-defined necessities rather than money to purchase an unimaginable array of commodities (Holbraad 2000: 9).

Before the legalization of hard currency (US dollars) in 1993 (converted to the Cuban convertible dollar, CUC, in 1998), the communist model seemed to function in Cuba as intended, if one ignores the periodic specter of the black market. Farmers and the state maintained a barter-like relationship (exchanging in kind), just as workers labored for state tokens used to buy provisions. In a sense, food and household items represented money or wealth during this period.

The situation in post-1993 Cuba is drastically different. Food is now a commodity, competing with its role as an entitlement in the state's value system (Wilson 2009). Very low daily wages (approx 10 pesos, or $0.52) earned in highly-devalued pesos (1 peso = 1/24 CUCs) are still exchanged for staple items intermittently available through the state subsidized system, such as rice and soap. Food *commodities* like export quality rum are sold in hard currency, their prices set largely by supply and demand. These luxury items are only available to privileged Cubans with access to CUCs. The CUC's value is—in theory if not in practice—determined entirely by its exchange value, as set against global dollar exchange rates. The Cuban peso's value rests on an entirely different value system: that of hard work and asceticism.

The Local Moral Economy of Provisioning: Ethnographic Examples

I have argued that the Cuban economy is linked not only to a global market driven by individual preferences and rules of supply and demand, but also to a national value system: the product of Cuba's particular political and intellectual history. While Cubans have partly incorporated the consumerist culture of their powerful northern neighbor, they are also influenced by ideas that have shaped Cuban society over time. As I found in my research, Cubans (like most other people) have "multiple, conflicting social identifications" (Davis 2004: 14, in reference to Folbre 1994), only some of which conform to the idea of the individual maximizing his personal benefits in the market. Below I provide ethnographic examples of food provisioning processes in Tuta, starting with production and ending with consumption. Despite my analytical distinctions, we shall see that these economic arenas are interrelated in practice.

Production

As Sir Henry Maine noted in 1861, property and ownership are always embedded in the "total range of rights and obligations" (von Benda-Beckmann *et al.* 2006: 17, in reference to Gluckman 1965) of any particular society. People with land in Cuba must balance their rights: partial subsistence, credit, technical and other social assistance—*notably more significant rights than those of many other smallholders in Latin America and the world*—with the moral obligation to work the land to meet the alimentary needs of society. Such was true not only for *campesinos* (peasants) and workers in the early years of the revolution, but also for recipients of land under the latest two agrarian reforms, in the period of 1993–6 and presently (from July 2008 to the date of writing, December 2011), as plots of land are distributed to Cubans in usufruct to produce food for their families and for sale (see Funes *et al.* 2002; Wright 2008). Driven by a political drive for food sovereignty (as well as economic necessity), the current rise in domestic food production is a great benefit for traders or 'intermediaries', but also for smallholders whom I have already noted to be better off than most other people in society: "I don't know what the people do in town who do not have land like I do. I am old [90 years old], but I still work the land for food."

As I found during fieldwork, it was not just communist norms that prompted people to work in agriculture for social ends, as illustrated by Eduardo's farming family, who received land from the Cuban state in 1993.[2] Eduardo's wife or *mujer*, Mariela, emphasized social over monetary aspects of their farming business. One day she expressed her anger with a woman who had come to the house to buy produce. While the woman who had visited *could* have brought milk from her family's goat as a gift to Eduardo's family, which would have been exchanged for produce, the woman was "stupid" as she brought only money. Mariela stressed that they always preferred to help others with what they produced, and were happy when people brought items of use to the family. In her terms: "it is not money, it is the feeling one gets knowing you are helping someone." As moral economy theorists of peasant societies (Scott 1976; Edelman 2005) have shown, the way people value food in Cuba is as related to sociality as price.

Though Eduardo did engage in market transactions by selling produce to visitors, like his wife he preferred personalized exchanges. He claimed that his farm was more successful because of these exchange relationships, which combined market and non-market or barter transactions. One example that stands out is the relationship between Eduardo and one of his (illegal) buyers of mint. In exchange for the latter's continued business, Eduardo said that he "controlled" the mint-buyer's *mujer*. He made me understand that the mint-buyer had several *mujeres*, and that, in order to keep this secret, his wife would need to be "controlled" by invitations to the farm or other distractions.

The official account of productive work in Cuba is tied to social values like national sovereignty, but at the everyday level, farmers engage in social relations to continue long-term, localized relations. Social exchanges in production such as the above examples also allow producers to reap economic benefits from their new position as small farmers. While producers of food may have an economic

FOOD,
CULTURE &
SOCIETY

VOLUME 15

ISSUE 2

JUNE 2012

advantage over state workers, all the Tutaños I interacted with were aware of the moral and political obligation to be generous and sociable, at least with everyone in their community.

Exchange

Among the non-farming public, there also seemed to be a fine line between true solidarity and the political requirement to help neighbors when they were in need. As Tutaños indicated, people were always watching others' behavior: "*La gente son chimosa*" (People are gossips). Clara (my Cuban "mother") told me this when someone asked her if she was buying beef from the street vendors for "the girl" (me). According to Clara, an affirmative answer to this question is dangerous as word might spread that one is buying beef illegally.

Because of this strong system of neighborhood watch, people such as Clara and Jorge (my Cuban "parents") also felt an obligation to be sociable and giving to their neighbors, even if they did not otherwise feel close to them. When the neighbors in front of Clara's house celebrated their daughter's second birthday, Clara felt obligated to buy her a *vulgaria* (a little something) though she would not usually care to spend time with the family. Another day I heard Jorge and Clara whispering excitedly about something in the kitchen. Because the two are as close as family, I asked them what they were talking about. Clara responded:

> We are talking about María [the next door neighbor]. She asks for everything! Today she asked for sugar, *which I had to buy* [in the CUC store; usually enough sugar is available via the neighborhood state store where quotas of cheap, basic food are distributed] … They are asking us for things but they are better off [financially] than us!

Despite their hidden annoyance, my Cuban "parents" ended up giving María a bit of sugar.

While the political pressure to be sociable and generous may direct some neighborly actions, other forms of exchange reflect a cultural solidarity that stems, at least in part, from the historical formulation of values in Cuban society. As a woman of marriageable age, my initiation into Tutaño society would have been impossible unless I learned how to provision for the household, and this could not happen until I learned the location of houses or places where staple items such as tomato purée were sold legally and illegally. Knowledge about where to find foodstuffs was just as important as knowledge about people, as determinations of quality were based mostly on personal relationships rather than consumer choice. It mattered from whom one bought meat, for example. "Everyone" (*todo el mundo*) knew that *el chino* (the Chinese man) sold better quality meat at the market than *el gordo* (the fat man). The criterion of trust in evaluating market traders is partly based on values embedded in Cuban ideas of community that have formed over time. Traders who charge too much money or sell poor-quality items at prices recognized as unfair are referred to as *abusadores* (abusers). By contrast, trusted *particulares* (traders) engage in the market sphere but do not place their own interests in money over the need to offer food at fair prices to their community.

In post-Soviet societies such as Cuba and Russia (as well as capitalist societies), "social relations ... are both a means to procure and exchange goods, and ... a means to evaluate the worth of goods" (Caldwell 2002: 299). Anthropologists of post-socialist states such as Caroline Humphrey (1998) have argued that, in contexts where social relations of trust replace a generalized trust in the national currency, personal relations characteristic of barter override the "all-pervasive links of a monetary system" (cited by Trouillot 2001: 128). As in all centralized economies, supply-constrained (Verdery 1993: 174) consumers in Cuba survive mostly by working around the system, and an essential element of social capital is acquiring information about where to find goods as well as people who may help in times of need (Humphrey 1998; Verdery 2003: 62). Constant communication about where one may find a second-grade item such as fodder "taken" from a factory floor, characterizes the "acquisitionmanship" (vs. "salesmanship"; Verdery 1993: 174) of such "economies of shortage" (Kornai 1980). Indeed, Cubanologist Anna Cristina Pertierra argues that personal relationships in consumption and exchange are more prevalent in socialist societies such as Cuba:

> Consumers in all societies, whether socialist, capitalist or otherwise can be seen to cultivate personal relationships that defuse the social distance that trade is often seen to create. Nevertheless, the emphasis in socialist states on the state-managed distribution of goods does seem to have a particular counter-effect in that many socialist consumers value even more highly their personal networks as a resource to offset state-imposed constraints. (Pertierra 2007: 121)

As in our own globalized economy-society, credit-worthiness in everyday Cuban exchange is linked to trustworthiness in social exchange: "Individualism is predicated on the social order" (Hart 1986: 648). Like Jane Guyer's example of gasoline sellers in Nigeria,[3] local idioms map out when and how to cross the line between self-interest and collective morality. My final example, which considers exchange as well as consumption, further illustrates this point.[4]

Consumption

When one day I wanted to buy rum to drink with my Cuban family we had several choices:

FOOD,
CULTURE &
SOCIETY

VOLUME 15

ISSUE 2

JUNE 2012

- to buy a bottle of Havana Club™ in the hard currency store for $3.25 CUCs (a significant amount for most Tutaños who usually earn about $0.50 a day);
- to buy one from a man living nearby who periodically sold rum on the black market for the equivalent of $1.75 CUCs in pesos (he could afford this). This rum was of a lower quality than Havana Club, but better than the final option;
- *La gasolina*, a very poor-quality rum (as the name implies) available from a neighbor.

Though the above distinctions in quality of available rums may imply a one-to-one relationship between taste and socio-economic standing (Goody 1982; Bourdieu 1984 [1979]), this hierarchical scheme is not entirely valid for the Cuban context, for determinations of consumer choice in Cuba do not always correlate with the satisfaction of individual desire. Indeed, though Jorge could have easily accepted my offer to buy the highest quality rum, he decided to bring back that of the lowest quality. I asked him his reasoning and he responded:

J: I could have got a bottle from a black market dealer [he had the money to do this], but I got this amount of *gasolina* because I worked for our neighbor down the street [the price of the Havana Club bottle placed it out of his range of choices].

M: Did you get paid to work for your neighbor?

J: No! One is not paid to help construct a neighbor's house … Their *mujer* serves bread with egg, and you may get some rum, but you are not paid in *money*.

M: And this rum was also given to you for working?

J: Yes. We drank a bit there, but they gave me this too because I worked extra hard. It is not as nice as the others, but it is for *everyone*.

M: What do you mean?

J: This rum is cheap, it comes from *them* [the state]. Everyone can buy it. It is good because of this. And everyone got a bit of it at our neighbor's house, but I asked for a small bottle for tonight and worked harder. Now I know my neighbor will come and work for us when we need it.

In speaking of his act, Jorge cited José Martí: "The wine is sour, but it is *our* wine." This oft-quoted adage points to ideas and actions at play in both national and local moral economies. As with Jorge, Cubans with whom I interacted sometimes preferred the universal distribution of lower-quality goods to commodities bought in the market, especially if the objects in question implicated social relationships. As I have argued elsewhere (Wilson 2009: 37), the prevalence of social over monetary or quality-based motivations for consumer behavior "call into question Veblenian assumptions about the universal desirability of 'luxury' goods" (Wilson 2009: 37).

Conclusion

Like the national moral economy in Cuba, which rests on ideas about the obligations and legitimate undertakings of state and citizens, the local moral economy in Tuta is linked to the interplay of rights and obligations between person and community. Cuban society is reproduced by the constant interplay of national and local levels, and this process involves both assimilation and contestation. As in Cuba, the production, exchange and consumption of food in all societies is a social event or performance, enacted for *particular* audiences and based on *particular* social rules for economic behavior. Economic anthropologists have used Karl Polanyi's (2001 [1944]) ideas and later theorists to show that even modern economies cannot be entirely explained by the market principle, as "coeval" (Gregory 1997)—or co-present and possibly contradictory—schemes of valuation are always at play. In a similar vein, critics of utilitarian economists (e.g. Williams 1973; Sen 1977, 2002; Davis 2003, 2004) have argued that social motivations such as commitment (Sen 1977, 2002) should not be seen as exogenous to economic processes (see Wilson 2010).

As recent reactions to the latest economic crisis indicate, suppositions embedded in our own "global" economy are as value-laden as ever. The announcement of the credit crunch coupled with that of generous bonuses granted to a few top bankers, was, at least on my radio, met with calls for an "unselfish capitalism" and talk of "bringing morality back into banking." More recently, the "Occupy" movement has spread across the globe as citizens demand their share of private and state-controlled assets. What such "counter-cyclic" (Polanyi 2001 [1944]) reactions to our market model illustrate is that, like the Cuban communist model, the "science" (Myrdal 1953: 57) of our modern economy is just as related to values as it is to an affirmation or negation of the Law of Value. Indeed, we cannot assume that people really desire the kind of general welfare offered by the neoclassical model, premised as it is on the moral imperative to increase one's consumption at all costs, and, inherently, to place the "sum total of happiness" above equal distribution (Myrdal 1953: 11, 41). But the opposite paradigm, weighed down on the collectivist side, is also inadequate, for categories and valuations set by each top-down model tell only part of the story. As Anna Cristina Pertierra writes in response to Cuban "transitologists":

> A study of consumption that unquestioningly reproduces a capitalist fantasy that all Cuban consumers crave Nike and McDonald's and dream of nothing more than moving to Miami, is as pointless to any genuine understanding of Cuban society as [is] a socialist fantasy that the revolution's provision of hospitals and schools has somehow erased all Cubans' desires for plentiful consumer commodities. (Pertierra 2007: 46–7)

While most economists rely on either/or (Shanin 1990: 86–91) ideological formulations (or, as current trends would suggest, artificial simulations)[5] to understand the way people choose to provision food and other commodities, anthropologists and other social scientists should look for the "residual components" (Dumont 1980 [1966]: 38–9) of historical values in everyday action.

Marisa Wilson is a lecturer in human geography at the University of the West Indies. Her principal research interests lie in political economic, moral and cultural ideas of food, ethical consumption and social justice at local, national and global scales, especially in regards to the uneven historical development of globalization. Her book, *Scalar Politics of Food in Cuba*, addresses the material and normative foundations of everyday food provisioning in a rural area of Cuba. Department of Food Production, University of the West Indies, St. Augustine Campus, St. Augustine, Trinidad and Tobago (marisawlsn@gmail.com).

FOOD,
CULTURE &
SOCIETY

VOLUME 15

ISSUE 2

JUNE 2012

Notes

1   See, for example, Hart (1986), Parry and Bloch (1989), Dilley (1992), Gregory (1997), Sayer (2000), Graeber (2001), Leyshon *et al.* (2003), Williams *et al.* (2003), Maurer (2006), Fuller *et al.* (2010), North (2010), Samers and Pollard (2010), Seyfang (2010).
2   This is part of a case study ("Eduardo") more thoroughly explained in Wilson (2010).
3   According to Guyer, in Nigeria there are locally-approved methods of earning a profit through sales of gasoline, but some forms of profit are considered unacceptable. The word *ojúlówó* ("normal price" or "all who want can afford") is morally distinct from *wón* ("expensive, scarce"), which, in turn, is contrasted with the very negative *ajeju* ("unnecessary profit, exploitation"), which is often associated with witchcraft (Guyer 2004: 104–5).
4   I have also referred to this ethnographic event in Wilson (2009).
5   Here I am referring to the latest fad of behavioral economics, which arguably strays less far from the dominant liberal paradigm as advocates would suggest. To my knowledge, the very important epistemological and practical distinction between "irrational" economic behavior in the lab and that in social reality has not yet been dealt with in economic anthropology.

References

Appadurai, Arjun. 1986. Introduction. In Arjun Appadurai (ed.).*The Social Life of Things: Commodities in Cultural Perspective.* Cambridge: Cambridge University Press, pp. 3–63.

Bloch, Maurice. 1989. The Symbolism of Money in Imerina. In Jonathan Parry and Maurice Bloch (eds) *Money and the Morality of Exchange.* Cambridge: Cambridge University Press, pp. 165–90.

Bohannan, Paul. 1955. Some Principles of Exchange and Investment among the Tiv. *American Anthropologist* 57: 60–70.

Bohannan, Paul. 1959. The Impact of Money on an African Subsistence Economy. *The Journal of Economic History* 19: 496–7.

Bourdieu, Pierre. 1984 [1979]. *Distinction: A Social Critique of the Judgement of Taste,* translated by Richard Nice. London: Routledge and Kegan Paul.

Caldwell, Melissa L. 2002. Taste of Nationalism: Food Politics in Post-Socialist Moscow. *Ethnos* 67(3): 285–94.

Cook, Ian. 2004. Follow the Thing: Papaya. *Antipode* 36(4): 642–64.

Davis, John. 2003. *The Theory of the Individual in Economics.* London: Routledge.

Davis, John. 2004. Identity and Commitment. Paper presented at the Workshop on Rationality and Commitment, University of St. Gallen, May 13–15.

Dilley, Roy. 1992. General Introduction to Market Ideology, Imagery and Discourse. In Roy Dilley (ed.) *Contesting Markets: Analogies of Ideology, Discourse and Practice.* Edinburgh: Edinburgh University Press, pp. 1–36.

Dumont, Louis. 1977. *From Mandeville to Marx: The Genesis and Triumph of Economic Ideology.* Chicago, IL: University of Chicago Press.

Dumont, Louis. 1980 [1966]. *Homo Hierarchicus: The Caste System and its Iimplications.* Chicago and London: University of Chicago Press.

Edelman, Mark. 2005. Bringing the Moral Economy Back in to the Study of Twenty First-

Century Transnational Peasant Movements. *American Anthropologist* 107(3): 331–45.

Fine, Ben and Leopold, Ellen. 1993. *The World of Consumption*. London: Routledge.

Friedman, Jonathan. 1994. *Cultural Identity and Global Process*. London: Sage.

Fulbre, Nancy. 1994. *Who Pays for the Kids? Gender and Structures of Constraint*. London: Routledge.

Fuller, D., Jonas, A.E.G. and Lee, R. 2010. *Interrogating Alterity: Alternative Economic and Political Spaces*. Surrey: Ashgate.

Funes, F., García, L., Bourque, M., Pérez, N. and Rosset, P. 2002. *Sustainable Agriculture and Resistance: Transforming Food Production in Cuba*. Oakland, CA: Food First Publishers.

Gluckman, Max. 1965. *The Ideas in Barotse Jurisprudence*. New Haven, CT: Yale University Press.

Goody, Jack. 1982. *Cooking, Cuisine and Class: A Study in Comparative Sociology*. Cambridge: Cambridge University Press.

Graeber, David. 2001. *Toward an Anthropological Theory of Value: The False Coin of Our Own Dreams*. New York: Palgrave.

Gregory, Chris. 1997. *Savage Money*. London: Harwood.

Guerra, Lilian. 2005. *The Myth of José Martí: Conflicting Nationalisms in Early Twentieth-Century Cuba*. Chapel Hill, NC and London: University of North Carolina Press.

Guevara, Ernesto "Che." 1971 [1965]. Man and Socialism in Cuba. In Bertram Silverman (ed.) *Man and Socialism in Cuba: The Great Debate*. New York: Atheneum, pp. 337–54.

Guyer, Jane. 2004. *Marginal Gains: Monetary Transactions in Atlantic Africa*. Chicago, IL and London: University of Chicago Press.

Hart, Keith. 1986. Heads or Tails? Two Sides of the Coin. *Man* 21(4): 637–58.

Holbraad, Martin. 2000. Money and Need: Havana in the Special Period. Presentation to the Annual Post-Socialism Workshop, University College, London.

Humphrey, Caroline. 1998. *Marx Went Away but Karl Stayed Behind* (revised edition of *Karl Marx Collective: Economy, Society and Religion in a Siberian Collective Farm*, 1983). Ann Arbor, MI: University of Michigan Press.

Leyshon, A., Lee, R. and Williams, C.C. 2003. *Alternative Economic Spaces*. London: Sage.

Kapcia, Antoni. 1997. Political and Economic Reform in Cuba: The Significance of Che Guevara. In Mona Rosendahl (ed.) *La situación actual en Cuba: desafíos y alternativas*. Stockholm: Institute of Latin American Studies, Stockholm University, pp. 17–48.

Kopytoff, Igor. 1986. The Cultural Biography of Things: Commoditization as Process. In *The Social Life of Things: Commodities in Cultural Perspective*, Arjun Appadurai (ed.). Cambridge: Cambridge University Press, pp. 64–91.

Kornai, János. 1980. *Economics of Shortage*. Amsterdam and London: North-Holland.

Martí, Jorge L. 1959. *Cuba: conciencia y existencia*. Havana: Editorial Libreria Martí.

Martí, José. 1977. *Our America: Writings on Latin America and the Struggle for Cuban Independence*, edited and translated with an introduction and notes by Philip S. Foner. New York and London: The Monthly Review Press.

Martínez-Alier, Juan. 1977. *Haciendas, Plantations and Collective Farms: Agrarian Class Societies, Cuba and Peru*. London: Cass.

Maurer, Bill. 2006. *Pious Property: Islamic Mortgages in the United States*. New York: Russell Sage.

Mauss, Marcel. 1954 [1925]. *The Gift. Forms and Functions of Exchange in Archaic Societies*, translated by Ian Cunnison with an introduction by Sir Edward E. Evans-Pritchard. London: Cohen & West.

FOOD,
CULTURE &
SOCIETY

VOLUME 15

ISSUE 2

JUNE 2012

Miller, Daniel. 1994. *Modernity, An Ethnographic Approach: Dualism and Mass Consumption in Trinidad*. Oxford: Berg.

Miller, Daniel. 2001. *The Dialectics of Shopping*. Chicago, IL and London: University of Chicago Press.

Mintz, Sidney. 1956. Cañamelar: The Subculture of a Rural Sugar Plantation Proletariat. In Julian H. Steward, Robert A. Manners, Elena Padilla Seda, Sidney W. Mintz and Raymond L. Scheele (eds) *The People of Puerto Rico*. Urbana, IL: University of Illinois Press, pp. 314–417.

Mintz, Sidney. 1961. The Question of Caribbean Peasantries: A Comment. *Caribbean Studies* 1: 31–4.

Mintz, Sidney. 1985. *Sweetness and Power*. Boston, MA: Penguin Books.

Myrdal, Gunnar. 1953. *The Political Element in the Development of Economic Theory*. London: Routledge and Kegal Paul Ltd.

Narotsky, Susana. 2005. Provisioning. In James G. Carrier (eds) *A Handbook of Economic Anthropology*. Cheltenham and Northampton: Edward Elgar, pp. 78–93.

North, Peter. 2010. The Longevity of Alternative Economic Practices: Lessons from Alternative Currency Networks. In Duncan Fuller, Andrew E. G. Jonas and Roger Lee (eds) *Interrogating Alterity: Alternative Economic and Political Spaces*. Surrey: Ashgate, pp. 31–46.

Parry, Jonathan and Maurice Bloch. 1989. Introduction: Money and the Morality of Exchange. In *Money and the Morality of Exchange*. Cambridge: Cambridge University Press, pp. 1–32.

Pertierra, Anna Cristina. 2007. *Cuba: The Struggle for Consumption*. Unpublished PhD thesis. University College, London.

Polanyi, Karl. 2001 [1944]. *The Great Transformation: The Political and Economic Origins of Our Time*. Boston, MA: Beacon Press.

Richards, Audrey. 1932. *Hunger and Work in a Savage Tribe: A Functional Study of Nutrition among the Southern Bantu*. London: George Routledge & Sons, Ltd.

Samers, Michael and Pollard, Jane. 2010. Alterity's Geographies: Socio-territoriality and Difference in Islamic Banking and Finance. In Duncan Fuller, Andrew E. G. Jonas and Roger Lee (eds) *Interrogating Alterity: Alternative Economic and Political Spaces*. Surrey: Ashgate, pp. 47–58.

Sayer, Andrew. 2000. Moral Economy and Political Economy. *Studies in Political Economy* 61: 79–104.

Scott, James. 1976. *The Moral Economy of the Peasant: Rebellion and Subsistence in Southeast Asia*. New Haven and London: Yale University Press.

Sen, Amartya. 1977. Rational Fools: A Critique of the Behavioral Foundations of Economic Theory. *Philosophy and Public Affairs* 6: 317–44.

Sen, Amartya. 1981. *Poverty and Famines: An Essay on Entitlement and Deprivation*. Oxford: Clarendon Press.

Sen, Amartya. 2002. *Rationality and Freedom*. Cambridge, MA: Belknap Press.

Seyfang, Gill. 2010. Time Banking: A New Economics Alternative. In *Interrogating Alterity: Alternative Economic and Political Spaces*. Duncan Fuller, Andrew E. G. Jonas and Roger Lee (eds). Surrey: Ashgate, pp. 193–206.

Shanin, Teodor. 1990. *Defining Peasants: Essays Concerning Rural Societies, Expolary Economies and Learning from Them in the Contemporary World*. Oxford: Basil Blackwell.

Silverman, Bertram (ed.) 1971. *Man and Socialism in Cuba: The Great Debate*. New York: Atheneum.

Strathern, Marilyn. 1999. *Property, Substance and Effect: Anthropological Essays on Persons and Things*. London and New Brunswick: Athlone Press.

Thompson, Edward Palmer. 1993 [1971]. *Customs in Common: Studies in Traditional Popular Culture*. New York: The New Press.

Trouillot, Michel-Rolph. 2001. The Anthropology of the State in the Age of Globalization: Close Encounters of the Deceptive Kind. *Current Anthropology* 42(1): 125–37.

Verdery, Katherine. 1993. Ethnic Relations, Economies of Shortage and the Transition in Eastern Europe. In C. M. Hann (ed.) *Socialism: Ideals, Ideologies and Local Practice*. London and New York: Routledge, pp. 172–86.

Verdery, Katherine. 2003. *The Vanishing Hectare: Property and Value in Post-Socialist Transylvania*. Ithaca, NY and London: Cornell University Press.

Von Benda-Beckmann, F., Von Benda-Beckmann, K. and Wiber, M. 2006. Properties of Property. In Franz von Benda-Beckmann, Keebet von Benda-Beckmann and Melanie G. Wiber (eds) *Changing Properties of Property*. Oxford: Berghahn Books, pp. 1–39.

Watts, Michael. 1999. Commodities. In Paul Cloke, Philip Crang and Mark Goodwin (eds) *Introducing Human Geographies*. Oxford and New York: Oxford University Press, pp. 305–15.

Weiss, Brad. 1996. *The Making and Unmaking of the Haya Lived World: Consumption, Commoditization and Everyday Practice*. Durham, NC and London: Duke University Press.

Williams, Bernard. 1973. Integrity. In J. Smart and B. Williams, *Utilitarianism: For and Against*. Cambridge: Cambridge University Press, pp. 108–17.

Williams, C. C., Aldridge, T. and Tooke, J. 2003. Alternative Exchange Spaces. In Andrew Leyshon, Roger Lee and Colin Williams (eds) *Alternative Economic Spaces*. London: Sage, pp. 151–67.

Wilson, Marisa L. 2009. Food as a Good versus Food as a Commodity: Contradictions between State and Market in Tuta, Cuba. *JASO (Journal of the Anthropological Society of Oxford)*, (NS) 1(1): 25–51.

Wilson, Marisa L. 2010. Embedding Social Capital in Place and Community: Towards a New Paradigm for the Caribbean Food System. In Gale T. Rigobert and Alam Asad (eds) *World Sustainable Development Outlook 2010*. Sussex: World Sustainable Development Publications, pp. 153–62.

Wilson, Marisa L. (in press). *Scalar Politics of Food in Cuba: Traversing State and Market*. London: Wiley-Blackwell.

Wright, Julia. 2008. *Sustainable Agriculture and Food Security in an Era of Oil Scarcity: Lessons from Cuba*. London: Earthscan.

FOOD,
CULTURE &
SOCIETY

VOLUME 15

ISSUE 2

JUNE 2012

FOOD,
CULTURE&
SOCIETY

VOLUME 15 | ISSUE 2 | JUNE 2012

The Opacity of Reduction
NUTRITIONAL BLACK-BOXING AND THE MEANINGS OF NOURISHMENT

Emily Yates-Doerr
New York University

Abstract

This article explores the process of consolidating technical and historically contingent ideas about nourishment into seemingly straightforward terms such as vitamins and minerals. I study the adoption of scientific principles of abstraction and reduction as a strategy of nutrition education in three Guatemalan highland sites: an elementary school classroom, a rural clinic, and the obesity outpatient center of Guatemala's third-largest public hospital. I show that despite its pretense of simplicity, the reductionism of nutritional black-boxing produces confusion. Moreover, dietary education not dependent upon simplified and fixed rules and standards may be more intelligible to people seeking nourishment in their lives.

Keywords: anthropology of nutrition, Latin America, obesity, reductionism, dietary education

Learning *Nutrición*

"I was so embarrassed when they referred me to a nutritionist. I thought they had it wrong. I thought nutrition was only for people who were starving, and, well, look at me."[1] Berta, a woman I had met at the obesity clinic of Guatemala's third-largest public hospital, located in the western highland city of Xela, was sharing her confusion about *nutrición* with me over a cup of coffee during one of my visits to her home. She continued: "I thought: 'I am plump. How could I need a nutritionist?'"

By the time I was sitting at Berta's table several months into fieldwork, I had heard many stories recounting confusion about the meaning of *nutrición*.[2] Like the people with whom I spoke, my own understandings had also shifted. When I arrived in Guatemala to study what scientists call "the nutrition transition" (Popkin 2001), I had conceptualized nutrition in broad terms. Geoffrey Cannon, secretary general of the World Health Policy Forum, writes that the word *diet* has origins in the Greek

2752/175174412X13233545145381
available directly from the
rs. Photocopying permitted by
nly © Association for the Study of
Society 2012

293

word *diaita,* which for centuries referred to a "way of life" or "way of being" (Cannon 2005: 701). The first definition given for nutrition in the *Oxford English Dictionary* also describes nutrition expansively: "The action or process of supplying, or of receiving, nourishment or food." "Diet" and "nutrition," as I had imagined them, encompassed the ability to care for oneself and others through the process of eating. Yet countless people I knew to be excellent cooks—including mothers who had raised several children—told me their knowledge of nutrition was murky at best.

I came to understand that in Xela *nutrición* referred not to a holistic conception of food, eating and nourishment, but to a nutrient-based approach to health centered upon vitamins and minerals. As a result, women who were skilled cooks nonetheless claimed ignorance about nutritional matters. Culinary knowledge—an awareness of the pleasures and tastes of food, the skill necessary to transform a limited budget into an abundant meal, an ability to give and receive food—had nothing at all to do with *nutrición*; *nutrición* was technical, scientific, precise.

Bruno Latour has famously written that "[t]he word black box is used by cyberneticians whenever a piece of machinery or a set of commands is too complex. In its place they draw a little box about which they need to know nothing but its input and output" (Latour 1987: 2). The controversies of its assembly, the complexities of its inner workings, and the commercial or academic networks that hold it in place do not matter: only the input and output count. We do not see the black box—the conduit of scientific objectivity—as problematic; taking it for granted, we often do not even see it. Yet while the black box presents itself as "unproblematic and simple," Latour suggests that it is always grappling with its Janus-faced twin: "science-in-the-making"—that is, the potentially fallible practices by which living complexity becomes reduced into theories, rules and facts (Latour 1987: 3). Moreover, Latour advises that by moving—in time and space—closer to places where black boxes are made, we will encounter controversies illuminating their process of assembly and their underlying complexity, as well as the means through which they gain their appearance of authority and immutability.

Following Latour, this paper explores a process that I call nutritional black-boxing— the process of consolidating technical and historically contingent ideas about nourishment and the myriad relationships surrounding dietary practices into seemingly unproblematic terms: a vitamin, a nutrient. Although nutrition educators are busy closing the black boxes of nutrition with their emphasis on seemingly objective facts—*nutrients are good, fats and sugars are bad; with the input and output established, what more is there to know?*—I show that their inner workings remain parts of the systems in which they operate. Self-evident labels might obscure the complexity of nourishment, but hidden within these categories are powerful ontological changes in people's relationships with their food, their environments, their bodies and their selves.

My examination of nutritional black-boxing in this article begins by looking at the adoption of scientific principles of abstraction and reductionism as a strategy of nutrition education in three sites: an elementary school classroom, a rural clinic, and the obesity outpatient center of Guatemala's third-largest public hospital.

Despite nutrition educators' claims that the black boxes of nutritional terminology facilitate simplicity—allowing for the abstractions of nutritional science to most easily benefit people's lives—I show how reductionism in nutritional knowledge produces understandings of nutrition that can be, given the rising rates of metabolic illness in Guatemala, dangerously opaque. Black boxes are imagined as stable, their meanings secured within them in such a way that they appear universal and objectively "detached from the individuality of [their] makers" (Porter 1999: 401). But, I will show in this paper that as they shift contexts, the information that they seem to hold in place transforms. Despite its pretense of simplicity, the reductionism of nutritional black-boxing produces confusion. Meanwhile, education about nourishment that encompasses diverse, complex experiences of hunger, satiety, pleasure and satisfaction—which cannot be easily reduced, generalized, or standardized into the soundbites of pedagogy—may be more accessible to people seeking and needing nourishment in their lives. At its broadest, the encounters I describe highlight the value of complexity, thereby making a case for the importance of ethnographic knowledge well beyond the domain of anthropology.

The Simplified Model

The Institute of Nutrition of Central American and Panama (INCAP) has operated out of Guatemala City since 1949.[3] Founded as a scientific research center, its earliest work focused on examining biochemical properties of food, studying metabolism, and collecting epidemiological profiles of population health. INCAP is widely recognized for its important longitudinal study of physiological development. With data collected between 1969–1977, 1988–1989, and 2002–2004, this study "continues to be one of the richest sources of information about the importance of nutrition for growth, development, and human capital in developing countries" (Ramirez-Zea *et al.* 2010: 397).

While it began as a research center, shortly after its inception, INCAP researchers began to respond to political pressure to translate their research into public health programs and policies. A newspaper article written at the conclusion of the first phase of the study paraphrases an INCAP scientist who stressed the need to define and execute national nutritional policies "at the country's highest political levels" while bringing these policies to people "through direct and simplified models" (David Oliva 1977). In 1991, after decades of working to formulate an official policy on educational outreach, INCAP officials approved the "Policy of Information and Communication," which formally recognized "the importance of facilitating access to information and communicating this information to the public as an core institutional function" (INCAP 2000: 31). In accordance with these goals, INCAP stresses that outreach programs and workshops should focus on "three *key components*" of nutrition: "a healthy home environment, basic health and nutrition with emphasis on school feeding, and health education with emphasis on developing life skills" (INCAP 2000: 21). It also emphasizes that to "strengthen knowledge" about food and nutrition in each of these arenas, the information to be communicated should be kept as "basic" as possible. In order to explore this strategy for nutrition educational further, I next trace three examples of what

FOOD,
CULTURE &
SOCIETY

VOLUME 15

ISSUE 2

JUNE 2012

happens to basic, impersonal knowledge about dietary practice, as this knowledge circulates between persons.

Scene 1: The Classroom

Nearly two decades after INCAP established its "Policy of Information and Communication," I sat in a small rural schoolhouse in a village outside of Xela, observing a nutrition class for fifth-grade students that was a result of continuing governmental efforts to transmit "basic" information about nutrition in a "direct and simplified model." Alfonso, the teacher, had received a degree in education at the public university in Guatemala City, and the notes for his lesson came largely from a textbook for children he had acquired in his training. He told me that most of the children and parents he worked with were *ignorantes sobre nutrición* (ignorant about nutrition). Because of this, he said it was important to keep his material as simple as possible.

With eighteen children aged ten to thirteen sitting in a circle around him he began the lesson by asking the students to name foods that were *comidas malas* (bad foods). Alfonso began the list: "Sugar is bad because it is sweet. Ice cream is bad because it is bad for your teeth." He paused and then asked: "Why are these foods bad?" The audience silent, he answered his own question: "They are bad because they don't have vitamins." During the next half hour, while the children sat quietly around him, he used hand-made cards to explain the meaning of the terms vitamin and mineral. His introduction to the concept of a vitamin was short: "They are in our blood and they help to keep us healthy." He then began to flip through the cards. He read from the front of the first card: "Vitamin A: A good source of nutrition." He turned the card over, revealing a picture of eggs, carrots and squash. "These are good for your eyes," he said. "Do you understand?" Heads nodded, silently. He moved to the next card: "Vitamin B: It keeps the body healthy." He had no examples of foods connected to vitamin B, so he moved to the next card, which was illustrated with pictures of lemon, orange and pineapple: "Vitamin C." Looking at notes he had written he explained: "It helps us be stronger. It helps our immunological system. It keeps us from catching a cold." He had grouped vitamins D and E on the same card, where he had written: "For keeping our body healthy."

He then turned to a discussion of minerals. "What is a mineral?" he asked the class. A few students, growing restless, tossed out suggestions in quiet voices: "A fruit?" "Water?" "No," he corrected them, "A mineral is something like calcium. It is good for our bones. We can find it in milk. It makes us strong. It is also in fruits and almonds." The next card read "Iron," which Alfonso said was good for strengthening the body, and was found in beans, spinach, vegetables, red meat, and cereal. He also explained, "Iron is good because iron gives you energy." Next came "Protein," a card that was illustrated with pictures of eggs, chicken, fish and red meat. He had the children recite the names for these images, a task they completed easily. The final card said carbohydrates. He asked where these came from; met with silence once again, he listed: "Wheat, rice, whole-wheat bread, corn, potatoes, bread."

With the initial material covered Alfonso quizzed the classroom: "What is a good food?" The students' silence encouraged him to monologue:

Carrots, for example, are a good food. Fruits and vegetables are good. They are good, and we should eat these three times a day, every day of the week. Why is this especially important for you? Because your bodies are growing. What else should you eat? Dairy. Three to four times a week, you should eat dairy. Cereals, you should have three to four days a week. Meat you should eat two to three times a week. To strengthen your body you should eat red meat and you should have cereals. You can tell your parents that I've taught you this. But do you remember what the bad foods are? The bad foods are cake, sugar, fat, coca cola. You shouldn't have any of these more than once a week. Why are they bad? They are bad because they don't have iron. They are bad because they have sugar and fat. Remember that sugar and fat are bad for the body. The good foods though, they are good because they have lots of vitamins and minerals. The good foods you should eat often: fruit, vegetables, pure water, boiled water.

Alfonso spent the last ten minutes of the class testing the students about the classifications of foods. The students did not miss a beat when asked how many drops of chlorine to add to a gallon of water to sterilize it (essential knowledge when washing produce), but there was considerable confusion about how to categorize food into various groups. It is important that while they spoke Spanish in school, most of the students were raised in K'iche' speaking homes. K'iche', as with other Mayan languages, has a word for plants (*k'yes*), but plants are not classified as "fruit" or "vegetables" as within public health nutrition programs. This classroom's classification of foods by vitamin and mineral content—intangible, invisible to the eye—was a similarly foreign form of knowledge, representing an unfamiliar way in which to understand, and to subsequently relate to the substance of food.

As a reward for sitting through the class, the students were each to receive half a banana, which Alfonso would only give them once they answered a final question. He paused for a minute before settling upon the question: "What is a good source of iron?" The shyness of the group had lessened and a few kids in unison shouted out an answer: "Sugar!" Alfonso, noticeably annoyed, promptly corrected them by listing beef, pork, beans and spinach as foods containing iron.

That night, while helping my home-stay family prepare coffee, I noticed the packaging on the sugar we used contained an image of a green cartoon triangle presenting the message: "Sugar with Iron." Indeed, following legislation enacted in 1974 (that became law in 1989), Guatemala's national government requires sugar companies to fortify sugar with Vitamin A, and many have also added zinc, copper and iron to the sugar they produce (Pineda 1998).[4] On several occasions when I watched people spoon sugar into their drinks, they clarified to me: "It's for the vitamins."

Although I have described a children's class here, it is representative of the nutritional education classes for adults that I also observed. The implicit

FOOD,
CULTURE&
SOCIETY

VOLUME 15

ISSUE 2

JUNE 2012

assumption made by health educators was that a vitamin-centered approach to eating was correct and that information about vitamins would help people make "healthy" eating choices. In the lesson, Alfonso became frustrated when his students' knowledge about iron did not conform to his pedagogical model, which categorized foods into simple binaries of good/bad and healthy/unhealthy. "Just Get the Facts Straight," says the black box of ready-made-science (Latour 1987: 7). Yet, straightening out "the facts" is not a straightforward task; the students were, after all, correct: their sugar did have iron. Here, the reductionist model of nutrition cannot handle the complexities of dietary practice, wherein the "health" of foods does not conform to fixed standards. In my next section I show that reductionism accompanying the classification of foods connects to other forms of nutritional reductionism; as food is divided into increasingly abstracted component parts, so are the relationships surrounding its production and consumption divided into discrete individuals. To illustrate this further, I turn to nutritional training at a rural health clinic.

Scene 2: The Rural Clinic

Nutrition education is part of the Guatemalan government's *extensión de cobertura* (health coverage extension), a program that sends doctors, *promotores* (health workers), medications, vaccines and food fortification packets to communities too small and remote to have health centers of their own.[5] The *extensión* that I became affiliated with during my fieldwork rotated between ten villages, attending to one each day. In the early morning, when the line waiting for a consult with the doctor was the longest, Eva, the program's certified health educator, would gather the group—almost exclusively women—together for a nutrition class. Eva told me when I began observing her lessons, "Since most of these women have never attended school, the information must be as simple as possible." Here again— a focus on the need for simplicity. Yet, as I will show, the pretense of simplicity masks the complexity of *nutrición*. While the metabolic operations of nutrition may appear self-evident to those raised in a post-Cartesian era where mechanistic explanatory structures are commonplace (Coveney 2006), the logic of nutrition in fact depends upon historically and culturally contingent understandings of food, bodies and life itself.

In the nutrition class I next describe, a class representative of the many months of instruction I observed, Eva stood in front of a group of Mam women holding a poster of *la olla de la alimentación de Guatemala* (the Guatemalan food pot), which divided foods into seven categories (sugars and fats; meats; dairy; herbs and vegetables; fruits; and grains, cereals and potatoes) to be consumed at various frequencies over the week (from once a week to every day).[6] "This is very important for our body (*nuestro cuerpo*)" she began, pointing to the poster. I often heard people speak of "our body" in this way— conveying the sense of a shared body among women in the community. Yet in Eva's teachings, this reference to a shared body, while common, countered her emphasis on an individual who must be responsible for her own diet. It is, I suggest, a momentary digression from the style of lesson-plan she is employing— an "epistemological survival" (Daston 2000: 36) of another way of relating to food. Next, following a pattern that more closely reflected the tone of the lesson, she asked one woman from the group: "What do you eat every day? Do you eat herbs? Do you eat proteins?" The woman did not respond, and Eva turned to address the group: "It is very important that you eat from all these categories. Do you know why?" Without waiting for an answer she continued: "Because food gives us energy. And this food here," she pointed to a section of the pot labeled herbs/vegetables:

> this food helps us with our defenses against the flu. It also helps our skin heal from infections. Why? Because our skin is fragile, and we need vitamins to help it repair itself. This food has vitamins that help the skin repair itself. These vitamins help us have beautiful, strong hair. They help make our skin strong and beautiful. They help strengthen our fingernails.

Eva next pointed to the area of the food bowl listing grains. "Some of your foods have what is called carbohydrates," she explained:

> Perhaps you aren't familiar with this term, but carbohydrates are our source of energy. If you don't eat them, you won't be able to get up. You won't be able to accomplish anything in the day. You won't be able to run. You won't be able to do your work. You won't be able to care for your children, even. So we need to eat these things [pointing to the illustration of carbohydrates] in order to have energy. Our body needs vitamins to keep going. We must feed ourselves well. At least two eggs a week … It's very important for your children's health that they get a bit of fat in their meals. And they need lots of vitamins as well. *Tiene que tener mucho cuidado. Mucho, mucho cuidado* [You must be very careful. Very, very careful].

With this message, her lesson ended.

It is important to note that discussions of food and health that focus on nutrients have only recently arrived to the region where I worked. Historically, communities throughout the Guatemalan highlands have followed a humoral/indigenous logic of wellbeing, where dietary health was conceived through sensory properties of foods and bodies (Adams 1952; Cosminsky 1975; Logan 1973; Redfield and Villa-Rojas 1971). Whereas the idea of balance is crucial to both nutritive and humoral logics of food and health, the abstract guidelines and international standards of nutrition are anathema to indigenous medicine, which depend on listening to, and making decisions around the state of the body and the immediate ecological context. What Foster calls "degrees of intensity" (Foster 1987: 368)—non-absolute classifications —are important to the determination of indigenous remedies. Many researchers have referred to a hot-cold *continuum* of humoral epistemologies (c.f. Cosminsky 1975; Tedlock 1984: 1074–5). Redfield and Villas-Rojas argued that it would be a mistake to try to overlay categories onto humoral beliefs as the "categories are blurred and run into one another" (Redfield and Villas-Rojas 1971 [1934]: 160). More recently, Weller has described the desire of healthcare professionals to create

FOOD,
CULTURE &
SOCIETY

VOLUME 15

ISSUE 2

JUNE 2012

"rules" out of humoral medicine, such as orange juice is cool, measles are hot (Weller 1983: 256). While healthcare professionals have sought to establish these rules to simplify and expand the delivery of healthcare services, these attempts misunderstand the workings of humoral medicine. From a humoral perspective, an individual food would never—could never—be understood as healthy or unhealthy on its own; rather, its health is determined through its relation to the different foods consumed and the state of the individual at the time of consumption. The *good* or *bad* character of foods would not be fixed but rather "dependent upon the condition of the person who eats them" (Redfield and Villa-Rojas 1971 [1934]: 161).

Eva's lecture, however, never mentioned sensory experiences or tastes. She focused not on internal sensations of the body—which resist standardization—but reductive properties of food (vitamins, carbohydrates) and external properties of bodies (hair, eyes). Even though her discussion of diet and nourishment clearly touched upon many areas of kinship and social life, her lesson focused on categories, particles and individuals: the parts, and not the whole. Moreover, Eva, in warning the women to "be very careful" and to pay attention to their consumption of carbohydrates or vegetables, was involved in a project much more abstract than the microscopic vitamins about which she spoke. She was encouraging a new kind of moral subject—a woman responsible for her health and her appetites. Moreover, this was not someone who should focus on the feelings of hunger and satiety, the flavors of food, or the broader experiences of eating, but someone who should learn to eat and to relate to food through abstract dietary guidelines.

Scene 3: The City Hospital

The nutritionists at the obesity outpatient clinic of Guatemala's third-largest public hospital, where I carried out much of my fieldwork, gave every patient a sheet of dietary recommendations. While nutritionists worked to personalize the recommendations to accommodate different metabolic illnesses, they also used a standardized template that listed foods in two columns: permitted and prohibited. Permitted foods included skimmed milk, low-fat yogurt, poultry without skin, whitefish, whole-wheat cereals, whole-wheat bread, boiled plantains, fresh fruits, fresh vegetables, olive or canola oil, diet or "fat-free" (in English) mayonnaise, mineral water, tea and coffee (without sugar). Prohibited foods included whole milk, butter, cream, cheese, pork (or anything pork-based), hamburgers, lasagna, any fried meats or fish, anything battered in egg, sweet cereals, fried potatoes, a long list of traditional foods cooked with lard, canned fruits, vegetables cooked in butter/margarine, most desserts, all oils (except olive and canola), hot chocolate, all alcoholic beverages, sodas, and a long list of snack foods. Nutritionists described permitted foods as *good*, emphasizing their vitamins or protein content. Prohibited foods—foods described as having fat and sugar—they described as *bad*.

After weighing the patient and then calculating his or her BMI, it was common for nutritionists to evaluate the patient's typical day of eating. The aim of the consultation was to produce a *dieta* that would list all of the foods a patient should consume over a given day, for each day of the week, including portion size and suggested time of consumption. To create the *dieta*, nutritionists again categorized certain foods as "good/healthy" and others as "bad/unhealthy." Sugar was bad. Fat was bad. By extension, foods associated with fats and sugars were also bad. Below, I present a substantial portion of one conversation between a nutritionist, a patient, and her grandson, so as to illustrate—as was also the case in the above example with Eva—that conversations about nourishment connect to broader themes of caregiving and kinship. Yet despite the diverse directions that interest in nutrition might travel, in this exchange foods ultimately become separated from the lived experiences in which they are consumed and treated as if they were solely functional and medicinal. As they are thus abstracted, they become endowed with fixed ontological properties—properties presumed to move with the foods across time and context. Sweets *are* bad. Fats *are* bad. Herbs *are* good. Like the universal and generalizable properties associated with numbers, food takes on absolute identities; judgments that might be made through taste and texture, and in conversation with kin or one's body instead become compressed into seemingly universal rules and standards.

The conversation progressed as follows:

Nutritionist:	Do you eat cakes, crackers?
Patient:	Yes, Ma'am. Sometimes I eat chocolate. It's a need. I am bad, aren't I?
N:	Ay! This isn't good Ma'am. Let's see. Well then, chocolate: no! Crackers: no! Jams: no! Honey neither. Cakes neither. Anything sweet: nope. Figs of whatever kind in honey: none of it. None of this can you eat. Only vegetables, fruits, meat and rice.
P:	Okay, rice and beans.
Grandson:	Bread?
N:	But no. It's the same with bread. Not very much. Yes you can eat it, but only every now and then. Except sweet breads. You must help your grandmother, so that she doesn't eat it. When she eats it you have to tell her: "No grandmother, don't eat this." Okay? Yes?
G:	[laughs]
N:	You must tell your cousins too—to watch that she doesn't eat.
G:	The young ones have all the responsibility.
N:	Yes! You tell your cousins, your uncles and aunts: "She can't eat this." Okay? You'll help me with this?
G:	Yes.
N:	Good! Very good. [Pause] Mazola oil or Canola oil. That's what you want—either of these is best. Okay? Herbs, whatever kind of herbs, you can eat. They're good.
P:	Soup with herbs?
N:	Yes, anything like that.
P:	Herbs with egg?
N:	We're going to avoid beets and carrots.
P:	These I can't eat?
N:	No because they're very sweet. No beets and carrots. They're bad.

FOOD,
CULTURE &
SOCIETY

VOLUME 15

ISSUE 2

JUNE 2012

P: Potato also?

N: No potato. No pasta either.

P: No pasta? What about mayonnaise?

N: No.

G: That is fat.

N: Excellent—that's right! He's got it! No hamburgers. No pizza.
        Nothing like that. No sausage. The worst is pork rind for all the fat
        it has. No cream. No cheese. Now you're thinking "Jeez, they
        haven't left me with anything to eat!" But we are leaving you
        something.

P: No cheese either?

N: No, it has too much fat. Perhaps *requesón* [a ricotta-like cheese].
        It's better—that you can eat. Okay?

Several of the hospital's nutritionists used colorful images of foods in the
consultations. As they conversed with the patients about their dietary habits, they
would assemble the images into three piles: healthy foods—to be eaten often;
unhealthy foods—to be avoided; and middle foods—to be consumed in moderation.
"These are confusing, complex diseases; income, family size, health history—this
all matters" one of the nutritionists told me when explaining why she used the
pictures. "They come in confused, and because we don't want to confuse them
further, we try to keep the lessons as simple as possible. You see, they might speak
another language [not Spanish], but they will certainly recognize that this is a
tomato and this is a carrot."

Yet despite attempts made toward reductive categorization, many of the foods
resisted easy placement into the piles by being low in fat (good) but high in sugar
(bad), or high in some vitamins (good), but also high in simple carbohydrates (bad).
The nutritionists often disagreed among themselves about where to place the
pictures. Eventually they always chose a pile, which they then presented to the
patient as an inflexible fact, but the root of the disagreement would not disappear:
the "health" of a food can never be fixed into a category of good, bad as health is
always dependent on the specificity of context. The apparently objective "view from
nowhere" (Nagel cited in Daston 1999: 111) that seemed to materialize through
the classification of foods into three piles, would always be a view from somewhere.

Indeed, when I visited patients at their homes, the confusion that the
nutritionists aimed to attenuate through their simple classificatory schema would
resurface. Many patients were preoccupied with the details of the food rules they
had learned, afraid they had confused healthy with unhealthy foods. They received
messages about nutrition from a variety of sources: the hospital, friends and kin,
radio, television and newspapers. Each source employed reductive simplicity,
labeling some foods as good and others as bad. Porter writes that people commonly
view it as desirable "in cases of difficulty to have clear standards rather than to
depend on judgment" (Porter 1995: 35). Yet seemingly straightforward valuations
of foods as healthy or unhealthy collided into one another when their reductive
categorization spread out into the everyday experiences of eating. You see,

avocados are high in fat (bad), but also high in vitamins (good); carrots are high in vitamins (good), but also high in sugar (bad); potatoes are low in fat (good), but high in simple carbohydrates (bad) … and so on. "Clear standards" are, after all, still made of judgments.

Nutritional Reductionism

Although my research focused on Guatemala it is not my desire to emphasize a distinction between "Guatemalan" and so-called "Western" nutrition education strategies. Instead I aim to show how nutrients are black-boxed through a recursive logic that cares not for location or context—a logic that expands the significance of terms like vitamins and minerals, while also making it difficult to pinpoint what they are, and how they operate. The nutrients I encountered in my fieldwork—though small and invisible under most circumstances—both presume and produce calculative, quantitative and reductive forms of value. As is the case with historian Mary Poovey's numerical "modern fact," they reflect and circle back upon understandings of material reality, thereby contributing to systematic knowledge about the world. They entail information about the self through which we learn to manage our relationships with others; they act as a mode of representation that embodies "available ways of organizing and making sense of the world"; and they do all of this while appearing to be disinterested free-floating signifiers without an interpretive dimension (Poovey 1998: xv).

A nutrient-based understanding of human energy has been traced to Descartes' efforts to explain bodily movements in mechanical terms. According to Cartesian explanations, digestion entailed a heat-induced separation of food particles, "the coarsest descending, ultimately to be expelled through the rectum, and the finest particles flowing through appropriately sized pores to the brain and organs of reproduction" (Shapin 1996: 48). Central to this belief was the idea that bodies, like machines, were composed of smaller and smaller parts. The interaction of these parts produced the qualities of the whole—its tastes, colors and smells (Jardine 1999: 94–6). Yet though Descartes' mechanistic theories laid a foundation for a nutrient-based vision of food and bodies, a view of nutrients as elements in food required in a "balanced ration for life" would still be centuries in the making.[7]

Nutrition scientist Kenneth Carpenter describes the laborious processes by which the mysterious workings of nutrition became a reputable science. He provides the memorable example of US Director of Public Health Joseph Goldberger, who in 1916 used his own body to test whether pellagra—which was causing epidemic rates of death in the American south—was infectious: "He received subcutaneous injections of blood from patients [with pellagra], then had skin eruptions rubbed into his nasal mucosa, and finally ate some of their excreta" (Carpenter 2003: 3027). Goldberger did not become ill, giving credibility to the idea that pellagra was not caused by the spread of microbes but by deficiencies of a small, invisible substance—what would later be known as niacin or vitamin B3.[8] In the 1930s, niacin—today called nicotinic acid—became mapped alongside other vitamins, which scientists began to understand to be organic compounds (defined as the substance arising from the combination of two or more atoms from different

FOOD,
CULTURE &
SOCIETY

VOLUME 15
ISSUE 2
JUNE 2012

elements) necessary for life. Between 1913 (with vitamin A) and 1941 (with folic acid), vitamins were dissected into chemical parts and then labeled and arranged by the activity of their compounds. Regardless of how foods are enacted in dietary practices, "they all end up at such scale that a few men or women can dominate them by sight; at one point or another, they all take the shape of a flat surface of paper that can be archived, pinned on a wall and combined with others" (Latour 1987: 227). Metabolic research on nutrients would soon be translated into the charts, graphs, and labels of recommended daily allowances (RDAs), which in turn began to accompany processed foods (Mudry 2009). Sociologists Espeland and Stevens suggest that commensurate systems—one of which, I suggest is the RDA—unite objects through a "shared cognitive system" where qualitative differences and similarities are transformed into quantities that can be expressed in magnitudes of more or less (Espeland and Stevens 2008: 408). That which is continuous and interpersonal comes to appear as impersonal, discrete and hierarchical. Nourishment becomes equated with elements; health begins to appear as the sum of elemental parts.

This method for valuing food was largely unfamiliar for the women with whom I lived and spent time. They had been raised to consider tastes and textures, a process that required engagement and adjustment. Their knowledge about food was not knowledge that could exist outside of the activities of cooking; they did not (and could not) answer my question of "what is good food" with words, but would invite me to sit next to them while they crafted their meals. They gave me tastes of what they prepared so I could develop awareness of their skill within me, as this was how their own culinary knowledge had been formed.

Historian Gyorgy Scrinis argues that increasingly complex nutritional technologies that have emerged since the late nineteenth century have led to a "biomarker reductionism" (Scrinis 2008: 42). In a process he calls *nutritionism*:

> Particular nutrients, food components, or biomarkers—such as saturated fats, kilojoules, the glycemic index (GI), and the body mass index (BMI)—are abstracted out of the context of foods, diets, and bodily processes. Removed from their broader cultural and ecological ambits, they come to represent the definitive truth about the relationship between food and bodily health. Within the nutritionism paradigm, this nutri-biochemical level of knowledge is not used merely to inform and complement but instead tends to displace and undermine food-level knowledge, as well as other ways of understanding the relationship between food and the body. (Scrinis 2008: 40)

The argument I have been advancing about nutritional education in Guatemala is that nutritional reductionism obscures foods' intricate social histories and complicated physical interactions. Absent from the classificatory categories of nutrition is attention to taste, pleasure and awareness of all of the social relations inherent in the production and consumption of any meal. What remains is a focus on biological functionality—"a way of looking at and encountering food as being composed of nutrients, which overwhelms other ways of encountering and sensually experiencing food" (Scrinis 2008: 46). It is not that social context itself becomes irrelevant; rather it becomes obscured by the abstraction of a meal's value into its biochemical parts, parts that themselves come to appear as the whole source of a meal's value to the body. Though reductive language camouflages the complexity that underpins the "epistemological units" (Poovey 1998) of nutrients, this complexity remains—resurfacing in the confusion that arises when people attempt to incorporate universalized food rules into the unpredictable and often-contradicting demands of everyday life. This confusion about eating does not result *in spite of* an effort to present food in a simplistic form, but *because of* this presentation.

Everything Good is Harmful: Misunderstandings in Nutrition Communication

In my fieldwork I encountered numerous situations where an idea of value, presumed by health educators to be stable, transformed from one context to another. For example, I saw that patients at the obesity outpatient clinic of Xela's hospital often expressed confusion about vitamins. In nearly every consultation, nutritionists advised patients suffering from metabolic illness to eat more vegetables. *Vegetables have a lot of vitamins and are healthy* the nutritionists would say. The advice sounds simple; who could become confused? Yet when I spent an afternoon with a patient, Gloria, in her home, I noticed that she avoided eating the vegetables she served for lunch. When I later asked her about this, she told me that vegetables had too many vitamins. Asking further, I learned that at a health training that she had attended at her children's grade school, the teacher advised her to feed them lots of vegetables. "Vegetables have vitamins," Gloria had learned from the teacher, whose knowledge mirrored that of the nutritionists. Yet, in this context the teacher had encouraged Gloria to feed her children vitamins because vitamins would help them to gain weight. Many children in Xela remain malnourished, and although concern about childhood obesity is increasing (Groeneveld *et al.* 2007), childhood weight gain is still tightly linked with wellbeing. Gloria, however, had been treated for hypertension and was trying to lose weight. Associating vegetables with vitamins, and vitamins with weight gain, she was consequently avoiding their consumption.

The following exchange between a hospital nutritionist and a patient with diabetes illustrates another example of the potentially harmful effects of nutritional reductionism. Here, fears about food have caused the patient to avoid drinking atoles/cereals entirely; instead she drinks only purified water. The nutritionists told me that one of the largest obstacles they encountered was that patients attempted to diet by skipping meals or not eating enough. Nutritionists almost always advised patients to eat a snack between meals to stave off hunger, and they found unsweetened atole to be a popular, convenient, and inexpensive snack. Yet the patient here, uncertain and scared about what to eat, finds safety only in total avoidance:

> Nutritionist: Cereal? Do you drink any kind of cereal? [In Guatemala, cereal is consumed as a beverage]

FOOD, CULTURE & SOCIETY

VOLUME 15

ISSUE 2

JUNE 2012

Patient:	No, I only drink purified water, that's all I drink, doctor.
N:	Just purified water? You don't drink atole any more?
P:	I don't drink atole any more.
N:	Not at all?
P:	No
N:	Why? Do you not like it?
P:	Well I like it, but it scares me.
N:	No, atole is okay.
P:	Ah, that's good, doctor.
N:	So, what we are going to want to drink, we're going to have two tablespoons of *mosh* (dry oatmeal).
P:	That's how I make it.
N:	That's how you make it? When?
P:	Before breakfast.
N:	Okay. And how much … how much mosh do you add?
P:	I add three teaspoons.
N:	I see. And in how much water? In one cup?
P:	In my cup of water, I add about three teaspoons of mosh, and I drink it before breakfast.
N:	Okay, that's very good. Don't stop doing that.
P:	Very well.
N:	Because that's very good, and it will take away all the fat you have in your body.
P:	Very well doctor.

Although nutritionists commonly bemoaned the tendency of patients to think in "all or nothing" terms, I suggest that the pedagogical framework they employed contributed to this tendency. In the example above, the nutritionist might have taken the opportunity to direct the patient toward an awareness of the specificity of the taste of the atole (i.e. if it is sweet, do not drink it); or she might have talked about the circumstances surrounding its consumption. Yet instead of discussing the context of the meal, the nutritionist circumscribed the patient's diet into a carefully measured prescription: two teaspoons of dry oatmeal with one cup of water. Removing the context from mealtime experiences, she leaves the patient with other absolutes: "it's very good," and "it will take away all the fat you have in your body"—the obvious implication being that fat is very bad.

A reductive valuation of foods as good or bad has the additional effect of assigning to individuals the personal responsibility of following these ostensibly self-evident rules. Eva's warning in the nutrition class above—"you must be very careful"—locates responsibility for health within the individual. Similarly, I often heard health educators scold their students when the students admitted to eating "bad" foods. Viewing nutritional advice as simple and therefore easy to follow, health educators described to me their students' decisions to eat fats and sweets as willfully "non-compliant." Patients and students, on the other hand, spoke to me about conflicting pressures they faced when eating. Eating fat might be "bad" from the vantage of a nutrition class, but it was also "bad" socially to forego eating what a friend or family member had prepared. However, because food rules were presented through simplistic and individualized frameworks, educators were often ill-equipped to help their students negotiate the complicated interstices of lived dietary experiences where "goods" and "bads" exist as continuums-in-conversations and not as absolutes. Moreover, a reductive understanding of foods as good or bad has the effect of situating illnesses as the result of "simple" food choices, with the expectation that treatment lies in equally "simple" changes in dietary behaviors. In the following exchange we see a patient who, despite desiring foods she believes to be fattening, is following a recommended diet. Unable to map the patient's illness to an obvious dietary failing, the nutritionist can offer no further assistance:

Patient: I have to tell you that I love fried plantains with refried beans. And cream.

Nutritionist: And cream?

P: But from a distance, because I know they're harmful, right? Everything good is harmful.

N: Yes, that's right.

P: I also don't make fried chicken.

N: No, absolutely not. That's forbidden.

P: No. I told you I never ever have it. Only boiled or stewed. But most importantly, with no fat.

N: Exactly.

P: Now, it's me with my problems.

N: [Pause, turns to chart. Picks up again 30 seconds later to ask about a typical day of food.]

Underlying many nutritional miscommunications is the polysemic character of the commonly invoked notion of "health." *¡Vamos a Comer Sano!* (We're Going to Eat Healthy!) was a slogan for many governmental health classes, which educators reiterated in their lessons by identifying specific foods as *sano* or *saludable* (Spanish synonyms for health). Yet as I have been showing, "health" is not a property that can be fixed within a food; existing instead in the specificities of dietary practices, it is a process to be enacted, not an object to hold.

Within my field notebook I carried a picture of a local fruit stand. The photograph showed sliced pineapples, papaya and melon, to be served with lime, salt and chili powder for 13 cents a bag. In the background was a *comida chatarra* (junk food) stand, where for the same price, vendors sold bags of chips packaged in colorful plastic wrapping. During an afternoon conversation with Brenda, one of the first women with whom I lived, who became a friend I visited often, the picture slipped out of my notebook. Brenda, who was familiar with my project, picked it up and as she handed it back to me, smiled cleverly. She pointed to the fruit and then the chips and then asked me: *Which of these do you think is healthier?*

I had observed enough health education classes by that point to know that the "correct," answer was the fruit. "Fruit is good and healthy"—I had heard this

FOOD,
CULTURE&
SOCIETY

VOLUME 15

ISSUE 2

JUNE 2012

mantra hundreds of times. Yet despite a rubric of standardizable, reductive guidelines, there was no clear answer to Brenda's question. The fruit might have been sitting on the street for hours absorbing the exhaust of traffic, the knife used to cut it might not have been clean, it might have been grown in polluted water. These were all possibilities that Brenda, who had two young children, pointed out as she told me that she did not allow her children to eat fruit from the street because it could give them diarrhea. She said that when she was away from home, she thought chips were a healthier snack for her family than fruit because they would not make them sick. *Not in the short term, anyway*, she laughed.

Not all potential misrecognitions were humorous. Many of the people I worked among were terrified by the changes happening within their bodies: the pain or numbness in their limbs, the violent and unfamiliar urges of appetite or thirst, the repetitive need for urination even when they had not been drinking, the unusual palpitations of their hearts, or heat felt in their chests. While metabolic illnesses such as diabetes and heart disease have existed in small numbers in Guatemala for some time, the rates at which they are now occurring are unprecedented (Mendoza Montano *et al.* 2008). People could not turn to their parents or relatives for stories to place the illnesses in a historical context. Scared, they listened carefully to the ideas of nourishment that came from nutrition educators. That people easily reinterpreted nutritional guidelines—adding extra sugar to drinks because it was fortified with iron, avoiding broccoli because they associated its vitamins with weight gain, eating chips because they were safe from microbes—was not the result of their lack of interest or attention. It was instead a result of the sheer impossibility of translating the sensations, emotions, and relationships of eating into abstract food groups and eating guidelines.

Conclusion

Latour writes that knowledge is understood to be "familiarity with events, places and people seen many times over" (Latour 1987: 220). Yet knowledge, he clarifies, must also account for the "whole cycle of accumulation" (Latour 1987: 220). Most health educators I worked among would be judged as knowledgeable given the first part of this definition: they can match certain foods to certain vitamins; they can arrange foods into piles according to their quantities of fats and carbohydrates; they can explain a carbohydrate in the terms in which they have learned it (*if you do not eat them, you will not have energy*). And yet, their knowledge of nutrition is cut off from the accumulation of nutritional knowledge. They are like the scientists Latour describes who hold a piece of information, having "the form of something without the thing itself" (Latour 1987: 243). As a result, nutritional black boxes eventually lead to the tautologies of recursive definitions: *a vitamin is a vitamin*.

Nutritional black boxes give an appearance of stability to the otherwise processual experiences of nourishment; this stability allows them to travel around the world, so that even in the remote highlands of Guatemala people are learning to value food and eating on the basis of nutrients. Nutritional black boxes also make formerly separate objects—take the classically incommensurate apple and orange—appear in like terms. We no longer consider: *How do they taste?* We instead ask: *How many vitamins do they have?* We presume that the sum of the parts will equal the whole, and we consequently count the nutrients in apples and oranges to know their value. Yet when we relate the apparently "immutable and combinable mobiles" (Latour 1987: 227) of nutrients to one another through equations derived from dissected parts, we lose sight of the *relationships* formed in eating, which can never be accurately fixed and measured. Nourishment will never simply be nutrients.

Humoral/Indigenous beliefs about health are no longer present in Xela, and I want to be clear that I am not advocating for their reintroduction. I draw attention to them because they help us to imagine other ways in which to communicate dietary health, and they provide a window into the existence of other—potentially many other—ways in which people might come to *know* their food and their bodies. It is relevant that in K'iche', the experiences of desire and pleasure (*utz*) must be expressed through three other sensory experiences— sight, feeling (which encompasses touch, taste and smell) and sound. Instead of simply saying "I like," as we do in English (in Spanish, *gustarse*), K'iche' speakers linguistically conjugate the experience of pleasure with reference to these three different sensory experiences, identifying whether something pleases their sense of sight (*ilo*), their sense of feeling (*na'*), or their sense of sound (*ta*). I do not intend to create a false sense of difference between K'iche' cosmologies of pleasure and the beliefs of those who speak only Spanish or English. We also experience pleasure through sight, touch, taste, smell and sound. But, I suggest that the pedagogical and discursive models that surround *nutrición* minimize awareness of varied forms of pleasure in eating. In a complex world, these models present rigid grids and reductive language. It is from these reductions that people begin to say: this food is bad/unhealthy; this food is good/healthy. Such ideas appear simple, and at first glance they may even appear to be more intelligible. But this reduction obfuscates our diverse experiences of food, bodies, communities and ourselves.

It is important to my argument that in most nutritional education classes I observed, those who were being "educated" remained quiet. Whether classes were directed toward children or adults, the assumption built into the pedagogical approach of the courses was that the audience had no nutritional knowledge of its own. Rarely did instructors ask about—or by extension value—the understandings of nourishment held by their audience. Porter argues that in democratic societies, institutional classroom instruction has supplanted the "kind of wisdom that comes from long experience, which is often passed on from parent to child or master to disciple" (Porter 1995: 7). Formal instruction, he suggests, appears "more open and less personal" (Porter 1995: 7) thereby appearing more objective. In a similar vein, Daston has argued that aperspectival objectivity—the removal of individual idiosyncrasies central to nutritional black-boxing—became a scientific value when scientific knowledge had to be communicated across boundaries of nationality, training and skill. She writes:

Indeed, the essence of aperspectival objectivity was its communicability, narrowing the range of genuine knowledge to coincide with that of public

FOOD,
CULTURE &
SOCIETY

VOLUME 15

ISSUE 2

JUNE 2012

knowledge ... aperspectival objectivity may even sacrifice deeper or more accurate knowledge to the demands of communicability. (Daston 1999: 112)

As I have argued, within nutritional education in the Guatemalan highlands, a "deeper" form of knowledge is sacrificed to an ostensible demand of communicability—with the unfortunate consequence of infelicitous communication. As is the case with nutritional knowledge—and potentially many other forms of knowledge—nourishment must necessarily be *personal* (and familial, and communal).

The example of research on pellagra I described in my earlier discussion of the history of nutritional science connects to my argument in a revealing way. "Outbreaks" of pellagra often occurred in communities around the world where corn was a staple food, yet the illness of pellagra was mostly absent in Mesoamerica, the ancestral homeland of corn. Nonetheless, it took scientists nearly two centuries to move from this observation to the knowledge of pellagra as a deficiency in niacin. Meanwhile, Maya peasants with no knowledge of *nutrición* continued to mix their corn with lye-filled *cal*, the lye helping to transform the niacin in corn to an unbound form that could be utilized by the body, thereby preventing the illness. Lacking a periodic table of elements—indeed lacking the concept of vitamins—they nonetheless followed careful culturally regulated tortilla-making practices that staved off sickness and subsequent death.

My research suggests that nutrition educational strategies have much to learn from listening to and valuing the knowledge that people already possess, even when this knowledge takes the inconvenient, ineffable form of practices, engagements and diverse sensory experiences: even when this knowledge resists reductive simplicity. As difficult as it might be, public health nutrition might work to develop knowledge of and communication about nutrition that is deeply connected to the "cycle[s] of accumulation" through which this knowledge is produced. It might also find a way to value the tastes, pleasures, relationships and ways of knowing oneself and others that emerge through eating and feeding. This approach will be more complex than the educational strategy currently employed, with its black boxes of vitamins and nutrients. But this complexity may resonate with people in a way that is less confusing and more intelligible than contemporary models of nutritional reductionism. Nourishment is not cybernetics; it is not mathematics; it will never be "a modern fact." No matter how hard educators work to distill the flesh of experience from the black boxes of nutrition, nourishment will remain the domain of bodies and lives.

Acknowledgments

I conducted the research upon which this article draws with support from a Wenner Gren research grant and a Fulbright Hays dissertation research award. Support from an SSRC IDRF fellowship and a Tinker grant enabled preliminary research between June and August of 2006, and NYU's Doris M. Ohlsen Award for Latin American Scholarship allowed me to further develop my project through the summer of 2007. I thank the participants of Emily Martin and Rayna Rapp's *Science*

Ethnography workshop for their comments on an earlier version of this article. I also thank Marion Nestle, Krishnendu Ray, Emily McDonald, Pilar Rau, Andrew Roper, and Damien Stankiewicz for their suggestions. I am deeply grateful to Dr Noel Solomons, Gaby Montenegro, Jose Gramajo, and the researchers at CeSSIAM for their support during my fieldwork, as well as to the nutritionists, educators, and patients, who made my research possible. Finally, members of the ASFS community, including FCS editors Ken Albala and Lisa Heldke, have informed this article with their intellectual contributions and lively debates.

Emily Yates-Doerr is a postdoctoral fellow in the department of Sociology and Anthropology at the University of Amsterdam. She is part of a European Research Council-funded interdisciplinary research project titled *Eating Bodies in Western Practice and Theory*. Kloveniersburgwal 18, 1012 CX Amsterdam, The Netherlands (ejfyd@nyu.edu).

Notes

1 The use of quotes indicates that I recorded, transcribed and translated the conversation cited. When I refer to what people say in italics and without quotes this indicates I recorded the conversation in field-notes shortly after it took place. I recorded all hospital interactions, with consent from the nutritionists and patients following my university's protocol for research with human subjects.

2 During the 16 months of the fieldwork upon which this article is based (January 2008 to April 2009), I conducted participant observation ethnography two days a week in the obesity outpatient clinic of the Xela's public hospital, traveled with health educators to rural communities two to three days a week, and lived in the homes of twelve local families.

3 INCAP was established following the Universal Declaration of Human Rights (1948), which identifies access to adequate food as both an individual right and a collective responsibility. Since its founding, the institute has been connected to the Pan American Health Organization—an offshoot of the United Nation's World Health Organization—as well as the national ministries of health from the countries it represents.

4 Sugar meets the important international health criteria of being a processed food that is widely consumed and whose production is relatively centralized in just a few refineries (corn, while widely consumed, is processed in hundreds—if not thousands—of sites) (Dary *et al.* 2005).

5 Like many health services in Guatemala, these programs are funded by the government but coordinated by non-governmental organizations, making them both governmental and non-governmental.

6 INCAP designed this graphic in 1998, and it has since been incorporated into health and hygiene classes throughout Guatemala.

7 It was not until the early twentieth century that the *Oxford English Dictionary* linked nutrients with dietary rations. According to the entry from 1903, "a balanced ration is one which contains a sufficient amount of nutrients from a variety of foods to meet the requirements of the animal."

FOOD,
CULTURE &
SOCIETY

VOLUME 15

ISSUE 2

JUNE 2012

311

8   The medical physiologist Albert Szent-Györgi, widely credited with the discovery of Vitamin
     C in the 1930s, defined vitamins saying: "A vitamin is a substance you get sick from if you
     don't eat it" (Gratzer 2005: 163). While this may today appear to be obvious, the idea that
     illness could be born of lack (and not the presence of a pathogen or toxic agent) countered
     the scientific paradigm of the nineteenth century.

References

Adams, Richard. 1952. *An Analysis of Medical Beliefs and Practices in a Guatemalan Indian
     Town*. Guatemala: Instituto Indigenista Nacional De Guatemala.

Cannon, Geoffrey. 2005. The Rise and Fall of Dietetics and of Nutrition Science, 4000 BCE–
     2000 CE. *Public Health Nutrition* 8(6a): 701–705.

Carpenter, Kenneth J. 2003. A Short History of Nutritional Science: Part 3 (1912–1944).
     Journal of Nutrition 133(10): 3023–32.

Cosminsky, Sheila. 1975. Changing Food and Medical Beliefs and Practices in a Guatemalan
     Community. *Ecology of Food and Nutrition* 4: 183–91.

Coveney, John. 2006. *Food, Morals and Meaning: The Pleasure and Anxiety of Eating* (2nd
     edn). London, New York: Routledge.

Dary, O., Martínez, C. and Guamuch, M. 2005. Sugar Fortification with Vitamin a in Guatemala:
     The Program's Successes and Pitfalls. In Wilma B. Freire (ed.) *Nutrition and an Active
     Life: From Knowledge and Action*. Washington DC: Pan American Health Organization, pp.
     43–59.

Daston, Lorraine. 1999. Objectivity and the Escape from Perspective. In Mario Biagioli (ed.)
     The Science Studies Reader. New York: Routledge, pp. 110–24.

Daston, Lorraine. 2000. *Biographies of Scientific Objects*. Chicago, IL: University of Chicago
     Press.

David Oliva, Saul. 1977. 900,640 Niños Desnutridos. *Diario de Centro America*. August 23.

Espeland, Wendy Nelson and Stevens, Mitchell L. 2008. A Sociology of Quantification.
     European Journal of Sociology 49(3): 401–36.

Foster, George M. 1987. On the Origin of Humoral Medicine in Latin America. *Medical
     Anthropology Quarterly* 1(4): 355–93.

Gratzer, W. B. 2005. *Terrors of the Table: The Curious History of Nutrition*. Oxford and New
     York: Oxford University Press.

Groeneveld, I. F., Solomons, N. W. and Doak, C. M. 2007. Nutritional Status of Urban
     Schoolchildren of High and Low Socioeconomic Status in Quetzaltenango, Guatemala. *Pan
     American Journal of Public Health* 22(3): 169–77.

INCAP (ed.). 2000. *Inform Anual*. Guatemala City: Instituto de Nutricion de Centro America y
     Panama (INCAP/OPS).

Jardine, Lisa. 1999. *Ingenious Pursuits: Building the Scientific Revolution*. New York: Random
     House.

Latour, Bruno. 1987. *Science in Action: How to Follow Scientists and Engineers through
     Society*. Cambridge, MA: Harvard University Press.

Logan, Michale H. 1973. Humoral Medicine in Guatemala and Peasant Acceptance of Modern
     Medicine. *Human Organization* 32(4): 385–96.

Mendoza Montano, C., Estrada, K. Chávez, A. and Ramírez-Zea, M. 2008. Perceptions,
     Knowledge and Beliefs about Prevention of Cardiovascular Diseases in Villa Nueva.

Prevention and Control 3: 1–9.

Mudry, Jessica. 2009. *Measured Meals: Nutrition in America*. Albany, NY: SUNY Press.

Pineda, Oscar. 1998. Fortification of Sugar with Vitamin A. *Food and Nutrition Bulletin* 192: 131–6.

Poovey, Mary. 1998. *A History of the Modern Fact: Problems of Knowledge in the Sciences of Wealth and Society*. Chicago, IL: University of Chicago Press.

Popkin, Barry M. 2001. The Nutrition Transition and Obesity in the Developing World. *Journal of Nutrition* 131(3): 871S–73.

Porter, Theodore. 1992. Quantification and the Accounting Ideal in Science. *Social Studies of Science* 22(4): 633–51.

Porter, Theodore. 1995. *Trust in Numbers the Pursuit of Objectivity in Science and Public Life*. Princeton, NJ: Princeton University Press.

Ramirez-Zea, M., Melgar, P. and Rivera, J. A. 2010. Incap Oriente Longitudinal Study: 40 Years of History and Legacy. *Journal of Nutrition* 140(2): 397–401.

Redfield, Robert and Villa-Rojas, Alfonso. 1971. *Chan Kom, a Maya Village*. Chicago, IL: University of Chicago Press.

Scrinis, Gyorgy. 2008. On the Ideology of Nutritionism. *Gastronomica* 8(1): 39–48.

Shapin, Steven. 1996. *The Scientific Revolution*. Chicago, IL: University of Chicago Press.

Tedlock, B. 1984. An Interpretive Solution to the Problem of Humoral Medicine in Latin America. *Social Science & Medicine* 24(12): 1069–83.

Weller, Susan C. 1983. New Data on Intracultural Variability: The Hot-Cold Concept of Medicine and Illness. *Human Organization* 42(3): 249–57.

FOOD,
CULTURE &
SOCIETY

VOLUME 15

ISSUE 2

JUNE 2012

FOOD,
CULTURE &
SOCIETY

VOLUME 15 | ISSUE 2 | JUNE 2012

(Re) Focus on Local Food Systems through Service Learning

EMPOWERING PEDAGOGY IN A HUMAN NUTRITION DEGREE PROGRAM

Laurie A. Wadsworth
St. Francis Xavier University

Christine Johnson
St. Francis Xavier University

Colleen Cameron
St. Francis Xavier University

Marla Gaudet
St. Francis Xavier University

Abstract

Recent nutrition professional discourse has emphasized reintegration of food and society concepts into undergraduate programs currently entrenched in the intricacies of nutritional science. To reintroduce this macro-approach, a community–university partnership was developed to address the strengthening of local food systems to improve community food security. Service learning, an experiential pedagogical technique, allowed students to work with a community agency on a community defined problem and emphasized connection of classroom theory to real-world situations. Two courses integrated service learning opportunities for forty-seven students in eighteen projects that developed awareness-building and advocacy tools for community organizations. Evaluation of these course components included written reflections of the experience, shared learnings in classrooms, instructor reflections and community feedback. A thematic analysis organized these data into empowerment domains for community capacity development. Results indicated that service learning and community–university

?752/175174412X13233545145147
available directly from the
s. Photocopying permitted by
nly © Association for the Study of
Society 2012

315

partnerships can be key tools for enabling empowerment of future nutrition professionals, while integrating food systems into courses.

Keywords: service learning, empowerment, nutrition professional training

Introduction

> DC [Dietitians of Canada] strongly encourages dietitians to educate themselves about the issues and processes to achieve food security through social change, to use empowering strategies in community-based food programming, to conduct and apply research, and to participate in coalitions that advocate to create the conditions in which all Canadians can achieve food security. (Power 2005: 43)

Social responsibility and community service have been integral to the dietetics profession in Canada from the outset. In the late nineteenth century, the matriarch of the Canadian profession, Lillian Massey, began the first School of Household Science and Art as part of her father's mission in downtown Toronto (Brownridge and Upton 1993). By 1902, this became the first Canadian degree-granting program of its kind through the University of Toronto. The impetus behind the nascent profession was simple—food insecurity. Massey witnessed poverty and its resultant inequities firsthand in the Toronto core area and chose to act. Not only did she personally work with community women to improve living conditions through education, but she facilitated the university training of others to carry on similar community work (Brownridge and Upton 1993).

Not surprisingly, acceptance of the household science degree by the university community was not a smooth road (Brownridge and Upton 1993). One of the first instructors in the University of Toronto program, Annie Laird stated, "There is no thought that the universities are to become cooking schools, but that the subject of right living, including the right nutrition of the human race, is to be given its legitimate status in the world of science" (Brownridge and Upton 1993: 25). Perhaps it was this lack of acceptance by academe that resulted in the refocusing of nutrition and dietetics programs to become more "rigorous" through greater dependence on medical science.

A century later, nutrition and dietetics programs throughout North America have begun to look at ways to reintegrate the social roots of the profession. Acknowledgment of the lack of course content concerning foods and societal systems has been examined at conference sessions for both Dietitians of Canada and the American Dietetic Association (Derelian 2006; Rankin *et al.* 2006). These presentations served as springboards for formal and informal discussions within the profession. The need to revise university curricula to include a more "macro" or systems approach is clear. The possible strategies are many.

Service learning, one approach to reintroduce the social roots of the nutrition profession into education and training by framing within a broader food studies approach, has emerged with the growing emphasis on community–university partnerships. Both Canadian and American nutrition programs have expanded the use of service learning within curricula (Chabot and Holben 2003; Charbonneau 2004). As an alternative pedagogy, service learning combines experiential learning with learning that builds connections between course content and community. The goal of this approach involves providing service that supports and fortifies learning, while learning does the same for improved service (Eskow 1979, cited in Lazarus *et al.* 2008). In effect, service learning is a process. It involves active participation in well-planned service experiences that meet real community needs. It becomes integrated into the academic curriculum, providing students structured opportunities to reflect on their service experiences. It provides opportunities for students to put into action the theoretical knowledge learned in the classroom. Finally, it moves student learning outside the classroom and into the community, further cultivating the sense of social responsibility inherent to the nutrition profession (National Service Learning Clearinghouse 2005–2008; Stanton 2008).

A broad theoretical foundation exists for a pedagogy of local engagement (Lazarus *et al.* 2008; Winter *et al.* 2006), much of it based in critical theory and the resultant expectation of social change (Freshwater 2000). Different service learning models exist, ranging from experiences within courses, to outside class time, to week-long immersion events (University of British Columbia Public Affairs 2006; Stanton 2008). Regardless of the model, planning for an effective experience will be similar. Pedagogical principles for developing sound service learning experiences have been outlined (Howard 2001; Lazarus *et al.* 2008; Stanton 2008). Academic credit is earned through demonstration of learning, such that academic rigor is not compromised. Reflection is central to this process as it helps students to situate their experiences in the larger contexts of community structure and learning processes (Lazarus *et al.* 2008). Learning objectives for service experiences match objectives for the course. Orientation to learning from the community should be provided for participating students (Howard 2001), to enhance integration of observations, reflections and learnings of students within the classroom environment. Such critical thinking is central to the service learning process and may require the instructor to move outside the classroom comfort zone to facilitate rather than direct the learning process within the community setting (Howard 2001). This may involve a perceived loss of control with the student's learning outcomes, due to variations in student experiences and their personal reflective processes. However, results of service learning components have shown that despite the increased workload for faculty members, many positive, if not enthusiastic responses arise from students, faculty and community partners (Chabot and Holben 2003; Kim and Canfield 2002; Whelan *et al.* 2007). Fusner and Staib (2004) found that nursing students discovered the broader role of the practicing nurse, a role that went beyond caregiver. These students began to comprehend better their roles as health advocates. It is not beyond reason then for nutrition students participating in service learning also to clarify the wider responsibilities of professional service. Adoption of this altered pedagogy for dietetics education would incorporate a greater food studies approach and could bring many benefits for the students, educators and communities involved.

FOOD,
CULTURE&
SOCIETY

VOLUME 15

ISSUE 2

JUNE 2012

St. Francis Xavier University in rural Nova Scotia introduced its Service Learning Program in 1996, the first Canadian university to do so (Service Learning Program 2008a), thus advancing the university's history of engagement. The curricular service learning model emphasizes engagement with mainly non-profit community organizations and service that focuses on community-determined needs (Service Learning Program 2008b), clearly separating it from traditional extension and outreach approaches (Gaffikin and Morrissey 2008; Stanton 2008). Within the Department of Human Nutrition, students in the dietetic stream are encouraged to complete two service learning experiences prior to graduation, while limiting these opportunities to no more than one per half term (Department of Human Nutrition 2003). In 2006, with funding from an internal grant[1] designed to enhance service learning delivery and research (Service Learning Program 2008c), members of the Departments of Human Nutrition and Earth Sciences, the School of Nursing and a local community food network (Voices Antigonish) undertook a collaborative research project. This larger project aimed to strengthen linkages between the community and the university, and thus enhance service learning opportunities related to building food security for students in human nutrition courses.

Purpose

This paper centers on the service learning components of the larger project as offered in two upper-level courses—Community Nutrition (HNU 365) and Food Availability (HNU 405)—during the 2006/7, 2007/8 and 2008/9 academic years. The purpose of this paper is to clarify the impact of service learning on capacity development, specifically empowerment at the individual level of the students.

Methods

Service learning opportunities were offered over three academic years (2006/7, 2007/8 and 2008/9) in two human nutrition courses commonly taken by students in their third and fourth years of study (Community Nutrition [HNU 365] and Food Availability [HNU 405]). Specific projects were identified by community partners that included Voices Antigonish, a community food security network, the Nova Scotia Nutrition Council, the Student Union Environment Office, a local food security research project, and the local food bank. All projects involved working on building local food security using capacity building and redesign strategies. (Toronto Food Policy Council 1994) and addressed course objectives related to working in the community and understanding of food insecurity, namely:

- to understand the role of the nutrition professional as a partner in social change;
- to create student awareness of nutrition professional and citizen roles in policy development;
- to introduce community-based and institutional initiatives to alleviate food insecurity;
- to develop critical thinking skills to assist with analysis, interpretation and reporting on world food issues;

- to participate in discussions surrounding various domestic and global food issues;
- to explore specific food issues in-depth;
- to develop an understanding of food insecurity and its possible solutions;
- to develop critical thinking skills to assist in analysis and reporting on nutrition-related health problems in the community.

Data for this project were gathered from student evaluations of their service learning experiences. Student reflections were shared verbally within the classroom and in meetings with the course instructor, who noted these in a personal course journal. The instructor included her reflections on the learning processes based on her interactions with the students and community partners. Students' written reflections were integral parts of the weekly updates and final reports for the course projects. The course syllabus included information on the reflective process as well as opening questions to begin the exercise. Students were encouraged to examine their individual roles in the project through understanding what they learned about themselves working in a team setting, how the experience might affect their future health practices, how they would advise other health professionals undertaking similar tasks, what worked well, what failed to go as they thought it might, and whether they could have used a different approach to problem solving to be more effective. Other data were gathered through the completion of a written evaluation form from the Service Learning Program. This involved several open-ended questions regarding motivations for choosing a service learning opportunity, perceived benefits of the experiences, and potential improvements for future opportunities. These reflective questions enabled the gathering of information on capacity development as understood from the student viewpoint.

The tools used to gather these data were part of a larger evaluation of the Service Learning Program to understand outcomes of engaged learning experiences and to determine best practices for engaged teaching. For this reason, an ethics submission to the St. Francis Xavier University Research Ethics Board was not required. Students had the option to participate or not participate in the evaluation process. Those completing the anonymous process were deemed to have provided assent. Any possible identifying information was removed by the Service Learning Program personnel prior to supplying a typed copy of comments to the course instructor.

Data Sources and Analysis

FOOD,
CULTURE &
SOCIETY

VOLUME 15

ISSUE 2

JUNE 2012

An action research paradigm drove this project, which strove to build community through participatory processes designed to enable participants to become empowered through individual and group capacity building (MacAulay et al. 1999). Qualitative data were gathered from students and the course instructor by the Service Learning Program as part of their program evaluation process. Reflective comments from students as included in their final report submissions for each course provided further insights into their perceptions and experiences as did the personal reflections of the course instructor. An inductive analysis occurred using an interpretive hermeneutic process to generate and construct meaning of the service learning experiences to participating students. In an iterative process, data were systematically read, reflected upon, annotated and organized into themes. Themes were organized according to a typology involving Laverack's (2006a) empowerment domains for community capacity development in a health promotion context (see Table 1).

Trustworthiness of Interpretation

Adequacy of interpretation was established through the use of several techniques as described by Lincoln and Guba (1985). Credibility (truth-value) of findings was enhanced through prolonged engagement with the project to add scope and persistent observation of participants to add depth. Debriefing sessions occurred between the instructor and community members to clarify and explore patterns emergent from the data. Triangulation of data sources through examination of perceptions from students, instructor and community partners augmented credibility of findings (Janesick 1994). Thick description of the context within which findings occurred enables others to determine transferability (applicability) of findings to other situations. Clear organization of raw data and analysis products provide a decision-making trail for a future research audit, thus establishing confirmability (neutrality) of findings.

Results and Discussion

Participants and Projects

One instructor taught both courses in which service learning opportunities for this project were offered. A total of forty-seven students participated in eighteen projects over the three academic years (thirty students and ten projects in Community Nutrition HNU 365; seventeen students and eight projects in Food Availability HNU 405). Five community partners participated with Voices Antigonish, the major partner from the outset. Other partners were added over time including a provincial nutrition advocacy organization, student union office, food security research project and local food bank. Specific service learning opportunities centered on understanding local food systems, such as:

- development of a newsletter template and newsletter content for use with a Good Food Box program;
- assistance provided for organization of annual public forums to discuss aspects of local food availability;
- development of a pamphlet that discussed impacts of shipping foods over long distances;
- development of a local food producer listing and map;
- assistance with community survey research project;
- development of an advocacy tool for use in provincial elections that highlighted questions to determine how platforms of political parties addressed the determinants of food insecurity.

Table 1: Capacity Building Domains

Domain	Definition
Participation	Community and stakeholder participation indicate capacity building processes. Participating in groups or organizations may improve individual ability to define, analyze and act on issues of general concern for the broader community. Participation also may increase individual self- and social-esteem.
Resource mobilization	The ability to mobilize personal and community resources can improve self and social-esteem. This is a necessary component of program sustainability.
Forming networks	Strengthening equitable links with others is essential for capacity building. Alliances between individuals and organizations need to be formed to address community needs.
Problem identification and assessment capacity	This includes identification of problems, solutions, and actions within groups. It is the rationale for using participatory approaches to build capacity. These abilities may assist individuals in reaching their autonomy through increased capacity for assessing problems that affect their lives.
Relationships with outside "other"	Relationships between outside agents and communities must be equitable. The role of outside agents such as health promoters in community programs involves assistance, while power is transferred to the communities.
Ability to ask why	This concept reflects higher levels of success in the ability to think critically rather than in the ability to retain factual information. An individual's ability to critically assess causes of inequalities is necessary to develop effective change strategies.
Leadership skills	This domain is linked to aspects of participation. Leadership needs a strong participant base and participation requires the direction and structure of leadership.
Building organizational structures and local management control	Organizational structures contain elements that represent ways people come together to socialize and address concerns. Empowering organizational structures facilitate participation. Shared decision making among community members is necessary for program management. This requires clearly defined roles and responsibilities of all participant groups.

FOOD,
CULTURE &
SOCIETY

VOLUME 15

ISSUE 2

JUNE 2012

Definitions adapted from Laverack (2006a) and Labonte and Laverack (2001).

Findings and Analysis

Capacity building goes hand-in-hand with health promotion programming, which aims to enable people to gain control over and improve health status (First International Conference on Health Promotion 1986). Capacity building is both a method to address health promotion and an outcome of such programming. Addressing capacities of individuals, communities and systems is central to strengthening community action, one of the five health promotion strategies outlined in the Ottawa Charter for Health Promotion (First International Conference on Health Promotion 1986). This approach involves "development of skills, organizational structures, resources, and commitment" to social action (Hawe *et al.* 2000). Laverack (2006a) has conceptualized this form of empowerment through the definition of nine empowerment domains (see Table 1). Findings have been presented within this framework applied to individual-level capacity building.

Participation

The theme of "participation" encompasses aspects of experience known to foster capacity building and enable empowerment of individuals and groups (Laverack 2006b). Perceptions of service learning experiences most often focused on aspects of community participation. Students perceived the participatory nature of their experience as one of the most resonant benefits. Comments centered on understanding of the roles of various agencies and students' roles as citizens and nutrition professionals. For example:

> If it had not been for this project I would not have considered going to the [community] meeting. I was so impressed by the way the meeting flowed, the ideas generated, the networking that occurred, and the positive attitude. It was a great feeling to be part of a group in which everyone was so focused on a common goal. (S1FA08)[2]

> I feel closer to the [town and university] communities by applying my knowledge of food security and how to effectively [communicate] information about nutrition and services. (S2FA08)

Development of social support became apparent to students through participation. This increased awareness of connection and involvement with the community (Laverack 2006b) seemed to empower students by giving them permission to become involved. Nnakwe (1999) reported significantly increased motivation to participate expressed by students after a similar community service experience. In this study, all student responses stated that they would recommend a similar experience to others, indicating optimism and trust based on a positive participation experience (White-Cooper *et al.* 2009). Several student comments showed a budding comprehension of the potential role of nutrition professionals within community growth and development. For example:

[The experience] showed the responsibilities [dietitians] have in food security issues. (S3FA07)

A reported benefit of service learning experiences with university health professional students included exposure to future career roles (Pittman *et al.* 2000) and a survey of nursing students showed increased awareness of professional service roles (Bentley and Ellison 2005). In this study, students noted the potential professional roles in the field of food security, though without reference to the usefulness of the experience to their specific career paths. As reflection does not end when the service learning opportunity ends, it is possible that integration of the experience into personal career goals may occur with time. Shorter-term career goals were highlighted by some students who reported the perceived "requirement" of a completed service learning experience for application to dietetic internship programs as the impetus for their choice to pursue these opportunities. While this could be construed as a less positive motivation for choosing to participate in service learning opportunities, i.e. simply a means to an end, it does show some forethought to their careers. This student perception, though, appeared to be based on a misconception of the departmental policy "encouraging" but not "requiring" students to undertake such experiences (Department of Human Nutrition 2003).

Resource Mobilization

Selected students began to recognize not only their capacity to work with community groups but the integration of course content with the experiential learning. This actualized learning showed recognition of personal ability to learn by doing and linking coursework with practice. These students saw themselves as active participants in the learning process. As such, they exhibited an improved understanding of method to use their personal resources (i.e. skills, abilities, knowledge) in a community setting. For example:

We learned the importance of planning, developing objectives and aligning the objectives to meet our goals. As a group we discovered that it takes a lot of effort, review and revision to communicate our message effectively. (S4CN06)

[I] learned that a small contribution can help. (S1FA08)

[I] learned more about local food issues and extended my written communication skills. (S5FA08)

FOOD,
CULTURE&
SOCIETY

VOLUME 15

ISSUE 2

JUNE 2012

Similar findings occurred in a group of nursing students where 80 percent of participants showed improved understanding of course content after the service experience (Bentley and Ellison 2005). Increased concern about food insecurity issues has occurred in nutrition students after community service experiences (Nnakwe 1999).

One student spoke to an awareness of personal learning style:

For me, the "hands-on" learning is more effective than just writing a paper for a professor to read. (S6FA08)

Often students state this as a desire "to do something" not just "to learn about it." While this seems contradictory on the surface, it does note the beginnings of an ability to articulate personal needs in the learning process. While critical theory was designed for an outcome of social change, the development of skills and abilities also constitutes a form of empowerment, as not all empowerment must have externalized behaviors attached (Freshwater 2000). As noted by Laverack (2006b), the ability to recognize and use resources from within such as technical knowledge and personal skills, as well as from outside oneself, such as acquisition of new knowledge, constitutes resource mobilization. Students in this project clearly recognized their personal capacities and ways in which these could be used to the benefit of themselves and others.

Forming Networks

The sense of satisfaction brought to students by the participatory process was apparent. Evaluations stated that students would "highly recommend" service learning to their peers as a method to be involved with a "real" community group. This connection with the off-campus community was clearly important to the students. Becoming part of a network and forming relationships with community partners provided them with a direction for and clarification of their future roles. Example comments included:

The most satisfying aspect of doing this project is that I have contributed something tangible to the community … Working with a "real" organization, learning about and meeting members of the community … has given me a more memorable learning experience. (S7VFA08)

Gave us an insight to the experience by exposing us to other people's personal experiences. (S8CN06)

[I] was able to meet new people who provided a lot of support and information and learned a lot about a topic covered in my course which I didn't know. (S3FA07)

Service learning experiences with other university students found their sense of connectedness to the off-campus community increased (Raspberry 2006) and they reported formation of meaningful relationships with community members (Scott *et al.* 2005). Described benefits of service learning opportunities have included increased student awareness of community-determined needs and increased willingness to be a part of solution building (Bentley and Ellison 2005; Nnakwe 1999). Networks among students and community agencies serve to build capacity through opportunities to enhance skill sets. Skills include communication, understanding a situation, teamwork and connection with others (Laverack 2006b).

Learning to strengthen links with others empowers individuals and groups and facilitates development of trust (Gingras 2005; White-Cooper *et al.* 2009), thus enabling further organization to address social issues.

Problem Identification and Assessment Capacity

Understanding local issues from the viewpoint of those living with them, is a central component of community development (Laverack 2006b). This communication skill requires a high degree of self-efficacy to perceive how others understand and interpret the world (Lazarus *et al.* 2008). This appeared to be difficult for students in their first community-based experience. Academic institutions traditionally engender an approach grounded in control and power, leaving students feeling disempowered (Freshwater 2000). One particular group service learning experience identified a problem, yet encountered difficulties finding a solution, which appeared based in lack of communication. Early in the term, students had met with the community partner contact to clarify the project needs. No further contact was initiated until near the end of term when the community contact appeared to have changed the project focus. Confusion existed on both sides due to the lack of regular communication. It was clear that the resultant difficulty was identified yet neither the students nor the community partner seemed able to move forward to a solution without outside assistance. For example:

> Our advisor from the agency went back and forth on the task he wanted us to complete; it was confusing sometimes. (S9CN06)

Instructor reflections noted the stated confusion and bewilderment experienced by this student group. The misunderstanding with the project that had been agreed upon was not communicated to the students until a week before the project was due for the course:

> The anxiety felt by the students was palpable. They were nearing a state of panic, but were unable to move into a problem-solving mode. I assured them they did not need to redo the project, nor could they in the time remaining in the term. With some discussion and a couple of quick phone calls to the Service Learning Coordinator and the community contact person, the misunderstanding was resolved. (ICN06)

> Upon reflection, there may be a need to revisit the guidelines for weekly updates from the project teams. Providing a more specific outline of expected content might catch potential problems before they become larger issues. Besides including communication of what was completed in the previous week and what is planned for the coming week, clarification is needed of when group members were communicating with the community agency or any outside resource people. (ICN06)

This experience made clear that not all situations can be handled by students and community partners alone, as "power is resource dependent" (Laverack 2006b:

FOOD,
CULTURE
SOCIETY

VOLUME 15

ISSUE 2

JUNE 2012

325

114). The service learning coordinator and course instructor are meant to be involved throughout an experience. In this situation, the students had adopted an "assignment" approach to the project, expecting that they should complete the work on their own for course credit. Assisting with the problem-solving process during this experience could enable them to approach future problems with greater self-efficacy. However, the motivation to change lies within the individual and cannot be imposed from outside (Laverack 2006b).

Relationships with Outside "Other"

Most student groups encountered an equitable relationship with the community partner. Sample comments included:

> It benefits students and community; both are resources for the other. (S10FA08)

> [Our community partner] allowed me to think beyond simplicity and perform more in depth or "outside of the box" thinking. (S11FA08)

The goal of development of equitable relationships with outside agents involves a power-sharing approach for trust development. In some experiences, course instructors and community partners were perceived by students to be in the power positions. As such, it became important to assess whether each partner was directing, facilitating or enabling the service learning process (Laverack 2006a). The latter two roles would be useful given the level of self-efficacy held by student groups. While community partners, instructors and students received orientation information on expectations during a placement, more guidance may be necessary for beginners in the service learning process. Relevant comments included:

> I find that there was a lack of contact between myself and my group members and our [community] contact person. We met with her only once due to her busy schedule and upon our completion of our draft tool, she didn't get back to us in time [for us] to change any of her suggestions. (S12CN06)

> Perhaps [the community contact person] could work more with the students in preparation of tasks instead of just being available for consultation and revisions. (S2FA08)

Power sharing differences exist even within organizations and individuals. Constant tensions occur between the top-down and the community-driven approach to programming (Anderson 1998; Laverack and Labonte 2000). Students and professionals struggle between the roles of expert and partner. Power-sharing involves elevating the status of one person or group, while at the same time diminishing that of another (Laverack 2006b). Instructors and program coordinators are perceived to be in a more powerful position than students or community members, but it is the intent that the former strive to enable empowerment of the latter. From the context of these experiences, perhaps more attention needs to be given to building community partners' capacities to transform power relationships.

Ability to Ask Why

Development of a critical awareness of food insecurity and its broader social determinants occurred with many of the students. For example:

> In my recent visit to Cuba, via [immersion] service learning, I was also able to draw parallels with the [project] methods and Cuban culture. Their vast knowledge of sustainable organic agriculture and respect for the environment was a lesson that should be learned by all. I feel like these values were presented in the brochure [we developed]… (S11FA08)

> I guess I never really took into consideration where my food came from, how it got to my table, and the cost of doing so. (S13FA08)

Other students wrote about insights into the lives of others that arose through self-questioning and reflection:

> When reflecting on the hard labour that farmers do, the challenges they face daily, seasonally and yearly, I wondered how they accomplish all they do (family, production, promotion, paper work, etc.) and what is their driving force. Then I reflected on my own life. I thought about the number of people that questioned why I have come back to school (at this stage of my life) putting myself through all the work and stress that goes with school. At the end of the day, it all comes down to following your passion, giving to others, and doing the best you can and that really doesn't feel like work, it is living life. (S7FA08)

Increased ability to critically assess contextual issues within the community leads to empowerment (Laverack 2006b). This involves reflection on the viewpoints of others and appreciation of other lifestyles (Lazarus *et al.* 2008). In this study, students showed the ability to apply the life contexts of community members to their own lives and experiences. This critical thinking led to altered intentions to act, such as attending the farmer's market and learning more about local food systems. Service learning experiences facilitated students' professional development through the questioning of existing concepts, gaining new knowledge, and changing their own behaviors, all fundamental to service learning pedagogy (Lazarus *et al.* 2008).

FOOD,
CULTURE &
SOCIETY

VOLUME 15

ISSUE 2

JUNE 2012

Leadership Skills

Students exhibited varying degrees of leadership during service learning experiences. As their leadership skills increased, so did their participation (Laverack and Labonte 2000). Power structures influence leadership style; as power sharing increases so does the partnership approach (Laverack 2006b). Students with more experience seemed more ready to work as a partner rather than an expert

(Anderson 1998) when leading others through the project, as noted by the course instructor reflections:

> The more experienced students showed a greater degree of confidence in their abilities. The same students used their communication skills more effectively to guide or facilitate processes rather than direct them. Perhaps greater self-actualization is playing a part in their capacity to act as expert or partner as required. (ICN08)

> Some students, new to community participation, approached the project as they would any other course assignment. They seemed uncomfortable making the transition to a less structured process. In one case, a student wasn't able to see another instructor as a community partner volunteer, but only as an instructor, even though the relationship was addressed by two or three people to try to clarify for her. This strongly held perception led to her reporting, "We did not have a real placement." As an instructor, this situation caused me to rethink how I present myself to students. There needs to be an understanding by students that I wear many hats besides that of "professor" and they are active participants in the learning process. (ICN06)

Again, the traditional power structures inherent in university education may cause a less satisfactory service learning experiences for some students. Changes in dietetics education towards a more participatory learning experience should be addressed during first-year courses. This may help students move beyond traditional didactic learning styles.

Building Organizational Structures and Local Management Control
As noted earlier, some of the capacity-building constructs require a degree of empowerment to put into practice. Student participants carry control that they may not recognize—power to improve course structures. Comments and reflections by students and the instructor led to a number of suggestions for improvement of the service learning components of human nutrition courses:

> Ensure professor, community organization and student have the same goals, objectives and expectations. Group meeting with all three parties initially. (S14FA08)

Several comments pointed to the need for improved communication structures. As many of the community partners in this study were new to the service learning process, some misconceptions of roles and responsibilities of all involved may have occurred as in another study (White-Cooper *et al.* 2009). Without clear role definition, projects may not meet their potential. Strong and continual communication links between all parties are necessary for trust development (White-Cooper *et al.* 2009) and thus successful experiences.

The instructor noted that student reflection on experiences and perceptions of professional roles throughout the service learning experience might be necessary for all partners:

> Student reflections in final reports can be insightful or simply a laundry list of what occurred during their experiences. To move them closer to the self-exploration that would be ideal, I may need to include more structured responses, especially for those who aren't yet comfortable with the introspection necessary. I will try adding reflective components to the first-year course to begin the process that they will encounter throughout their four years here. (ICN&FA08)

The need to tailor service learning requirements to student skill level was noted by Rasor-Greenhalgh *et al.* (1998). Reflections should clearly connect course learning objectives with community experiences (Chabot and Holben 2003). Pomson (2008) described four types of common reflective responses—summative, evaluative, analytic and subjective. Reflective practice requires parts of each of these with an emphasis on critical thinking and understanding of personal experiences and their links to the learning process and professional growth. This may require a more structured outline of written expectations for some students, as described by Ash (2003). In HNU 365, weekly updates were required that dealt mainly with the chronology of the project. Addition of reflective components throughout the experience may further facilitate personal connections as might reflective journaling (Fusner and Staib 2004).

Instructor reflection highlighted the personal and professional benefits of offering service learning opportunities within courses:

> It is fantastic to see the light bulbs go off as students begin to integrate classroom material with practical experiences! You can see it in their demeanour—they just look different—and they smile a lot. It's obvious that they feel great having made the connections. As with the integrated internship process, when students bring that new-found realization to the classroom things become much more interesting for everyone. (ICN&FA08)

FOOD, CULTURE & SOCIETY

VOLUME 15

ISSUE 2

JUNE 2012

Integration of student service learning experiences in classroom settings provides an enhanced learning environment for all students. This sharing leads to an ever-changing classroom. While challenging for instructors, the participatory nature of the varied examples and discussions forces constant reworking of course structure, resulting in a more salient, dynamic atmosphere for students and instructors (Champagne 2006; Chabot and Holben 2003). An additional benefit to faculty is the increased opportunity to remain connected to their own professional practices (Pittman *et al.* 2000).

Facilitating service learning in course instruction is not without its challenges, such as the workload requirements:

Guiding service learning opportunities can be exhausting. It adds considerably to the course prep time and student contact time. There are days when it seems much easier to just ask them to write a paper. However, these opportunities keep me connected to the community and professional practice. (ICN06)

That service learning enriches the classroom experience for students and faculty is clear (Chabot and Holben 1999; Champagne 2006). One challenge remains for faculty who plan to integrate this learning model in courses—that of recognition of the time required (Champagne 2006; Stanton 2008; White-Cooper *et al.* 2009). University institutional structures seem slow to adopt inclusion of service learning within faculty evaluation. This is particularly problematic for professional programs that strive to include "real-world" experience along side theoretical course content. Here, one of the comments was particularly salient:

When I applied for tenure and promotion, my pioneering of service learning components within the courses I taught was not fully appreciated. While it enhanced the education process and the preparation of quality professionals, it took time away from research and publication, which seemed to be the main measuring sticks for advancement at that time. (ICN&FA07)

It must be noted that changing academic institutional structures will not be easy. Tensions exist between the "bureaucratic traditions" (Gaffikin and Morrissey 2008: 101), and the engaged institution. Valuation differences between traditional science-based and experiential-based knowledge pose barriers to change (Liquori 2001). Financial pressures exist that place greater attention on more "financially enriching" pursuits over those less likely to yield financial gain (Gaffikin and Morrissey 2008). However, the movement to a fully engaged institutional model will benefit research, scholarship and preparation of high-quality professionals (Stanton 2008), through collaborative discovery and application of knowledge (Gaffikin and Morrissey 2008). Recognition of faculty members involved in curricular and research-based service learning within institutional reward and promotion systems is a key component to developing a valued, sustainable service learning program (Gaffikin and Morrissey 2008; Stanton 2008).

Summary

A limitation of these analyses is that it was not possible to include the voices of all the students as some chose not to participate fully in the evaluative process. Future evaluation of service learning components should include individual interview data to add further depth to the findings. Breadth could be added through interviews with students, course instructors, community partners and program staff. Actions, both internal and external to the individual, based on insights gained through a service learning experience are also limited by the desire of the individual to act on the newfound knowledge (Freshwater 2000).

This project gave voice to the student experience in service learning components focused on building local food security. Analysis highlighted the empowering nature of such experiences for both students and course instructors. Planning for service learning integration in dietetics education requires adequate orientation of all parties involved, reflective and reflexive discussions and writings, and a planned evaluation process. Organizational change may be necessary to enhance uptake of this influential pedagogical approach. Building student capacity to participate in community settings as a professional and an enlightened citizen is central to choosing this transformative learning process.

Acknowledgments

This project was completed with the financial support of an internal grant from the Service Learning Faculty Development and Research Support Fund, with grant funds secured from the J.W. McConnell Family Foundation. The authors wish to thank the students and community partners for their enthusiasm and assistance in strengthening the community–university partnerships.

Laurie A. Wadsworth is an associate professor at the Department of Human Nutrition, St. Francis Xavier University. Her academic work is influenced by over 12 years working in public health in Saskatchewan. Her teaching and professional interests include food systems analysis, global food insecurity, health advocacy for policy development, community health frameworks and qualitative research methods. Laurie's research and professional service aim to inform social and health policy directions and to effect change in education and training of health professionals. Department of Human Nutrition, St. Francis Xavier University, Box 5000, Antigonish, NS, B2G 2W5, Canada (lwadswor@stfx.ca).

Christine Johnson is an assistant professor at the Department of Human Nutrition, St. Francis Xavier University. She is actively involved in research focused on approaches to addressing food insecurity including mapping food security status, food access and food security assets in the local community. This work has been used to incorporate service learning components into undergraduate honors degree thesis projects. She has also incorporated service learning into course instruction. Department of Human Nutrition, St. Francis Xavier University, Box 5000, Antigonish, NS, B2G 2W5, Canada (cjohnson@stfx.ca).

Colleen Cameron has worked internationally as a nurse in clinical, community and emergency relief work. She currently teaches and supervises nursing students in clinical settings and teaches courses in community development and health, gender and development, and gender and health for community development workers from countries of the South. Colleen incorporates service learning in a gender and health course for nursing students, which is cross-listed with women's studies. She has been co-Chair of Voices Antigonish, a volunteer advocacy group for food security, since its inception. Coady International Institute, Box 5000, St. Francis Xavier University, Antigonish, NS, B2G 2W5, Canada (accamero@stfx.ca).

Marla Gaudet currently focuses on management of a community-based, experiential learning program where undergraduate university students from all disciplines have the

FOOD,
CULTURE &
SOCIETY

VOLUME 15

ISSUE 2

JUNE 2012

opportunity to provide service to the community that is directly related to the field of study. Her research activities include investigation of the costs and benefits of service learning to the community, best practices for involving faculty members in service learning, and the use of student leaders to facilitate community–university partnerships. St. Francis Xavier University, Box 5000, Antigonish, NS, B2G 2W5, Canada (mgaudet@stfx.ca).

Notes

1   In 2005, the J.W. McConnell Family Foundation funded a new internal granting program at St. Francis Xavier University. This funding was designed to enhance delivery of service learning within courses and to expand research in the area of service learning. The resulting Service Learning Faculty Development and Research Support Fund provided funds for conducting the research project, Mapping Food Security and Access to Food in Downtown Antigonish: A Community–University Partnership, as well as travel grants for researchers to present aspects of the findings.

2   The citations with each quotation in the paper follow the format of Speaker/Course/Year, where Speaker is designated as S (student) with each individual respondent noted through the use of an numeral, or I (instructor); Course is designated as CN (Community Nutrition HNU 365) and FA (Food Availability HNU 405); and Year is designated by the last two digits of the year in which the course was held.

References

Anderson, B. 1998. Reflection on Practice: Dietitian as Partner or Expert? *Canadian Journal of Dietetic Practice and Research* 59(3): 138–42.

Ash, S. 2003. Integrating Service-learning into a College-level Nutrition Course. *Journal of Nutrition Education and Behaviour* 35(3): 161–2.

Bentley, R. and Ellsion, K. 2005. Impact of a Service-learning Project on Students. *Nursing Education Perspectives* 26(5): 287–90.

Brownridge, E. and Upton, E. 1993. *Canadian Dietitians. Making a Difference.* Toronto, ON: The Canadian Dietetic Association.

Chabot, J.M. and Holben, D.H. 2003. Integrating Service-learning into Dietetics and Nutrition Education. *Topics in Clinical Nutrition* 18(3): 177–84.

Champagne, N. 2006. Service Learning: Its Origin, Evolution, and Connection to Health Education. *American Journal of Health Education* 37(2): 97–101.

Charbonneau, L. 2004. Educating Citizen Jane: Community Service Learning, a Teaching Model that Combines Volunteer Service With Academic Work, Aims to Instill in Students a Sense of Citizenship and Civic Engagement. *University Affairs* 45(2): 12.

Department of Human Nutrition, St. Francis Xavier University. 2003. *Dietitians of Canada Accreditation Report.* Antigonish, NS: Department of Human Nutrition.

Derelian, D.V. 2006. Where Have all the Foodies Gone? Paper presented at ADA Food and Nutrition Conference and Expo, Honolulu, HA, September 16–19, 2006.

First International Conference on Health Promotion. 1986. The Ottawa Charter for Health Promotion. Available from: http://www.who.int/healthpromotion/conferences/previous/ottawa/en/print.html (accessed May 14, 2010).

Freshwater, D. 2000. Crosscurrents: Against Cultural Narration in Nursing. *Journal of Advanced Nursing* 32(2): 481–4.

Fusner, S. and Staib, S. 2004. Students and Senior Citizens Learning from Each Other. *Journal of Gerontological Nursing* 30(3): 40–5.

Gaffikin, F. and Morrissey, M. 2008. A New Synergy for Universities. *Education, Citizenship and Social Justice* 3(1): 97–116.

Gingras, J. 2005. Evoking Trust in the Nutrition Counsellor: Why Should we Be Trusted? *Journal of Agricultural and Environmental Ethics* 18: 57–74.

Hawe, P., King, L., Noort, M., Jordens, C. and Lloyd, B. 2000. *Indicators to Help with Capacity Building in Health Promotion*. Sydney: New South Wales Health Department. Available from: http://www.health.nsw.gov.au/pubs/2000/pdf/capbuild.pdf (accessed May 14, 2010).

Howard, J.P.F. (ed.). 2001. *Service Learning Course Design Workbook. Journal of Community Service Learning*. Ann Arbor, MI: Edward Ginsberg Center for Community Service, University of Michigan, pp. 16–19.

Janesick, V.J. 1994. *The Dance of Qualitative Research Design: Metaphor, Methodolatry, and Meaning*. In N.K Denzin and Y.S Lincoln (eds) *Handbook of Qualitative Research*. Thousand Oaks, CA: Sage Publications, pp. 209–19.

Kim, Y. and Canfield, A. 2002. How to Develop a Service Learning Program in Dietetics Education. *Journal of the American Dietetic Association* 102(2): 174–6.

Labonte, R. and Laverack, G. 2001. Capacity Building in Health Promotion, Part 1: For Whom? And for What Purpose? *Critical Public Health* 11(2): 111–27.

Laverack, G. 2006a. Using a "Domains" Approach to Build Community Empowerment. *Community Development Journal* 41(1): 4–12.

Laverack, G. 2006b. Improving Health Outcomes through Community Empowerment: A Review of the Literature. *Journal of Health, Population and Nutrition* 24(1): 113–20.

Laverack, G. and Labonte, R. 2000. A Planning Framework for Community Empowerment Goals within Health Promotion. *Health Policy and Planning* 15(3): 255–62.

Lazarus, J., Erasmus, M., Hendricks, D., Nduna, J. and Slamat, J. 2008. Embedding Community Engagement in South African Higher Education. *Education, Citizenship and Social Justice* 3: 57–83.

Lincoln, Y.S., and Guba, E.G. 1985. *Naturalistic Inquiry*. Newbury Park, CA: Sage Publications.

Liquori, T. 2001. Food Matters: Changing Dimensions of Science and Practice in the Nutrition Profession. *Journal of Nutrition Education* 33: 234–46.

MacAulay, A., Commanda, L., Gibson, N., McCabe, M., Robbins, C. and Twohig, P. 1999. Participatory Research Maximises Community and Lay Involvement. *British Medical Journal* 319: 774–8.

National Service Learning Clearinghouse. 2005–2008.What is Service Learning? Available online at: http://www.servicelearning.org/what_is_service-learning/service-learning_is/index.php (accessed May 14, 2010).

Nnakwe, N.E. 1999. Implementation and Impact of College Community Service and Its Effect on Social Responsibility of Undergraduate Students. *Journal of Family and Consumer Sciences* 91(2): 57–61.

Pittman, K., Wold, J., Wilson, A., Huff, C. and Williams, S. 2000. Community Connections: Promoting Family Health. *Family and Community Health* 23(2): 72–8.

Pomson, A. 2008. "Close to Home': Reflections at the Intersection of Teaching and Research. *Reflective Practice* 9(2): 157–65.

FOOD,
CULTURE
SOCIETY

VOLUME 15

ISSUE 2

JUNE 2012

333

Power, E. 2005. Individual and Household Food Security in Canada: Position of Dietitians of Canada. *Canadian Journal of Dietetic Practice and Research* 66(1): 43–6.

Rankin, J., Kasten, G. and Waisman, M.S. 2006. Putting Food Back into Food and Nutrition. Paper presented at DC National Conference, Marketplace for Your Mind! Halifax, NS, June 7–10.

Raspberry, C. 2006. Teaching Nutrition Concepts through Service Learning. *Journal of Nutrition Education and Behaviour* 38(1): 59–60.

Scott, S., Harrison, A., Baker, T. and Wills, J. 2005. Interdisciplinary Community Partnership for Health Professional Students: A Service-learning Approach. *Journal of Allied Health* 34(1): 31–5.

Service Learning Program, St. Francis Xavier University. 2008a. Service Learning for Faculty. Available from: http://www.mystfx.ca/academic/servicelearning/Information%20for%20Faculty/Faculty%20Home%20Page.htm (accessed May 14, 2010).

Service Learning Program, St. Francis Xavier University. 2008b. Service Learning for Community Partners. Available from: http://www.mystfx.ca/academic/servicelearning/Information%20for%20Faculty/Faculty%20Community%20Partners.htm (accessed May 14, 2010).

Service Learning Program, St. Francis Xavier University. 2008c. Service Learning Faculty Development and Research Support Fund. Available from: http://www.stfx.ca/academic/servicelearning/Research%20Grant/Research%20Grant%20Home%20page.htm (accessed May 14, 2010).

Stanton, T.K. 2008. New Times Demand New Scholarship. *Education, Citizenship and Social Justice* 3(1): 19–42.

Toronto Food Policy Council. 1994. Reducing Urban Hunger in Ontario: Policy Responses to Support the Transition from food Charity to Local Food Security. Toronto Food Policy Council Discussion Paper Series, Discussion Paper #1.Toronto, ON: Toronto Food Policy Council. Available from: http://www.toronto.ca/health/tfpc_hunger.pdf (accessed June 27, 2011).

University of British Columbia Public Affairs. 2006. Not Your Typical Spring Break. Hundreds of UBC Students Sign up for Community Service. Available from: http://www.publicaffairs.ubc.ca/media/releases/2006/mr–06–019.html (accessed May 14, 2010).

Whelan, K., Thomas, J.E. and Madden, A.M. 2007. Student Research Projects: The Experiences of Student Dietitians, University Faculty Members, and Collaborators. *Journal of the American Dietetic Association* 107(9): 1567–74.

White-Cooper, S., Dawkins, N.U., Kamin, S.L. and Anderson, L.A. 2009. Community-institutional Partnerships: Understanding Trust among Partners. *Health Education & Behavior* 36(2): 334–47.

Winter, A., Wiseman, J. and Muirhead, B. 2006. University-Community Engagement in Australia. *Education, Citizenship and Social Justice* 1(3): 211–30.

NATURE'S PERFECT FOOD: HOW MILK BECAME AMERICA'S DRINK

BY MELANIE DUPUIS (NEW YORK: NEW YORK UNIVERSITY PRESS, 2002).

MILK: THE SURPRISING STORY OF MILK THROUGH THE AGES

BY ANNE MENDELSON (NEW YORK: KOPF, 2008).

MILK: A LOCAL AND GLOBAL HISTORY

BY DEBORAH VALENZE (NEW HAVEN, CT: YALE UNIVERSITY PRESS, 2011).

RE-IMAGINING MILK

BY ANDREA S. WILEY (NEW YORK: ROUTLEDGE, 2011).

Reviewed by Diana Mincyte, Yale University

DOI: 10.2752/175174412X13233545145462

FOOD,
CULTURE &
SOCIETY

VOLUME 15

ISSUE 2

JUNE 2012

Humanity's embrace of fresh animal milk as a source of food around the globe is a highly improbable event. Not only did it require fearlessness and ingenuity on the part of our ancestors to break into and capitalize on the feeding cycle of other (mammalian) species, but such an unusual food procuring practice had to coincide with the emerging genetic changes in some human populations who did not digest lactose well in adulthood. These phenomena were augmented by an unlikely historical confluence in early modern Europe and North America: the rise of beliefs that espoused values of "naturalness" and "freshness," urbanization, industrialization, the changing gender politics that pushed women to search for alternatives to breastfeeding, the success of hygienic movements that made milk safer to consume, and immense technological and scientific advances enabling this highly perishable food to become a stable industrial commodity. The list of social, religious, bacterial, political, geographical and economic forces working against milk is long, but despite this, fresh milk today is still considered as an indispensable food praised by nutritionists and found on the shelves of almost every grocery story around the world.

What is most fascinating about milk is not only the unusual twists and turns in its history, but also a sense that the process of its "domestication" is never complete. Pasteurized or raw, fermented or fresh, skim or whole, goat's milk or cow's milk, nature's perfect food or a Frankensteinian invention—are just a few dilemmas that have animated debates surrounding milk since ancient times, as was the case, for example, in North European Medieval cities where ale competed with cow's milk as the primary food for young children. Though milk seems to have won, its victories are fragile, and it continues to be enmeshed in ongoing battles over what constitutes the health of a nation, perfect bodies and diets, morality, tradition, sovereignty and agrarian politics.

The four excellent books covered in this review work to balance these two contradictory stories—that of milk's "conquest of space, energy, and dietary preferences" (Valenze 2011: 3), on the one hand, and ambivalence surrounding milk consumption and contestations over milk's universal "merits" (Wiley 2011: 30), on the other. They do so by showing how meanings, economic relations, religious beliefs and material and biological qualities of milk have been reconstituted at different historical junctions.

Collectively, the authors make a powerful point that what we think of as "milk" is not a homogenous entity, but a number of different things. Mendelson uses the term "label Babel" to highlight the diversity of milk products, exposing vast differences in dairy production practices, histories and geographies. By contrast, DuPuis critiques scientific representations such as graphs depicting the rise of milk production to argue that they mask significant differences in the quality of milk—including its taste, smell, color, microbial composition, geography, and its meanings—at different points in time. The ultimate message delivered by the authors is that milk should really be used as a plural term.

Sharing their commitment to tell a story of milk from a comparative-historical perspective, the four books are deeply interdisciplinary, making unusual connections, recombining methodological tools, and employing varied theoretical frameworks. Yet, when juxtaposed, the contours of four broad conceptual frameworks emerge, including a history of ideas, political economy, biocultural perspective, and practice studies.

Built on a wealth of historical materials including literary texts, popular press, philosophical treatises and travelogues, Valenze's book tracks how the culture surrounding milk has changed over the last 5,000 years. Opening with a reference to the Hindu myth of Churning the Ocean, the book follows the path of Western cultural history by highlighting Egyptian mythologies, the ancient Near East, Greek and Roman worlds, with brief detours into Mongolia and China. Later chapters tell fascinating stories of how milk functioned in Christian imaginaries, played into ideas about abundance, pleasure and restraint in Medieval Europe, and how it emerged as a commodity on both sides of the Atlantic. Valenze's analysis combines the history of ideas with analyses of food practices as well as broader discussions about gender, work and market politics in the Old and New Worlds to advance an argument that the history of milk is "a marker of the emergence of a peculiarly Western food culture and its path into the modern age" (Valenze 2011: 5).

The first part in DuPuis' *Nature's Perfect Food* echoes Valenze's approach, arguing that the history of ideas about milk is a proxy for the negotiations over what constitutes progress, health and perfection in particular social and historical settings. Focusing primarily on the eastern United States, DuPuis initially examines transformations of dairy production in the mid-nineteenth through twentieth century as embodying ongoing moral and social reforms. The second half of the book takes a political economy approach and offers a comparative analysis of dairy production in New York, Wisconsin and California to show that the popular ideas about perfection had specific social, political, economic and material consequences. An analysis of the changing geography of milk production is particularly illuminating in that it reveals how the boundaries of milksheds changed in relation to new transportation technologies, regulatory regimes and social norms. *Nature's Perfect Food* is a deeply theoretical book that engages and challenges classical social theory positions, including those of political economy.

Wiley's *Re-imagining Milk* is a concise and easily accessible introduction to the history and anthropology of milk. Yet, the issues discussed in the book are anything but simple. *Re-Imagining Milk* explores intricate connections between nutritional science, the health claims in food marketing, export of Western cultural ideals to other parts of the world, outright racism, and body politics. Wiley grounds the political economy of milk production in a biocultural perspective. The book starts with an explanation of the biochemical processes involved in digesting milk to show how claims about universal goodness of milk go against variations in human ability to digest lactose beyond childhood. Wiley's analysis also illuminates the embeddedness of nutritional science, in particular national and political contexts to show, for example, that Finnish nutritional scientists suggest devoting 25 percent of the entire food intake to dairy, while Singapore's diet guides do not specify milk as a necessity, and in China's food guide "pagoda," milk and legumes share the same food category.

Mendelson takes a global perspective on milk's geography and, by so doing, further complicates the view of milk as an inherently Western commodity. In carefully demarcating the boundaries in culinary cultures and milk animal cultivation zones, Mendelson identifies four dairy regions: the Diverse Sources Belt (or Yogurtistan) that spans vast swaths of Eurasia from the Balkans to western Mongolia, the Indian subcontinent, Northeastern Europe and Northwestern Europe. In linking the history and geography of milk production to environmental and animal histories, *Milk* tells a rich story that combines a biocultural approach and practice studies, with interludes of social history. The second part of the book offers 120 recipes, from Chinese fried milk to cold blueberry soup, that also include short histories and helpful tips. In inviting the readers to work with milk, Mendelson adds an important performative dimension to studying milk, showing how its history and geography can materialize in our own kitchens.

When read together, the four books represent what could be termed as social studies of milk, a burgeoning field exploring milk's histories and cultures (e.g. Atkins 2010, Patton 2004). The challenges that these authors face are similar to those that others in the field are encountering, namely, in what ways milk is different (and

FOOD,
CULTURE &
SOCIETY

VOLUME 15

ISSUE 2

JUNE 2012

similar) to other single food commodities as well as what gets obscured (and gained) by focusing on a single food item. More importantly, should we approach milk as a lens to understand social processes, or should it be considered as an agent in and of itself transforming these processes? If it is an agent, then how does it impact and change social and economic relations, institutions and landscapes? In advancing the theoretical framework of this field, it may also be worth reflecting on how milk studies relate to the established disciplines in social science and the humanities. How do milk studies in particular, and food studies more broadly, challenge and extend the ongoing scholarly debates?

In terms of audiences, all four books are aimed at mixed audiences, including academic and wider audiences. Academic historians and those interested in food history would benefit greatly from reading DuPuis and Mendelson, and especially Valenze's book. Since its publication, *Nature's Perfect Food* by DuPuis has already been included in curriculums across a wide spectrum of disciplines, including sociology, environmental studies and geography, while Wiley's *Re-imagining Milk* is an excellent introduction to milk from anthropological and global perspectives. Mendelson's work speaks to interdisciplinary audiences as well as curious practitioners who are eager to test the recipes while learning their rich stories.

References

Atkins, Peter. 2010. *Liquid Materialities: A History of Milk, Science and the Law*. Surrey: Ashgate.

Patton, Stuart. 2004. *Milk: Its Remarkable Contribution to Human Health and Well-Being*. New Brunswick.

LIQUID MATERIALITIES: A HISTORY OF MILK, SCIENCE AND THE LAW

BY PETER ATKINS (FARNHAM, SURREY: ASHGATE PUBLISHING LTD, 2010).

Reviewed by Deborah Valenze, Barnard College, Columbia University

DOI: 10.2752/175174412X13233545145507

Milk as material has seldom been the subject and main character of academic study. It is the "stuff" (quite literally) of history, which, as Atkins points out in a compelling preface and first chapter, food historians often overlook, substituting instead other subjects and agencies surrounding the product itself. Atkins is well known to those interested in milk; trained as a historical geographer, he is the author of a great many articles and essays on the subject. This book represents something of a departure from his earlier work: in a more theoretical vein, he sets out to trace the career of milk through the matrices of modernity mainly in urban localities, laboratories and court rooms, where its identity has been perpetually shaped and transformed by technologies, laws and expert opinion. Milk presents a particularly suitable subject for this quest, given its changeable nature under any circumstances; its qualities are distinctive according to location, the passage of time, and imposition of varying environmental conditions. As important to Atkins is the tendency of modern society to act upon milk through a particular grid having less to do with milk, *qua* milk, than issues peculiar to a larger project, that of "redraw[ing] boundaries between nature and society" (pp. xix). For the first half of the nineteenth century, "milk was an 'epistemic thing,'" Atkins explains. "Certainly, until the First World War, milk remained what [H.-J.] Rheinberger has called a 'question-generating machine' that inspired investigation, reflection and frequent redefinition" (p. 60). The concerns of the period—dirt, disease, scientific knowledge, market quality and nutrition—presented milk with very particular opportunities. The liquid appropriated qualities that gradually became understood as essential and normative to its nature. So, Atkins points out, the story of milk replicates the story of "the modern object" (p. 14).

It is impossible to review the myriad arguments proposed within this valuable book, which is densely written and heavily footnoted. The overall plan offers a sense of an even larger project at work (to be completed with the publication of three more volumes) on other aspects of milk's complex trajectory through primarily a British setting. In a brief chapter highlighting a courtroom drama of 1876, in which a New York City judge tried to rule on what the condition of commercial milk ought to be, Atkins guides us through the search for milk in laboratories of the nineteenth century. An array of chemists and public analysts appear in quick succession, equipped with lactometers, microscopes, photomicrographs, refrigeration techniques and centrifuges. Science, technology, the laboratory and commercial interests engaged in a struggle with milk, emerging with fragmentary knowledge at best. What was milk, but a mutable liquid whose fat content seemed to matter more than anything else? Atkins savors the irony of this fact in light of the fanfare at the beginning of the twentieth century, when the discovery of vitamins prompted nutritional scientists to seize upon the importance of butterfat for its contribution to human growth. This happened to be the same constituent part of milk that marketers and consumers gauged carefully throughout the nineteenth century, given that buyers were well aware of the likelihood of a watered-down product on the market. But fat was anything but a stable property of milk: different types of cows produced different quantities of fat, and bovine diets could alter the amount, too. As Atkins shows in this and every chapter, the search for certainty and stability in the history of milk led repeatedly to ironies and paradoxes.

Atkins' discussion of the elusive nature of milk sets the stage for a discussion of how the "natural" aspects of milk were constructed through the latter part of the nineteenth century by way of considerable monitoring by public health legislation and the many experts who sampled and recorded the condition of milk in the marketplace. In "Legal ontologies and the performative realm of the law," Atkins demonstrates his argument by reviewing the attempts to regulate the sale of milk through the major Sale of Food and Drugs Acts of 1860, 1872, 1875, 1879, 1899 and 1928. "The law," he points out, "proved to be a blunt instrument in its inability to accommodate the slippery uncertainty of the question 'what is milk?'" (p. 211). Atkins considers the development of practices aimed at detecting

FOOD,
CULTURE &
SOCIETY

VOLUME 15

ISSUE 2

JUNE 2012

poisonous, alien, or fraudulent properties in milk. A variety of data is presented in several charts, showing that "the publicity surrounding the Sale of Food and Drugs Acts of 1872, 1875 and 1879 was probably responsible for a declining incidence of fraud in the 1870s, and in the 1880s a more general and effective legal enforcement took over" (p. 192). Given such improvements, Atkins surmises that consumers' expectations and trust increased, and so did milk consumption. In his final chapters, Atkins moves to the concern for clean milk, which persisted through the 1920s and 1930s, promoted and contested by laboratories, consumer groups and government agencies. The environment surrounding milk was slowly changing to accommodate the modern consumer and the conditions of modernity, namely, anonymous dealers operating in large, industrial cities.

Atkins' more subtle reflections are very much in the spirit of Bruno Latour's mordant insights into the problematic capabilities of allegedly "'value-free' science to equip administrators with technologies for such control" (p. 203). Unadulterated food, according to legal definitions, had "nothing added, nothing taken away," and refinement in the law also stipulated that the food must be regarded as "of the nature, substance and quality demanded" (p. 212). Appeal cases showed how inadequate these terms (and samples) would be in determining what constituted acceptable milk for the market. Gradually, judges learned a great deal of agricultural science from farmers, who in turn came to see themselves as victims of analysts, technologies, and generic terminology. In a final, ironic twist, cows became the ultimate arbiters of milk because their subsequent samples enabled the court to reconsider evidence of quality (and nature and substance). Milk once again triumphed as the elusive product of nature, capable of upending whatever human contrivance happened to be set in its path.

Scholars will appreciate and applaud the move that Atkins has made to pull food history into a theoretical discussion of materials and modernity. *Liquid Materialities* engages frames of reference drawn mainly from the social sciences; more humanistic historians may not recognize the many debates that crop up (sometimes referenced only by the surnames of scholars) in these pages. It will take some effort on the part of the reader, then, to bridge the gap between the concerns of this book and food history approached by way of political economy or social and cultural debates of the era. The reader will have to supply the missing parts played by the apparently naïve consumer, who thought she knew what milk was, or the pediatrician, who lobbied to save the babies, or the cagey capitalist, who fully embraced the task of manipulating milk's fungible nature. Perhaps future volumes of Atkins' project will more directly engage those agencies.

THE STRUGGLE FOR MAIZE: CAMPESINOS, WORKERS AND TRANSGENIC CORN IN THE MEXICAN COUNTRYSIDE

BY ELIZABETH FITTING (DURHAM, NC: DUKE UNIVERSITY PRESS 2010).

Reviewed by Jacqueline Geoghegan, Clark University

DOI: 10.2752/175174412X13233545145543

In 2001, scientists discovered transgenic corn at its origin in Mexico, even though genetically modified corn was prohibited in Mexico at that time. This book describes and discusses the debates surrounding this discovery as well as changing rural Mexican agriculturalists' activities and views, which are attributed to structural changes in Mexico's political economy, via economic reforms, including the increased integration of Mexico into the global economy. In reality, this book is two separate works, which the author implicitly acknowledges in structuring the book into "Part 1: Debates" and "Part 2: Livelihoods." The first part, which consists of two chapters, reviews the different policy and cultural implications of transgenic corn for Mexico, while the second part contains three chapters consisting of an ethnographic study of a group of corn producers in a town in central Mexico. Both parts of the books are well researched, documented and written, although the author's training, skills and talents particularly shine in the second part of the book.

Any study of corn in Mexico must entail a rich understanding and explanation of the role of corn, as more than "just" a staple food, for the people of Mexico. From early colonial days, Mexico has struggled with the changing racial and ethnic identity of its people over time. The author creates a wonderful, detailed introduction to these issues in the first part of the book and explains how the cultural context and self-identification of the residents of Mexico with regard to their relationship to corn has changed over time. With the background, the author describes the controversy and response to the discovery of transgenic corn in Mexico, in the context of the wider economic reforms and greater economic integration into the world economy that have affected the agricultural sector in Mexico. While this is an excellent introduction and overview of these issues, a weakness in this section of the book is the policy analysis of the economic reforms related to the North American Free Trade Agreement (NAFTA), although I acknowledge that as an agricultural development economist, that is the literature I am most engaged with and the lens through which I approached the book.

The second half of the book is an ethnographic study of thirty agricultural producer households in the town of San Jose Miahauatlan in the southern Tehuacan Valley in the State of Puebla in central Mexico, who the authored interviewed while living there during 2001–2002, and with subsequent field trips over the following six years. Given the title of the book, the biggest surprise upon reading the introduction is that "When fieldwork began I asked residents what they thought about *maiz transgenico*, but found that the controversy had not reached the valley

FOOD,
CULTURE &
SOCIETY

VOLUME 15

ISSUE 2

JUNE 2012

during my visits, despite the government study which found evidence of transgenes in its northern end" (p. 9). The author began her fieldwork around the time of the discovery of transgenes in local varieties of corn in Mexico (2001).

The second part of the book should really be titled "The struggle for water," as this is what it describes. There is a wonderful detailed description of the historic struggle for water in the studied community and how views of race and ethnicity have changed over time and how these have affected differential access to water and the related view of being an agriculturalist. As I have spent the past 15 years associated with a large interdisciplinary research project on agricultural land use and land use change in southern Mexico, it was interesting to read the "stories" of the agricultural families interviewed by the author and to compare them with the "stories" generated via our repeated interviews with approximately 200 families across ten villages in southern Mexico. While the access to resource issue is different, as in southern Mexico most agriculture is rain fed, the effects of economic reform on corn production and labor migration are similar between the two regions. Corn continues to be grown in southern Mexico for a mix of both economic and cultural reasons, and cyclical migration to urban hubs within Mexico as well as further to the United States is also the norm. This is similar to other research performed throughout Mexico, as the author also states in her conclusion:

> My research confirmed what several other studies had found elsewhere in central and southern Mexico—that maize cultivation is subsided by off-farm income and at the same time provides a safety net for rural producers as a dependable yet flexible crop used for subsistence food and cash income. (p. 230)

The author does make an attempt to link the two sections of the book. She argues that although none of the farmers she interviewed for her research knew anything about transgenic corn or the controversies surrounding it (the material of Part 1), because transgenic corn was inexorably part of the technology associated with economic reforms and globalization, therefore the ways in which farmers were responding to the changes in state support of corn as a result from NAFTA and increased migration from the region (the focus of the Part 2), were indicative of the changes caused by economic reforms and globalization. However, I found this argument to be unconvincing, as my reading of the first part of the book did not help inform my reading of the second part and vice versa. That said, each part of the book is well written and would be of interest to potentially different audiences. Readers interested in the economic, political, historical and cultural contexts and institutions related to the production and consumption of corn in Mexico will find an excellent introduction and explanation in Part 1 of the book, while readers interested in an ethnographic study of the role of race and ethnicity and the struggle for access to natural resources under changing political regimes will be happy with Part 2. Finally, the larger policy implications of the transformation of the Mexican countryside from a producer of different varieties of corn to a producer of migrant laborers for urban Mexico as well as the United States is an important theme of the book, but an even greater emphasis could have been placed on the biodiversity loss impacts of this transition and how these compare with other regions and their associated similar losses in the biodiversity of staple crops as a result of globalization.

GLOBALIZATION, FOOD AND SOCIAL IDENTITIES IN THE ASIA PACIFIC REGION

EDITED BY JAMES FARRAR (TOKYO: SOPHIA UNIVERSITY INSTITUTE OF COMPARATIVE CULTURE, 2010).

Reviewed by Zane Ma Rhea, Monash University

DOI: 10.2752/175174412X13233545145589

This collection of sixteen online papers epitomizes the collision of Arjun Appadurai and Immanuel Wallerstein with *Iron Chef*. Both eclectic and familiar, the works capture the rich pastiche of food traces that have become the modern, global, foodways of fast capitalism. Centered in Japan, and the outcome of a symposium on "Globalization, Food and Social Identities in the Pacific Region" held at Sophia University on February 2009, the project invites the reader to its smorgasbord of tasty, bite-sized entrées. This is not your full-blown sit-down dinner cum feast, *à la* the traditional "book," but rather it allows the reader to move among the papers, downloading, tasting, and digesting according to interest and pleasure.

The collection marks the importance of the Asia-Pacific region as a global, historically central, commercial hub, and seeks to establish the co-evolution of food studies and global studies, arguing successfully that food is an excellent subject by which to interrogate the complexities of globalization. Each food examined provides rich local history, is highly context-specific, and engages with its movement through national consumption and distribution networks and into the global trading and culinary systems, collectively creating a unified framework of understanding.

The theoretical reach of the collection is broad, crossing cultural sociology, urban studies, and food studies to examine social, national, and increasingly complex interconnected national food identities. Unlike those critics of globalization who warn of the homogenizing impact of American food products (fast food and processed industrialized foods), decrying the seduction of the global palate by Coca-Cola and McDonald's, these papers describe the nuanced emergence of globally aware, local food practices that are creative, formative, and to some degree signal a change in the global culinary tipping point towards Asia.

The collection is sectioned into three parts. The first focuses on particular foods and examines a range of issues around the concept of "local" food. The second examines food in a global perspective through a number of eclectic examples. The third section is well described by one of the contributors, Rossella Ceccarini, as an examination of the glocalization of foreign culinary products. Food is one of Appadurai's "things" that has moved with nomads and traders around the globe for centuries. The "origins" of a particular food are often lost, and over centuries their

FOOD,
CULTURE&
SOCIETY

VOLUME 15

ISSUE 2

JUNE 2012

presence in a community becomes so normalized that they become part of the local culture, gathering a social history and sometimes even achieving a nationalistic, ideological standing.

The first section of the book covers themes of tourism and nostalgia, raising questions about the porosity of the "local" and its usefulness in theorizing the social meaning of food. The chapter by Kenneth Riddle and Naomichi Ishige, "On the origins, diffusion and cultural context of fermented fish products in Southeast Asia," takes the concept of origins and diffusion and examines fermented fish foods. They argue that these foods were first developed in inland places because of the conditions they identify as necessary for the production of fermented fish products, namely, that there would be a marked seasonality in the availability of fish, and that there would be access to rice and salt. The paper highlights an important aspect of the "local" and "origins" debates, that humans have commonly shared good ideas about food and that a good discovery is rapidly copied in other local contexts where the necessary ingredients and conditions are present. Patricia Yarrow, in her chapter "'Here's looking at you': re-imaging saké locally and globally," charts the local slump in saké brewing and consumption in Japan in favor of beer. The paper discusses the movement of saké consumption away from its "local" context into the urban Japanese context where saké is considered to be an old man's drink by younger Japanese urbanites. Tourism, combined with high-end Japanese restaurants selling superior saké in America and across Europe, has enabled "outsiders" to savor specific locally-produced Japanese saké. It is now something that the global food market recognizes as quintessentially Japanese even as Yarrow questions whether the global audience understands the true meaning of the saké label. She fails, however, to question the possibility that it may be because of the exotic unintelligibility of the saké label that it has such cachet in high culinary circles. Yarrow asks instead if it will be because of the popularity of saké in culinary hubs such as Paris that Japanese urban youth will re-identify with it as a source of national identity and pride.

Hiroyuki Tani's paper, "From national symbol to economic goods: a brief history of maize consumption in post-revolutionary Mexico," addresses the "local" dimension of political meaning and the ideology of food in its examination of maize. Tani charts the history of the social meaning of maize from its elevated post-revolutionary days as a crop of the people to its present role as a poor person's food, ultimately showing that maize is no longer valorized as the food of "national identity." As Sidney Cheung's and Yarrow's discussions also show, food identities are not neutral; they have symbolic value that changes over time in the local context. Yarrow's question about whether saké will be taken on by Japanese youth because of its high status and popularity outside Japan extends the question of change to symbolic value by opening up the possibility of a recursive loop of revalorization. Could the same happen in Mexico with maize, given a new set of global conditions?

The chapter by Jun Akamine titled "Problems on sea cucumber conservation" raises another aspect of "local" food production and consumption—that of population pressure and the local consumption of wildlife by examining the

Japanese delicacy—sea cucumber. The species favored most in Japan is a scarce resource, commonly taken from the Galapagos Islands, processed there, and brought back to Japan. Akamine asks what happens when a "local" wild food, full of social meaning, is no longer available locally, but must be imported to satisfy the "local" demand. Modern, global sea harvesting practices have the potential and the capacity to strip the sea of edible "wild" foods, even more so for high-status (and high market value) food such as sea cucumber and abalone. The concept of the "wild" and of local rights to certain "wild" foods has drawn attention from national and international wildlife conservation agencies who are working with communities to establish sustainable farming and harvesting practices for these foods.

The problem of the availability of "wild" foods is not confined to local communities. Increasingly, big players in the global market are looking for clean, unprocessed foods for their niche, adding pressure on sources of "wild" food. Stephanie Assmann's chapter "Food Action Nippon and Slow Food Japan: the role of two citizen movements in the rediscovery of local foodways" brings this debate to the forefront as Japan considers its reliance on imported processed foods. Examining the issue from the perspective of food self-sufficiency and food safety, she discusses the fact that Japan is only 40 percent food self-sufficient, meaning that it can no longer feed itself on domestically produced foods. Her discussion highlights the vulnerability of populations to global food market fluctuations. David Wank's chapter "Culinary nostalgia and Chinese neo-liberalism: local dish restaurants in Shanxi province" approaches the question in the context of China, examining what he describes as "culinary nostalgia" in the local food movement in Shanxi province. He makes the point that while there might be a demand for foods that are considered "local," the actual ingredients in these dishes are often imported from around the globe.

James Farrer approaches his discussion of food in the globalized context and the emergence of new global cities in "Eating the West and beating the rest: culinary Occidentalism and urban soft power in Asia's global food cities." Focusing his chapter on Shanghai and Tokyo as two examples of this phenomenon, he examines their high-status culinary identities and the impact they are having on global culinary practices. What is fascinating in both this work and that of Michiko Kubo in "The development of an Indonesian national cuisine: a study of new movement of instant foods and local cuisine" is how global food production is keeping pace with an exponentially growing population. Kubo examines the demand by Indonesian women for instant foods that are less labor-intensive than traditional food, highlighting how traditional food preparation methods do not necessarily fit with modern life. While some markets will always cater to customers who prefer older-style food production and consumption methods, these chapters demonstrate that population growth and mass urban migration is leading to significant changes in food production methods and global culinary preferences, arguably tipping toward an "Asian" style of eating fast food.

FOOD,
CULTURE&
SOCIETY

VOLUME 15

ISSUE 2

JUNE 2012

Krishnendu Ray's chapter, "A taste for ethnic difference: American gustatory imagination in a globalizing world," echoes this change in the analysis of how American chefs are differentiating themselves as "taste makers." On a similar theme, Vanina Leschziner in "Cooking logics: cognition and reflexivity in the culinary field" examines food and high cuisine, where chefs can either be differentiated by taste or by originality, drawing on global inspiration to create "high cuisine" in global cities in America. Shoko Inai's chapter "Nobu and after: Westernized Japanese food and globalization" traces the successful transplantation of Nobu's Japanese restaurants into America, arguing that there is an emerging Americanized Japanese food that is an outcome of this process of transplantation. In "Four dances of the sea: cooking "Asian" as embedded cosmopolitanism," Jean Duruz discusses the new "Australian–Asian culinary citizenship," building on the common theme in this grouping of articles about the shift in the global palate to Asian-style food preferences. Ceccarini in "Food workers as individual agents of culinary globalization: pizza and pizzaioli in Japan" examines the reverse transplantation process, discussing the popularity of Italian pizza in Japan. Her work focuses on the role and practices of the food creators, both Italian and Japanese, opening up important avenues for research into the complex processes of exchange and acculturation of new food knowledge practices into a new environment through human agency.

In counterpoint to these chapters, "Malaysian cuisine: a case of neglected culinary globalization" by Kosaku Yoshino asks the question of why Malaysian food, a clearly Asian style of cuisine that already draws from its multiethnic communities for its richness, has not achieved the same global status as other Asian nations such as China or Japan. A chapter by Mauro Neves, "*Como Agua Para Chocolate* as a food film: food, family ties and emotion," examines the global film industry and the impact it has on newly emerging, globally connected, discussions about the food that humans are eating, how they are eating it, and what is driving the rich emotion behind new food practices.

Overall, this web-book successfully highlights how food, its creation, production, consumption and social identity are intimately imbricated with globalization, with implications for both public and private space. This collection raises many new and exciting possibilities for research, which are particularly relevant today when our knowledge about food—from harvesting to production to preparation to consumption to distribution—is entering a new phase where concepts such as "local," "wild," "sustainable," and "national" are being shaped and are shaping global food consumption and production patterns. This collection proposes that Asian culinary habits are achieving global prominence because they are able to meet the demands of a global society who now, more than ever, are aware of the array of food options available to satisfy their increasingly demanding palates.

ALIMENTARY TRACTS: APPETITES, AVERSIONS AND THE POSTCOLONIAL

BY PARAMA ROY (DURHAM, NC: DUKE UNIVERSITY PRESS, 2010).

Reviewed by Krishnendu Ray, New York University

DOI: 10.2752/175174412X13233545145624

Hunger has dominated the conversation on Indian food for a very long time. Slowly the terms are changing. Strong economic growth for the last two decades, the emergence of an assertive and better-off middle class (estimated to be the size of substantial nations), and the successes of the diaspora are adding new concerns. Michael Worboys (1988) and David Arnold (1994) have provided us with hunger's prehistory in British imperial concerns about diet and malnutrition and its relationship to colonial science from the 1860s to the interwar years. The nationalist response to this colonial "reconnaissance and categorization of India" (Arnold 1994: 4) developed hesitatingly and did not acquire full force until the third decade of the twentieth century. "By the late 1930s what had once clearly been a branch of colonial science *about* Indians … was becoming part of an Indian scientific research agenda *for* Indians" (Arnold 1994: 26). A robust thread of that discussion continues in Amartya Sen's Nobel Prize–winning work on the political-economy of hunger, which came out of those discourses and was developed within modern Western epistemologies (see Drèze *et al.* 1995). More recently in the United States, *Late Victorian Holocausts* (Davis 2001) is an inspired example of where such research can lead—as a critique of market–state relations within the frame of political-ecology. In some ways, Davis pursues the argument of the first generation of Indian nationalist economists such as Dadabhai Naoroji in *Poverty and Un-British Rule in India* (1901).

The two ends of this incongruent polarity, colonial hunger and postcolonial gastronomy, are surprisingly tied together by this remarkable book by Parama Roy. Heavily theorized and deeply entangled in the thicket of literary criticism, it is chronologically selective, hopping, skipping and jumping from the 1857 Indian Mutiny (against East India Company rule), to Gandhi's austere vegetarianism and spectacular fasting, through hungers of the low-caste poor in Mahasweta Devi's fictions, to the gastronomic reclamation of curry powder by Madhur Jaffrey. In doing so, Roy walks the fertile borderlands of the ethical and the aesthetic consequences of eating the other. In allowing the other to enter one's body without the desperate need of purgation, she expertly inverts the critique of hooks (1992), Heldke (2003) and Nandy (2003). She does this by drawing on Jacques Derrida's (1991) suggestion of anthropophagy, not as an abomination but as a "parabolic instantiation of unexpected somatic and ethical engagement with the other" where the "refusal to partake of the other is an important breakdown in or rejection of ethical reciprocity with the other" (p. 14).

Alimentary Tracts opens with some of the most seductive lines I have read about food and memory:

FOOD,
CULTURE &
SOCIETY

VOLUME 15

ISSUE 2

JUNE 2012

As a child in India I tended to dream of what I considered to be British food. Improbable at it seems now, I dreamed of potted meats (especially Spam), tinned tongue, jam tarts, ginger beer, pork-pies, and éclairs. I dreamed of gastronomic surprises nestled in tuck boxes and hampers of food, poised to reveal their bounty in the midnight feats I read about but never experienced in my own life. I longed especially for the singular delectation of eating my food out of a tin—to me the very sign of gastronomic avant-gardism, situated as I was in a global backwater and largely innocent of what I was to learn later were called "industrial foods." (p. 2)

Immediately that passage re-memorialized for me the deep pleasures of having read Sara Suleri's *Meatless Days* (1989) and Salman Rushdie's *Midnight's Children* (1980). These two texts most successfully convey the postcolonial structure of feeling about comestibles and colonialism that I have been struggling to articulate for over a decade. *Alimentary Tracts* now enters my study as a delectable trifecta of longing for the nation while fleeing from it. So one part of my excitement about this book then is the sheer pleasure of private reading. The other part, as a teaching tool it now joins *Appetites: Food and Sex in Post-Socialist China* (Farquhar 2002) as a well written and theoretically useful approach to difference—in terms of time, place and epistemology—for students who have mostly read Euro-American instances of food studies.

Roy argues that as the:

psychopharmacopoeia of empire—spices, opium, sugar, and tea—demonstrate, colonialism was in important respects a reconfiguration of the fantasmatic landscapes and the sensorium of colonizer and colonized, generating new experiences of desire, taste, disgust, and appetite and new technologies of the embodied self. (p. 7)

In doing so, she puts into relief the theoretical brilliance and empirical acumen of her genealogical predecessors Frantz Fanon (1963), Wolfgang Schivelbusch (1992), Sidney Mintz (1985), and Pierre Bourdieu (1987). The fact that British imperial consumption of India was book-ended by the Bengal Famine of 1769–70 and that of 1943–44 is put to good use by Roy. Thus, one could think of postcoloniality, she argues, as a promise of eating well.

The four substantial chapters in the book focus on an illustrative instance of each period: colonialism (and mutiny), nationalism (and Gandhi's fasting), decolonization (and tribal hunger), and finally postcoloniality (and diasporic appetite). Her first station on this arc is the Mutiny of 1857, one of the spectacular instances of anticolonial insurgency. Chapter 1, titled "Disgust. food, filth, and the Anglo-Indian flesh in 1857," ties roti (Indian flat bread) to rumor, in a prolific, Fanonist reading of the macabre violence and violation of mutiny and counter-insurgency, producing a subject with a peculiar constellation of love and hatred of the colony, the metropole, whiteness and color. In Chapter 2, titled "Abstinence: manifestos on meat and masculinity," she takes the scalpel to the vegetarian's body and casts it surprisingly and productively as "a body characterized by its hyperbolic visibility; it was a body characterized by its looked-at-ness and its status, first as freak [among the meat-worshipping imperialists] and then as holy spectacle" (p. 83). This spectacularization of the renunciant male body is most fruitfully investigated, successfully avoiding both the sentimentalism of the believer and the disdain of the carnivore. Chapter 3—the weakest chapter in my view—devotes almost exclusive attention to Gayatri Chakravarty Spivak's heroine Mahasweta Devi and the latter's fictions about what in India is referred to as "tribal" hunger, especially in "Shishu" (Children) (1993) and "Pterodactyl, Puran Sahay, and Pirtha" (1995), which searingly critique the failure of the decolonized Indian state to provide for, or even acknowledge, the hungers of the landless low-caste and tribal poor. Tribal "famine on a genocidal scale remains the inadmissible secret not just of the colonial Indian state, but of the postcolonial one as well" (p. 119). Here both the reader—me—and the writer—Roy—are, I think, so overwhelmed by Spivak's famous rendering of Mahasweta Devi's writing that we could not find a way to enter her work with any fresh perspective. It addresses, perhaps even trips over, the central question faced most pointedly by self-declared third-world, feminist, postcolonial theorists: how to make the silent subaltern speak and become the medium of that clairvoyance in spite of one's location in neoliberal networks. Furthermore, here Roy's theoretical language intrudes and becomes burdensome in conveying her point. The deeper I got into the chapter, the less I understood it. Thankfully, her lucidity and eloquence returned from the thicket of theorization in the substantial Chapter 4, "Appetite: spices redux," where she asks brilliantly how Madhur Jaffrey's "limpid prose and impeccable recipes can signify familiarity and comfort *and* exoticism and adventure as part of the same operation" (p. 178). After a sharp discussion about Jaffrey's initial disavowal and then full embrace of curry powder, Roy mischievously concludes:

> The career of Madhur Jaffrey and of her fabulous khansamah proves that despite manifold repressions and disavowals, curry powder repeatedly returns to the scene of Indian cooking, even if it is in the partially comic and partially guilty guise of Curry in a Hurry" (p. 190)

Nevertheless, in spite of its luster, given the weight of the issue of genocidal tribal hunger in the preceding chapter, the final one was bound to feel lighter, a problem that always confronts food studies in the presence of hunger.

Roy's attempt to yoke the political–economic to symbolic–aesthetic analysis remains exceptional, hence acquiring greater value for me. The field of engagement with Indian food is polarized into a number of discrete foci: one coalescing around crop science and development economics; another around culture; still another around nutrition and public health. Parama Roy's *Alimentary Tracts* is a necessary intervention in the creative breaking of a few established analytical pots. Roy's methodological trafficking across disciplinary boundaries accords well with her conception of the alimentary tract as both a fiercely policed and heavily traveled section.

FOOD,
CULTURE &
SOCIETY

VOLUME 15

ISSUE 2

JUNE 2012

References

Arnold, David. 1994. The "Discovery" of Malnutrition and Diet in Colonial India. *Indian Economic & Social History Review* 31(1): 1–26.

Bourdieu, Pierre. 1987. *Distinction: A Social Critique of the Judgment of Taste.* Translated by Richard Nice. Cambridge, MA: Harvard University Press.

Davis, Mike. 2001. *Late Victorian Holocausts: El Niño Famines and the Making of the Third World.* London: Verso.

Derrida, Jacques. 1991. Eating Well, or the Calculation of the Subject: An Interview with Jacques Derrida. In E. Cadava, J.-L. Nancy and P. Conner (eds), *Who Comes After the Subject?* New York: Routledge, pp. 96–119.

Drèze, J., Sen, A. and Hussain, A. 1995. *The Political Economy of Hunger: Selected Essays.* Oxford: Clarendon Press.

Fanon, Frantz. 1963. *The Wretched of the Earth.* Translated by Constance Farrington. New York: Grove Weidenfeld.

Farquhar, Judith. 2002. *Appetites: Food and Sex in Post-Socialist China.* Durham, NC: Duke University Press.

Heldke, Lisa. 2003. *Exotic Appetites: Ruminations of a Food Adventurer.* New York: Routledge.

hooks, bell. 1992. *Black Looks: Race and Representation.* Boston, MA: South End.

Mahasweta (Devi). 1993. Shishu. In S. Tharu & K. Lalita (eds), *Women Writing in India: the Twentieth Century.* New York: The Feminist Press at City University of New York, pp. 236–50.

Mahasweta (Devi). 1995. Pterodactyl, Puran Sahay, and Pirtha. *Imaginary Maps.* Translated by Gayatri Spivak. London: Routledge, pp. 95-196.

Mintz, Sidney. 1985. *Sweetness and Power: The Place of Sugar in Modern History.* New York: Penguin Books.

Nandy, Ashis. 2003. Ethnic Cuisine: The Significant Other. In G. Sen (ed.), *India. A National Culture?* New Delhi: Sage, pp. 246–51

Naoroji, Dadabhai. 1901. *Poverty and Un-British Rule in India.* London: Sonnenschein.

Rushdie, Salman. 1980. *Midnight's Children.* London: Jonathan Cape.

Schivelbusch, Wolfgang. 1992. *Tastes of Paradise: A Social History of Spices, Stimulants, and Intoxicants.* Translated by David Jacobson. New York: Vintage.

Suleri, Sara. 1989. *Meatless Days.* Chicago, IL: University of Chicago Press.

Worboys, Michael. 1988. The Discovery of Colonial Malnutrition between the Wars. In. D. Arnold (ed.), *Imperial Medicine and Indigenous Societies.* Manchester: Manchester University Press, pp. 208–25.

Notes for Contributors

Food, Culture & Society is published by the Association for the Study of Food and Society (ASFS). ASFS is a multidisciplinary international organization dedicated to exploring the complex relationships among food, culture, and society from numerous disciplines in the humanities, social sciences, and sciences, as well as in the world of food beyond the academy. Striving to represent the highest standards of research and scholarship in all aspects of food studies, we encourage vigorous debate on a wide range of topics and problems, such as:

  cross-cultural perspectives on eating behaviors
  gender and the food system
  the food voice
  recipes, cookbooks, and menus as texts
  philosophical and religious perspectives on food and the body
  social construction of culinary practices, beliefs, and traditions
  politics of the family meal
  dietary transitions
  psychological, cultural, and social determinants of taste
  methodological issues in food studies
  malnutrition, hunger, and food security
  commodity chain and foodshed analysis
  food in fiction, film, and art
  comparative food history
  social and cultural dimensions of food technologies
  political economy of the global food system
  food studies pedagogy
  plus original reviews of relevant books, films, videos, and exhibitions

Manuscripts will be subject to anonymous peer review by members of the FCS Board of Editors and ad hoc reviewers. If accepted for publication in this journal, the author(s) must agree not to publish it elsewhere in the same form, in English or any other language, without the written consent of the editors. Copyright will be held by ASFS.

Please send submissions electronically via email to both editors, Lisa Heldke: *heldke@gustavus.edu* and Ken Albala: *kalbala@pacific.edu*. The e-mail itself will serve as the submission letter and should indicate that the paper has not been published elsewhere, in whole or in part, and that it has not been submitted simultaneously for publication elsewhere.

Manuscripts should be no more than 9,000 words, including all endmatter. Please include an abstract at the beginning of the article, and a list of up to eight keywords. Label all files using a brief version of the title as the filename (e.g. fastfood.doc).

Please prepare manuscripts for anonymous review by removing all identifying references from text, notes and metadata. Authors must submit manuscripts in English. MS Word is the preferred software program. Please also submit in a separate file a 150-word biography including department, institution, e-mail, phone and street address, with file name as the brief title of the article and the word "author" (e.g. fastfood author.doc).

References and notes must conform to known citation style usually Chicago (history), MLA (literary) or APA (social sciences). For specifics, please consult Kate L. Turabian, *A Manual for Writers of Term Papers, Theses, and Dissertations* (latest edn).

Illustrations submitted should be clean originals or digital files. Digital files are recommended for highest quality reproduction and should follow these guidelines:

> 300 dpi or higher
> sized to fit on journal page
> submitted as separate electronic files (e.g. TIFF or JPG files) not embedded in text files

Color illustrations will be considered for publication only if the author agrees to pay the full cost of their printing and publication. Authors are responsible for obtaining permission to reproduce copyrighted material.

FCS reserves the right to make minor stylistic changes that, in the opinion of the editors, do not change the meaning of the article or the views of the author.
On publication, the first-named author will receive PDF of the final, published article for personal use.

Address all manuscript correspondence to the FCS editors: Lisa Heldke, Gustavus Adolphus College, St. Peter, MN 56082, USA (e-mail: *heldke@gustavus.edu*) and Ken Albala, University of the Pacific, Stockton, CA 95211, USA (e-mail: *kalbala@pacific.edu*).

Address all correspondence regarding books for review to the FCS book editor: Krishnendu Ray, Department of Nutrition, Food Studies and Public Health, New York University, 5th Floor, 411 Lafayette Street, New York, NY 10003, USA.

Authors need not be members of ASFS to submit articles. More information about becoming a member of ASFS may be found at: http://food-culture.org/